THE SPELT COOKBOOK

COOKING WITH NATURE'S GRAIN FOR LIFE

HELGA HUGHES

Avery Publishing Group

Garden City Park, New York

Cover Design: William Gonzalez
Original Illustrations: Vicki Rae Chelf
Typesetting: Bonnie Freid
In-House Editor: Joanne Abrams

Cataloging-in-Publication Data

Hughes, Helga.
    The spelt cookbook: cooking with nature's grain for life/
Helga Hughes.
    p.   cm
    Includes index.
    ISBN 0-89529-696-9

    1. Cookery.   2. Wild wheats.   I. Title.
TX652.H84 1995

641.6'1
QBI95-20216

Printed in the United States of America

10 9 8 7 6 5 4 3 2

Contents

Acknowledgments

First and foremost, I would like to express my thanks to Wilhelm W. Kosnopfl, president of Purity Foods, Inc., whose inspiration and encouragement made this book possible. Thanks also go to Purity Foods' domestic operations manager, Donald A. Stinchcomb, for the statistical information he provided.

I also wish to thank Dr. Ch.I. Kling of the Universität Hohenheim, and Professor William E. Barbeau of Virginia Tech for the invaluable information they supplied about grains; Anna Merighi, my patient cooking teacher, who paved the way for my culinary career; my cousin Luise and her husband, Wolfgang, who introduced me to the teachings of St. Hildegard of Bingen and her belief in spelt as a healing food; and Frau Ott of Störnhof, Bavaria, whose life is dedicated to growing and spreading the benefits of spelt.

As always, my thanks go to my mother, Anna; my godmother, Kuni; my sisters, Lore, Hannah, and Inge; and my cousin Erika for their generous support throughout the project, and for acting as guinea pigs.

Thanks also go to the many, many friends and acquaintances whose recipes, over the years, have found their way into my database and have been used and modified many times over.

I would like to express my appreciation to the Vita-Spelt competition winners whose recipes appear in this book. I trust they will accept the alterations I made, all of which were necessary for the purpose of creating a consistent work.

On behalf of all of us who enjoy spelt, I thank farmers everywhere who ensure that crops of this nutritious grain continue to be harvested in a world where wheat almost took over.

Joanne Abrams, my editor at Avery Publishing Group, deserves a special note of thanks for the vast amount of work she put into this book in order to ensure accuracy and consistency.

Finally, thanks go to my husband, Ken, for his support and for his computer skills, which kept my work in controllable order.

Foreword

Spelt is a member of the grass family of grains. It is thought to have originated in the Fertile Crescent, where it was first harvested over 9,000 years ago. In both the Middle East and Europe, spelt was the staff of life for many centuries. The Germans call it *dinkel,* the Italians refer to it as their beloved *farro,* and the French know it as *epeautre.*

To better understand spelt and how you might benefit from it, we must first address a few basic questions. The first is: What makes spelt different from other grains, and why is it a superior food? Spelt has a superior nutritional profile. It is a very good source of complex carbohydrates, protein, iron, and potassium. In its whole-grain form, spelt retains a delicious flavor—not a heavy, bitter taste like that of so many other whole grains. As such, this marvelous grain allows you to prepare high-fiber dishes without sacrificing taste. Spelt is also a good source of essential amino acids, components of protein that are not manufactured by our bodies.

Another basic question is: If spelt is such a superior grain, why haven't I heard about it before? Spelt fell into disfavor during the Industrial Revolution. As more people moved into the cities, the burden of food production fell more heavily on the shoulders of the remaining farmers. Spelt is a husked grain. This means that the kernel is tightly shrouded in a hull, which has to be removed mechanically. Because wheat does not have such a hull, it can be taken directly from the harvest fields to the flour mill. This convenience saved time and labor. So, with its high yield and lower costs, wheat replaced spelt.

What accounts for spelt's recent resurgence? The educated consumer knows that food should nourish and support the body, rather than compromise well-being in the interest of good taste. Food should be harmonious with health. Spelt is just such a food. Nature enfolded the spelt kernel in a husk, which protects the grain from the elements. And because the spelt kernel is very delicate, it is easily digested by people who are allergic to wheat. In fact, many naturopathic physicians include spelt in the diets of chronically ill patients, knowing that the last thing these people need is a product that is difficult to digest or a strain on the immune system.

Purity Foods' interest in spelt developed over time, first when a European customer expressed interest in organically grown spelt, and later when chronically ill individuals wrote to us about the need for this grain. Subsequent trips to Europe, where spelt is recognized as the preferred gourmet baking grain, further strengthened our resolve to bring spelt to the United States.

When we first took on the task of producing spelt products, we knew that it was vital to select the preferred baking variety of spelt for our growers. With this done, we brought the seed stock to the United States, and gave it to certified seed-growing farmers, who then produced sufficient seed stock for our organic growers. In 1991, we began to produce spelt products in earnest.

The task of making spelt available to American consumers borders on a spiritual experience, and is driven by the enthusiastic response of our many loyal customers. We have found that spelt's health benefits and great taste turn mild-mannered people into spelt zealots. In this day of overprocessed, nutrient-poor foods, spelt provides people with an energy and vitality they want to share with their friends and relatives.

The Spelt Cookbook is a wonderful resource for everyone who wants to enjoy the unique taste of spelt. Helga's numerous recipes highlight the versatility of spelt, and show everyone, from the person who is just discovering spelt to the true aficionado, how the many spelt products now available can be used with delicious results. For those who like to make dishes "from scratch," Helga explains how spelt flour and other spelt products can be used to make delicious breads, delightful homemade pastas, and many other treats. For those with less time to spare, Helga demonstrates how convenience products such as spelt bread mixes, spelt pancake mixes, and dried spelt pastas can be used to quickly create truly spectacular dishes designed to suit every taste and occasion.

As we learn more about human physiology, we begin to understand that simple decisions regarding how we fuel our body can have long-lasting effects on our quality of life. We at Purity Foods urge you to make informed choices and choose spelt—the grain for life.

Wilhelm W. Kosnopfl
President, Purity Foods

Preface

As a natural foods writer and cooking teacher, I know the importance of using whole foods that are both flavorful and rich in nutrients. Such foods allow you to create satisfying dishes that nourish the body and maximize your health. For this reason, I was delighted when spelt first appeared in health foods stores across the United States. Remembering spelt from my childhood in Bavaria, I looked foward to again enjoying crusty loaves of spelt bread, as well as other spelt-based foods. However, I quickly discovered that most Americans are unfamiliar with spelt, and so may be hesitant to use this new—yet ancient—grain in their recipes. *The Spelt Cookbook* is designed to guide you in cooking with this wonderful food.

The Spelt Cookbook begins by introducing you to the many different spelt products, including flours, bulgur, ready-to-make pastas, cereals, and bread mixes. You will also learn about natural sweeteners, low- and no-salt seasonings, dairy substitutes, and other ingredients that will help you create truly sensational dishes that are just as high in nutrients as they are in flavor.

Following this basic information, each chapter focuses on a specific meal or type of dish. Chapter 2 presents a wide range of recipes for brunch and breakfast treats, from Old-World Buttermilk Waffles to Muesli Breakfast Bars to Easy Mushroom Soufflé. Looking for a warming soup or a stick-to-your-ribs stew? Chapter 3 provides a tempting selection of soup and stew recipes, from White Bean Chili With Elbows to Minestrone. Still other chapters provide recipes for refreshing salads; hearty breads and muffins; enticing sandwiches; satisfying poultry, fish, and vegetarian entrées; savory homemade pastas, dumplings, and crêpes; and enticing side dishes. Finally, you'll find a dazzling array of desserts. And every recipe, from the easy-to-make Hazelnut Granola to the spectacular Raspberry Linzer Torte, shares a single ingredient—golden spelt.

It is my hope that this book will show you just how easy it is to add spelt to your diet. With its incomparable taste and its wealth of nutrients, spelt proves, once and for all, that every dish you serve can be both delicious *and* healthy.

The Story of Spelt

esearch indicates that *Triticum spelta,* or spelt, the earliest known bread wheat, first appeared about 9,000 years ago, some 3,000 years before the grain that led to modern wheat made its appearance. It is thought that spelt's birthplace was southwest Asia. As civilization spread, emigrants took spelt kernels with them. These travelers carried the kernels complete with their tough coverings, having learned that when planted in their sheaths, the plants better resisted the invasion of underground pests. In this way, spelt spread throughout Europe, until the plains became a shimmering sea of gently swaying stalks, slowly changing with the seasons from green to golden brown.

As the centuries rolled by, spelt grain became known farther and farther afield as it made its way from the farm lands to vessels that plied the Rhine and Danube. In Germany, spelt has always been called *dinkel*, and towns such as Dinkelsbühl, Dinkelhausen, and Dinkelrode took their names from it. In fact, the town of Dinkelsbühl has a museum devoted entirely to

spelt. In the city park, a life-size monument of a farmer holding a sheath of spelt greets the arriving traveler.

For hundreds of years, spelt was the most widely used grain in Europe. However, owing to its lower yield compared with that of newer varieties of wheat, and because of the need to dehull the grain before use, the popularity of spelt diminished during the Industrial Revolution. In fact, spelt has not been grown in Europe in large quantities since the nineteenth century. Nevertheless, today, a limited amount of spelt is cultivated by farmers in Bavaria, where I spent my childhood.

Hiking was a popular pastime in the country of my youth, and some of my fondest memories are of early morning hikes. We would wander from one village to the next, often stopping to warm our hands at the open-air bread ovens used by many farmers. Built of brick and resembling igloos in shape, these ovens were heated by a wood fire which burned in a central hearth. The farmers would extinguish the fire and then use long-handled wooden paddles to place rounds of spelt dough directly on the low brick shelf that surrounded the hearth. I will never forget the sight and aroma of freshly baked golden brown loaves coming out of the oven. Even better was when the farmer used a long-bladed pocket knife to slice pieces of the loaf, and then gave each of us a slice, still warm from the oven. Delicious!

Later, after moving to the United States, I lost touch with the grain. Then, a few years ago, I found spelt on the shelves of health food stores, and again became acquainted with this wonderful grain.

Why is spelt so special? Like most grains, spelt is a rich source of nutrients. But unlike wheat, the most widely used grain in the United States, spelt has an extremely fragile gluten content. This means that spelt is the perfect alternative for people who are allergic to wheat because of its high gluten content. And because the spelt kernel is surrounded by a very strong hull, the nutrients remain well protected until spelt is hulled and milled. In fact, because of the protective hull, pesticides are not needed for the cultivation of the grain.

For centuries, people familiar with spelt have observed the health benefits of this wonderful grain. Perhaps nowhere has spelt been so appreciated as at the Hildegard clinical practice in Constance, Germany. Built on the teachings of St. Hildegard of Bingen, a twelfth-century Benedictine abbess, the clinic follows many of St. Hildegard's dictums, but in particular her belief that the body must be detoxified before it can be healed; her almost 2,000 remedies and health suggestions; and her strong recommendations for the inclusion of spelt in the diet.

Of course, while we all want to eat a healthful diet, we also want our food to taste good. How does spelt taste? Spelt is a delicious grain, and is highly versatile in its cooking uses. Spelt flour has a deeper, richer color than whole wheat flour and a more pronounced flavor, suggestive of nuts. And spelt can be eaten in many forms. While many fine spelt products are readily available today, I have had greatest success using the products of Purity Foods, Inc., the leading manufacturer

of organically grown spelt products in the United States. Appearing under the name Vita-Spelt, these products cook up well and taste delicious. In addition to spelt flour, Purity markets spelt bread mixes, spelt pancake and muffin mix, hulled spelt kernels, toasted spelt flakes, a full range of spelt pastas, and spelt bulgur. These products make it easy to add spelt to your diet in dishes that are sure to please you and your family. In fact, many of the recipes that appear in this book were prize winners in a Purity Foods' recipe competition!

When cooking with spelt, both in my own kitchen and in the wheatless and meatless cooking classes I teach, I've found that spelt products lend themselves to the creation of imaginative recipes. Of course, spelt flour can usually be used as a substitute for wheat flour with excellent results. But spelt's uses are not limited to baked goods. This cookbook includes recipes for breakfast and brunch, for soups and stews, for salads, pastas, sandwiches, main dishes, and desserts. And all the recipes are made more delicious and healthful by the addition of spelt.

One of the reasons that it's been so easy to develop recipes for this wonderful grain is that spelt is a "natural" for American cuisine. As a health food writer in the United States, I have long been concerned that health-oriented people in this country lean too heavily on imported foods and foreign cooking styles. While this can certainly provide a welcome change of pace, sometimes the resulting dishes prove difficult to digest for those accustomed to Western foods, and fail to appeal to Western tastes. But, as you'll see when you begin cooking with spelt, this grain is beautifully compatible with American cuisine. It is a food that is grown in America, and that you can use to make healthy, down-to-earth American meals, as well as a variety of ethnic favorites.

I hope that you love cooking with spelt as much as I do, and that you and your family benefit from the delicious tastes and superior nutrition that spelt provides. Be adventurous, have fun, and enjoy your spelt meals!

1

In the Kitchen

*I*f spelt is new to you, you probably have a number of questions about cooking with this wonderful grain. In this chapter, you'll find out about the many different spelt products now available, and you'll see how you can enjoy success when cooking with these exciting new foods. You'll also learn about various sweeteners, some of which may be new to you and may well add a fresh dimension to your cooking. You'll then become acquainted with a few simple cooking techniques that will ensure good results each time you step into the kitchen to cook a spelt dish. Finally, because proper equipment is such an important part of the creative cooking process, you'll learn about the tools of the trade needed to make cooking easy, efficient, and enjoyable.

WORKING WITH SPELT

Even if you are an accomplished cook, spelt is likely to be a new addition to your pantry. Let's take a look at the various forms of spelt, and see how you can use them to make appetizing and nutritious meals.

Spelt Kernels

Because spelt kernels are whole and unprocessed, they contain all of their original nutrients, making them a delicious source of vitamins and minerals. But to use whole spelt kernels in certain recipes, you must first presoak and precook them, following these easy steps.

1. Rinse the kernels in a large sieve—not a colander, which might let some kernels fall through. Then transfer the kernels to a large bowl and cover them with water, using 1¼ cups of water for each cup of kernels. Allow the kernels to soak for 8 hours or overnight.

2. After soaking, discard any remaining water and again rinse the kernels in a sieve. Then transfer the kernels to a saucepan, adding water until the kernels are covered by 2 inches of liquid. Simmer for 20 minutes.

3. Remove the pan from the heat and allow the kernels to soak, uncovered, for an additional 30 minutes. Drain off any remaining water, and use the kernels in the recipe of your choice.

After the spelt kernels have been precooked, they can be dried and stored in the refrigerator for up to five days. Simply spread the kernels on a large baking sheet, and air-dry them for at least two hours. Then transfer them to an airtight container, and refrigerate for later use.

Precooked kernels may also be ground and added to soup stocks; substituted for rice in puddings, risottos, pilafs, and grain cakes; or steamed with vegetables for a quick and nourishing side dish. To grind the kernels, simply pass them through a food processor set to "grind," or use a power- or hand-driven grinder. If using a grinder, send a piece of dry bread through the grinder at the end, to push the last kernels through the machine. Stop grinding when the bread appears, but do not be concerned if a small amount of ground bread becomes mixed with the ground kernels. Keep in mind that 1 cup of whole precooked kernels will yield about ⅔ cup of ground kernels. Therefore, if your recipe calls for 1 cup of ground kernels, you will have to start with 1½ cups of whole kernels. The ground spelt kernels may be refrigerated in an airtight container, but total storage time, beginning with the presoaking stage, should not exceed five days.

Spelt Bulgur

Spelt bulgur is a time and energy saver because it is ready to use without precooking and pregrinding. To cook spelt bulgur, simply combine equal amounts of bulgur and boiling water or stock, and allow the mixture to soak for five minutes. Then serve as a substitute for rice, or simply add chopped vegetables and a dressing to create a quick bulgur salad. For a delicious hot cereal, add spelt bulgur to boiling low-fat milk or water, and simmer for a few minutes.

Some recipes require you to grind bulgur. When using such a recipe, simply place the uncooked bulgur in a blender or food processor, and grind for 1 minute at medium speed, or until the product is finely ground. You will find that 1 cup of regular spelt bulgur will yield about ½ cup of finely ground bulgur. Therefore, if you need 1 cup of finely ground bulgur in your recipe, you should start with about 2 cups of regular spelt bulgur. Once ground, the bulgur may be stored in an airtight jar at room temperature for up to a month.

Toasted Spelt Flakes

Spelt flakes, which come lightly toasted, are a wonderfully versatile food. When mixed with other ingredients and toasted again, spelt flakes make an excellent granola. When used right out of the box, these nutrient-packed flakes can be added to bread dough to create an interesting texture, or substituted for oat flakes in oatmeal cookies. Spelt flakes also make make a delicious topping for vegetable, tofu, and chicken dishes.

Some recipes list ground, rather than whole, spelt flakes among their ingredients. To grind these tasty flakes, simply place them in a blender or food processor, and grind for 1 minute at medium speed, or until the product is finely ground. You will find that 1 cup of spelt flakes will yield about ⅓ cup of finely ground flakes. Therefore, if you need 1 cup of finely ground flakes, you should start with about 3 cups of flakes. If you prefer, you may place the whole spelt flakes on a hard surface such as a wooden board and grind them with a rolling pin. Keep in mind, though, that while the resulting flakes will be fine for toppings, they will be too coarsely ground for use in coatings. Once ground, store the flakes in an airtight jar at room temperature for up to thirty days.

Spelt Pasta

In recent years, we've learned about the important part that whole-grain pasta can play in a healthful diet. Fortunately, spelt pasta—a delicious alternative to wheat-based pasta—is available in many varieties, including spelt-buckwheat spaghetti, elbow macaroni, egg noodles, lasagna noodles, angel hair, rotini, and medium and small shells.

To cook spelt pasta, fill a large saucepan or kettle with cold water, adding a few drops of oil to the water to keep the pasta pieces separate and to prevent them from sticking to the sides of the pan. A dash of salt may also be added. Bring the water to a rapid boil, add the pasta, and cook, stirring occasionally, just until the pasta is al dente—tender, but still firm. Drain the pasta, and serve immediately or use it in the recipe of your choice.

SWEETENERS

All natural sweeteners contain some form of sugar, but it is the form that counts. Refined white sugar, which is less complex than other sweeteners, enters the bloodstream in a rush, giving some people a "sugar high." White sugar has also been stripped of all nutrients, making it nutritionally bankrupt. The more complex structure of most other sweeteners causes them to be absorbed more slowly by the body, thereby eliminating the "high." In addition, the less processed the sweetener, the more likely it is to contain nutrients.

Because of its taste, I prefer turbinado sugar, and I specify its use in my recipes. But should you wish to use a more natural sweetener, you may want to try one of those described below. Following the list, a table of substitutions will allow you to use the product you prefer in any of the recipes found in this book, and in your own recipes as well.

Barley Malt Syrup. An extract of sprouted, roasted barley, this syrup is less sweet than many sweeteners, but is easily assimilated by the body, and does contain more nutrients than are found in other sweeteners.

Brown Sugar. Basically white sugar colored by the addition of molasses, brown sugar is little better than refined white sugar from a health point of view. When used sparingly, however, this sweetener provides a distinctive taste and color.

Honey. Although chemically much like refined white sugar, honey does contain some minerals and trace elements, and has the advantage of being sweeter than sugar so that lesser amounts are needed. Honey is also absorbed into the body more slowly than white sugar, and so provides a steadier supply of energy.

Maple Syrup. A natural sweetener with a distinctive flavor, this boiled-down sap of the maple tree is slightly less sweet than honey.

Molasses. A by-product of the sugar-refining process, molasses contains many useful vitamins and minerals, and adds a noticeable flavor and color to baked goods.

Rice Syrup. Having originated in Japan, this sweetener is made from fermented rice that has been boiled and evaporated, leaving the sweet rice syrup. It has a distinctive flavor.

Sucanat. A fairly new product in this country, Sucanat is made by evaporating the water from sugarcane juice. The result is a pure, natural sweetener.

Turbinado Sugar. When raw sugar crystals are washed with steam in a centrifuge, the result is turbinado sugar—coarse amber crystals with a delicate molasses flavor. Although it is 96 percent sucrose, turbinado sugar is close to being sugar in its natural state. Because it retains much of unrefined sugar's complex chemical structure, turbinado sugar enters the bloodstream slowly, providing a steady supply of energy.

Vanilla Sugar. Vanilla sugar is simply refined white sugar—granulated or confectioners'—that has been permeated with the fragrance of vanilla.

The following table should help you make sweetener substitutions within the recipes in this book. Of course, when making such substitutions, it's important to proceed with caution and common sense. Whenever liquid ingredients are substituted for dry ingredients, or vice versa, adjustments will have to be made to correct the consistency of the finished product. And, of course, while maple syrup may be substituted for honey, for instance, it will considerably change the flavor of the baked goods.

Sweeteners Equal to One Cup Turbinado Sugar
1 ⅞ cups Barley Malt Syrup
1⅛ cups packed Brown Sugar
¾ cup Honey
¾ cup Maple Syrup
¾ cup Molasses
1⅞ cups Rice Syrup
1⅛ cups Sucanat

EGGS AND EGG SUBSTITUTES

Now that we know the dangers of high cholesterol, and we understand the relationship between egg consumption and cholesterol levels, many people have given up eggs entirely, while others have greatly limited the use of eggs. And, of course, there are those who love eggs so much that although they have had to give up the egg, they refuse to give up egg taste and texture, and so have opted for egg substitutes.

In this book, most of the recipes that call for whole eggs also state that an egg substitute may be used. However, in some cases, you will find that only whole eggs or egg whites are listed. In these recipes, the listed ingredient does, in fact, work better than egg substitute. In the recipe for Whole-Grain Spelt Egg Noodles, for instance, eggs work better than egg substitute because of their ability to bind ingredients. Carrot Spelt Torte, too, must be made with whole eggs, as the use of an egg substitute will result in a "flat" torte. In still other recipes—specifically, when egg whites must be beaten until stiff—only natural egg whites are recommended. Unfortunately, egg substitute simply does not whip up like egg whites.

When substituting egg whites or egg substitute for whole eggs, use the following guideline for best results:

1 whole egg = 2 egg whites = $\frac{1}{4}$ cup egg substitute

OTHER INGREDIENTS AND COOKING AIDS

Aside from the ingredients already discussed, a number of other ingredients will prove invaluable whenever you cook with the goal of maximizing both taste and nutrition, whether or not your recipe includes spelt. Of course, most of these ingredients—canola magarine, for instance—are likely to be familiar to you, and can be found in almost any grocery or health foods store. But the following ingredients, which appear in many of the recipes in this book, may be new to you.

Herb Seasoning Salt

Often, a wise use of seasonings can reduce the amount of salt called for in a recipe, or completely eliminate the need for salt. One of the most helpful seasonings of this type is herb seasoning salt. This product—which is available under such names as Herbamare, Spike, and Vegesal—adds flavor with little or no salt. Vegesal contains no salt at all, in fact, but relies entirely on

vegetables and herbs for its flavor. Herbamare and Spike, on the other hand, contain sea salt plus vegetables and herbs.

In my own cooking, I prefer the taste of Herbamare. However, you may wish to try several of the available herb salts, and then choose the one that you and your family like best.

Low-Fat Cheeses and Cheese Substitutes

Fortunately for the health-conscious cook, a wide range of cheeses, from cream cheese to Parmesan to ricotta, is now available in low-fat and nonfat forms. These products allow you to enjoy the taste and texture of cheese while reducing the calories and fat. If you choose to avoid dairy products for any reason, feel free to use soymilk and nutmilk cheeses in any of the recipes in this book. You will find these products in your local health foods store and in some grocery stores.

Low-Fat Milk and Milk Substitutes

Like cheese, milk is now readily available in low-fat and nonfat (skim) forms. Do not hesitate to use the milk of your preference, whether low-fat, no-fat, or full-fat, in the recipes in this book. If you choose to avoid dairy products, look for soymilk and other nondairy milk substitutes in your health foods store.

Nonstick Cooking Spray

Traditionally, baking pans have been greased with butter, oil, or, more recently, margarine. Although a sparing use of low-fat butter or margarine may limit added fat, your best ally in the war against fat is still a nonstick cooking spray such as Pam. These products prevent sticking and allow browning. Better yet, a one-second spray adds an insignificant amount of fat to your dish.

Tamari Soy Sauce

A dark liquid with a rich fragrance and salty taste, soy sauce can enhance the flavor of a variety of dishes. Of the many types available in stores, I usually choose tamari soy sauce, a natural product made of water, whole soybeans, and sea salt. Tamari is quite concentrated, and so should be used sparingly. Look for it in health foods stores, gourmet foods stores, and some grocery stores.

Tofu

Tofu, which is sometimes referred to as bean curd or soybean curd, is a nutritious product made from whole soybeans. Because of its bland taste and ability to absorb the seasonings around it, tofu is a popular ingredient with many cooks, who use it in place of cheese, meat, and a variety of other ingredients. This versatile product is made in a number of consistencies, including extra-firm, firm, soft, and silken. You will find tofu in the refrigerated section of most health foods and grocery stores.

COOKING TECHNIQUES

Most of the recipes in this book require little prior knowledge about cooking. However, to get the best possible results, it's good to keep a few simple techniques and guidelines in mind. The following information should help you get the most from your kitchen adventures.

Altitude Cooking

Altitudes of up to 3,000 feet do not have a great effect on cooking, and even greater altitudes affect only boiling and baking.

Because pressure reduces with increasing altitude, water boils at progressively lower temperatures, making it necessary to either increase the cooking temperature or extend the cooking time. Keep checking the dish until it reaches the desired doneness.

In the case of baking, the lower pressure of high altitudes affects the way certain ingredients perform, and solutions are generally trial-and-error affairs. Generally, as altitude increases, you should progressively reduce the beating time for eggs, decrease the amount of double-acting baking powder used, and increase oven temperatures at the rate of 1°F per 100 feet. As you experiment, be sure to keep records until you find how to get the best results.

Crushing Garlic

Garlic is most easily crushed or mashed using either a mortar and pestle or a garlic press. If neither of these implements is on hand, simply use the tip of a knife to crush the unpeeled clove. Then remove the peel, and chop the garlic as fine as possible.

Making Bread Crumbs

Bread crumbs are used extensively in cooking, so it pays to always have some on hand, particularly if they're made from spelt bread. Whenever your spelt bread turns stale before you can use it up, wrap and freeze it. When you're ready to make the crumbs, thaw the bread, adding fresh bread if the quantity is too small for your needs, and carry out the easy steps that follow.

1. Crisp the spelt bread slices on a baking sheet in a 250°F oven. Do not allow the bread to start browning.
2. For small quantities of bread crumbs, grind the bread with a hand grinder or blender. For large quantities, use a food processor on a "coarse grind" setting.
3. Store the crumbs indefinitely in a container. The container need not be totally airtight, because in an airtight container, bread crumbs may mold if they have not been completely dried.

Measuring Spelt Flour

Measure spelt flour in a flush-rimmed measure that allows you to gauge an even cup. Do not pack the flour into the measure, and do not sift it before measuring. The consistency of spelt flour causes nutritious particles to be left in a sieve after the bulk of the flour has passed through, making sifting inadvisable. If spelt flour needs to be aerated, use your hands to "fluff" it in a bowl.

Measuring Sticky Ingredients

When measuring ingredients such as honey or syrup-based sweeteners, lightly oil the spoon or measuring cup to ensure that the correct quantity of the ingredient flows off the measure. This technique also makes subsequent cleanup far less messy.

Separating Eggs and Beating Egg Whites

If you have never separated egg whites from egg yolks or beaten the whites for use in recipes, you may find the steps that follow helpful.

1. Remove the eggs from the refrigerator, and allow them to reach room temperature.

2. Set out two small bowls and a medium to large bowl with a well-rounded bottom. Then tap the center of an egg firmly on the edge of one of the small bowls to make an even crosswise break. Alternatively, crack the egg with the back of a knife blade.

3. Using both hands, break the egg into two halves over one of the small bowls. Some egg white will drip into the bowl, designating it as the bowl you will use to collect the whites.

4. Carefully pour the egg yolk from one shell half to the other, allowing as much egg white as possible to drip into the bowl. Continue until only the egg yolk is left in a shell half. Do not allow any yolk to get into the bowl.

5. Transfer the egg yolk to the second small bowl. Then repeat for as many additional eggs as called for in the recipe.

6. Transfer the egg whites to the larger bowl. Then, using a wire whisk or a hand-held mixer, beat the egg whites until they form stiff peaks.

The vigor of the beating strokes and the coarseness of the wires of the whisk will determine how much air is trapped in the beaten whites and, therefore, will also determine volume. The best results are obtained by using a whisk made of many thin wires and by beating lightly.

Many professional chefs swear by a copper bowl for this task, and it is a bowl used for nothing else. It is said that using a copper bowl causes the beaten eggs to develop greater volume, which means that they won't quickly collapse. The bowl is 10 or 12 inches in diameter, fully rounded on the bottom, and usually fitted with a ring that you can hold to stop the bowl from spinning as you whisk. Unfortunately, copper bowls tend to be expensive.

Skinning Tomatoes

To skin tomatoes easily, place them in boiling water for one to two minutes. Then remove the tomatoes using a slotted spoon, and either pour cold water over them or plunge them into a bowl of cold water. You will then be able to remove the skin with a sharp knife.

Testing Baked Goods for Doneness

When testing cakes, muffins, breads, and other baked goods for doneness, three means may be used to determine if the dish is ready to be removed from the oven.

A probe, such as a wooden toothpick or a thin bamboo skewer, is an effective means of testing many baked goods. If after insertion the probe is withdrawn clean, the food is done. If particles adhere to the probe, the food requires more cooking.

Color should also be considered when testing for doneness. Most baked goods are done when they take on a rich golden color.

The feel or sound of the cake or bread is also an indication of doneness. When baking bread, the loaf should sound hollow when tapped. When baking a cake, lightly press the top. If it springs back, it is done.

EQUIPMENT

Cooking becomes far more easy and pleasurable when the proper equipment is on hand. I recommend that you stock your kitchen with the following items, which will help you prepare the dishes in this book. Of course, your own cooking preferences should always serve as a guide when outfitting your kitchen.

Power Food Preparation Appliances

There are many power food preparation appliances on the market—blenders, mixers, grinders, slicers, shredders, etc.—and each has its own character and idiosyncrasies. Consider the following products for use in your kitchen.

Blenders. Blenders are ideal for puréeing, chopping, and blending. You'll find a good many high-quality blenders on the market with a wide range of features.

Electric Mixers. Electric mixers may be either hand-held or standing. If you bake only occasionally, a hand-held mixer will probably fill your needs by allowing you to easily beat eggs, whip cream, and blend sauces. If you do a lot of baking, a standing table mixer may prove to be an invaluable appliance.

Food Processors. This appliance chops, beats, minces, shreds, and purées. In addition, most models knead dough and grind. If you do a lot of cooking, a food processor may help speed food preparation. And with so many models on the market, you're sure to find one to fit both your cooking needs and your counter space.

Cookware

The vast amount of cookware available today makes it difficult to be precise about size when writing instructions for a recipe. I have tried to use the most common sizes, but if you do not have what I specify, choose the next bigger size, providing the difference is not too great. Some of the more frequently used items are described in the list that follows, which also specifies common sizes.

Baking Pan. A baking pan has vertical sides varying in height from 3/4 inch upwards, and is used most often for runny batters. The most popular pans are the 9-x-13-x-1-inch and the 16-x-11-x-1-inch sizes.

Baking Sheet. A baking sheet has either very low sides or no sides, and is used for stiff batters and doughs. There are many sizes available, with the 9-x-13-inch and 17-x-14-inch sheets being most common.

Broiler Pan. This pan, usually supplied with the broiler section of a household stove, consists of a rectangular pan and a serrated insert. Sizes suit that of the broiler, with a 14-x-12-inch pan being the most common.

Cake Pan. A cake pan usually has straight sides ranging in height from 1½ to 3 inches. Recipes generally call for 8- or 9-inch pans in square or round shapes, or an 11-x-7-inch rectangular pan.

Casserole Dish. This multi-purpose dish is usually designed so that it can be taken to the table for serving. Sizes vary, ranging from a 2-cup size to 2- and 4-quart dishes.

Cookie Sheet. This versatile sheet is rectangular in shape and has no sides or very low sides. The best cookie sheets are made from two sheets of metal divided by an air cushion. The air in the cushion diffuses the heat so that the bottom of the cookies do not burn. Unfortunately, many cookie sheets do not have this air cushion design. Sizes vary, with 14-x-9½-inch and 16-x-14-inch sheets being the most common.

Crêpe Pan. This special type of skillet has curved sides and a defined bottom that gives the crêpe its sharp edge. If used only for crêpes, and especially if it has a nonstick coating, this pan does not need to be washed after use, but needs only to be wiped clean with a paper towel touched in oil. Sizes range from 5 to 9 inches, with 6- and 7-inch pans being the most common.

Double Boiler. Designed for foods that need protection from heat, a double boiler consists of a pair of saucepans, with the upper one fitting into the lower one so that a space is left between the bottoms of the two pans. The food is placed in the upper pan, and water is placed in the lower pan. The food is then cooked by the heat of the water, rather than by more direct exposure to the heat source.

Griddle. Useful for cooking pancakes, eggs, and similar foods, a griddle is a thick, flat pan with a trough instead of raised sides. Food is cooked on the griddle using no more than a touch of oil. Griddles come in 12- and 14-inch squares, 12- and 14-inch-diameter circles, and 18-x-12-inch rectangles.

Kettle. Also called a Dutch oven, this pot is generally larger than a saucepan and is fitted with two small handles so that the filled pot can be lifted with two hands. The lid is often deeper than a saucepan lid. This pot can be used for many types of cooking, but because of its large size, is most often used for cooking soups and stews and boiling pasta. Sizes range upwards from 4 quarts.

Loaf Pan. Used to make yeast breads and quick breads, most loaf pans measure 9 x 5 x 3 inches, although many other sizes are available. Loaf pans are most often referred to by the weight of the loaf produced by that pan, although this can be complicated by varying bread densities. The standard loaf pan yields a 1-pound loaf.

Muffin Pan. Most muffin pans have either six or twelve wells, each of which has a height of about 1½ inches.

Pie Pan. Whether metal or ceramic, pie pans are round and have sloping sides. Sizes range from 8 to 10 inches in diameter, with sides of 1 or 2 inches in height.

Ramekin Dish. This ceramic baking dish is designed for single servings of about 6 ounces in size.

Saucepan. This versatile pan is used for making sauces, cooking vegetables, and melting margarine and other solids. A saucepan ranges in size from 2 cups to 6 quarts and has a single handle.

Skillet. The word "skillet" is used to describe all types of frying or sauté pans. A skillet has a flat bottom and flared sides, and a single long handle. Common diameter measurements are 8, 10, and 12 inches.

Springform Pan. This round metal pan consists of a round base (similar to a round baking sheet) and a separate continuous side. The side is attached before the pan is filled with batter, and then released after baking. The cake may be served on the base, or may be removed from the base with a spatula or by inverting the finished cake. Sizes range from 6 to 12 inches in diameter.

Steamer. Some specialized steamers allow large quantities of food to be cooked by the direct application of steam. However, most household steaming needs can be satisfied by a round, fan-type, folding metal insert, sometimes known as a steamer basket. The insert, which is placed inside a kettle or large saucepan, has short legs that raise the colander-style body above the water in the pot. Because of the fan-type construction, these steamers fit in most pots and pans.

Now that you are familiar with spelt, and with the equipment and techniques that will make cooking with this delicious grain so rewarding, you are ready to begin using spelt in dishes as diverse as Spelt-Kernel Winter Muesli and Chicken Amandine Casserole. May your venture into the world of spelt be appetizing, healthy, and exciting!

2

Breakfast and Brunch

ookbooks that include a special section on breakfasts sometimes refer to it as "Good Beginnings," and, indeed, a hearty breakfast is a good beginning to the day. After you have spent ten or twelve hours without food, breakfast refuels your body for the morning's activities, and especially if these activities are to be strenuous, breakfast must be nutritious and satisfying. An old proverb suggests that the day should start with a breakfast fit for a king—which is fine, as long as the meal is not full of empty calories. The spelt products used in these recipes will not only provide you with the fuel you need to carry you through the morning, but will also create meals that are truly fit for a king.

The recipes in this chapter have been designed with your busy lifestyle in mind. Most of the dishes can be made ahead of time, so that you can cook them when your schedule permits and refrigerate them until needed. And, of course, any leftovers can be frozen for later reheating.

Because breakfast cereals are great favorites, and are wonderful time-savers as well, this chapter includes recipes for a number of cooked and dry cereals that use plain, toasted, or ground spelt flakes and kernels with delicious results. Hazelnut Granola, made with spelt flakes, is crunchy with nuts and sweet with fruit and maple syrup. Hot Cream of Spelt Bulgur is a stick-to-your-ribs breakfast that will keep you satisfied until lunch. The hearty whole grain flavor of these cereals allows them to stand alone, with few if any toppings needed. But, of course, milk may be added for even more nutrition. And for those who like to moisten their cereals with something other than cow's milk, soy, coconut, almond, and hazelnut milks make excellent substitutes, as does sweet rice nectar (amazake). Or you might want to try my own Sweet Spelt Oat-Milk on your next breakfast cereal, and double the spelt goodness of your meal.

When weekends provide you with a little extra time, you probably like to surprise your family with special breakfast treats such as pancakes topped with honey or maple syrup, or blintzes stuffed with a fruit or cheese filling. Spelt flour—as well as Vita-Spelt Pancake/Muffin Mix, the basis for many recipes found throughout the book—will help you make tempting breakfasts that will win raves from every member of your family.

Perhaps your family prefers waffles to pancakes. My Old-World Buttermilk Waffle recipe has seven variations. The cheese variation is ideal for brunch, while the gingerbread variation is perfect for a cool autumn morning.

The bread recipes presented in this chapter include a wide range of bread-basket treats, from scones to English muffins to biscuits. Served fresh from the oven with the spread of your choice, these breads make a great light breakfast on their own, or can be paired with other spelt dishes for heartier morning fare.

French toast, an all-time favorite of young and old alike, is not forgotten in this book. Vanilla French Toast—a new and healthy version of the dish—is baked in the oven, allowing you time for other morning chores. Apple-and-Spelt Bread Crisp, a splendid way to use up leftover spelt bread, is especially popular with younger children. Muesli Breakfast Bars are not limited to the breakfast menu, but can be packed in lunch boxes and briefcases for healthful snacking throughout the day.

Brunch, a meal that combines breakfast and lunch, may have originated in colonial times, although it was not then called by its present name. For many people in those days, workday breakfasts were eaten very early, with the main meal of the day being served between two and three o'clock. The long interval between the two meals was often filled with a second breakfast, more filling than the first. Now, brunch is a popular Sunday-morning activity, and is a favorite meal for entertaining. Dishes such as Overnight Spinach Breakfast Casserole, Easy Mushroom Soufflé, Sweet Onion and Tofu Quiche, and Seafood Eggs Benedict will be winners with friends and family alike. So go ahead, and delight everyone with these new and delicious spelt creations.

No discussion of breakfast and brunch is complete without at least a brief mention of the egg. For many people, in fact, breakfast isn't breakfast without the ubiquitous egg. Of course, we now know that eggs, though popular and versatile, are also high in cholesterol. Fortunately, in most recipes, egg substitutes and egg whites can be used with good results. In the following recipes, feel free to use a quarter cup of commercial egg substitute or two egg whites for each whole egg.

As you try the recipes that follow, you'll find that spelt makes a delicious and healthful difference in everything from granola to pancakes to waffles to French toast to quiche. And whatever dish you choose, as long as spelt is an ingredient, your family will have all the energy they need to start their day.

Spelt Breakfast Beverages

At breakfast time, the versatility of spelt becomes delightfully apparent. Of course, spelt makes hearty breads, crisp waffles, and crunchy cereals. Surprisingly, though, spelt also makes a delicious milk alternative, as well as a satisfying alternative to coffee. These healthful beverages are not only welcome additions to the breakfast table, but can be enjoyed throughout the day.

Sweet Spelt Oat-Milk

Sweetened with maple syrup, this oat-milk has a delightfully nutty taste.

Yield: 4 cups

½ cup toasted spelt flakes

½ cup rolled oats

8 cups water

2 tablespoons maple syrup

1. Place all the ingredients in a heavy 5-quart kettle, cover, and cook over medium heat for 1 hour.

2. Remove the pot from the heat. Place the pot, still covered, in the refrigerator, and allow to cool overnight.

3. The next day, place the mixture in a blender or food processor, and process on "purée" for 2 minutes, or until the mixture is smooth. Strain the liquid through a large sieve.

4. Use immediately, or place the oat-milk in an airtight container and store in the refrigerator for up to 5 days.

Variations

• For a creamier consistency, thicken the oat-milk by adding ¼ cup of instant nonfat dry milk. Mix well in your blender or food processor.

• Whenever a dessert recipe calls for cream, place 1 cup of the oat-milk, ½ cup of instant nonfat dry milk, and ½ teaspoon of vanilla extract in a blender or food processor, and whip at high speed for about 4 minutes.

• Whenever a soup stock or gravy recipe calls for cream, prepare the cream as explained above, but omit the vanilla. Pour any leftover oat-milk cream into ice-cube trays and freeze. The frozen cubes may be added to hot soups and gravies whenever needed. (They will dissolve instantly in the hot mixture.)

• For delicious ice milk, freeze the oat-milk in an airtight container until it reaches the desired consistency. For a more flavorful ice milk, freeze the oat-milk only partially. Then remove the oat-milk from the freezer, and whip in fresh fruit pieces or berries. Return the mixture to the freezer until it reaches the desired consistency.

Spelt Coffee

Yield: 1 cup spelt coffee kernels

1 cup washed and dried spelt kernels

This alternative to regular coffee is adapted from Dr. Wighard Strehlow's book "The Wonder Food Spelt."

1. Place the kernels in a heavy 8-inch nonstick skillet, and brown over medium heat, stirring frequently. Transfer all but 2 tablespoons of the kernels to a bowl, and continue roasting the remaining kernels until they are very dark in color, but not burned. Remove the kernels, and mix with the lighter brown ones.

2. To make 2 cups of spelt coffee, place 2 cups of water in a 1-quart saucepan, and bring to a boil. Add 3 heaping tablespoons of the roasted kernels, and boil for about 10 minutes, or until the water is brown in color.

3. Strain the brew, reserving the kernels, and serve.

4. Add a few roasted spelt coffee kernels to the old kernels each day, until some kernels start to fall apart. Then discard them and roast a new batch.

Carrot‑Raisin‑Pecan Muesli

Yield: 2 servings

½ cup toasted spelt flakes

½ cup rolled oats

¼ cup barley flakes

½ cup low-fat milk, or almond or soymilk, heated but not boiled

2 tablespoons honey

¼ teaspoon vanilla extract

1 cup coarsely grated carrot or apple

⅓ cup chopped pecans

⅓ cup golden raisins

1 teaspoon fresh lemon juice

Dash ground cinnamon

At the turn of the century, the now famous Dr. R. Bircher-Benner, founder of a health clinic in Zurich, Switzerland, served for breakfast a mixture of oats, apples, and nuts, sweetened with honey. The doctor called his cereal Birchermuesli, naming it after himself. Since then, muesli has become a breakfast favorite in many countries. This recipe and the one that follows illustrate muesli's delicious versatility.

1. Place the spelt flakes, oats, barley flakes, milk, honey, and vanilla in a 1-quart bowl. Mix thoroughly, cover, and refrigerate the mixture overnight.

2. Remove the muesli from the refrigerator, add the carrots or apple, pecans, raisins, lemon juice, and cinnamon, and mix thoroughly.

3. Place equal portions of the cereal in 2 individual serving bowls. Add additional milk and honey or a sprinkling of turbinado sugar if desired, and serve.

Spelt-Kernel Winter Muesli

This satisfying cereal allows you to enjoy fruit throughout the year by taking advantage of the ready supply of dried apricots, papayas, pears, and prunes.

1. Place the kernels in a blender or food processor, and process on "grind" for 2 minutes, or until the kernels are coarsely chopped.

2. Transfer the broken kernels to a 1-quart bowl, add the water and dried fruit, and mix thoroughly. Cover, and allow the mixture to absorb the water overnight at room temperature.

3. Drain off any excess water. Add the lemon juice, honey, yogurt, banana, and almonds, and mix gently.

4. Place equal portions of the muesli in 2 individual serving bowls, top with additional yogurt if desired, and serve.

Yield: 2 servings

¾ cups spelt kernels

¾ cup water

¼ cup chopped dried fruits

¼ cup fresh lemon juice

2 tablespoons honey

¼ cup plain nonfat yogurt

1 banana, peeled and sliced

2 tablespoons chopped almonds

Serving Suggestions

• For added taste and nutrition, top the muesli with ground roasted nuts, such as hazelnuts, pine nuts, cashews, walnuts, pecans, or peanuts.

• For an unusual and equally nutritious topping, try a mixture of finely chopped hulled sunflower, pumpkin, and squash seeds.

Variations

• For a more robust flavor, add freshly grated carrots.

• Take advantage of the summer harvest by substituting fresh berries or other fruits for the dried fruits.

Summer Spelt Cereal

Yield: 4 servings

3 tablespoons canola margarine

2 cups toasted spelt flakes

1/4 cup turbinado sugar (or other sweetener)

1/2 cup chopped walnuts

2 tablespoons toasted wheat germ

4 peaches, peeled and coarsely chopped

4 cups kefir, any flavor*

1/4 cup plain nonfat yogurt

Peaches, sometimes referred to as Persian apples, together with kefir and plain nonfat yogurt, give this cereal a true peaches-and-cream flavor.

1. Place the margarine in a 10-inch skillet, and melt over medium heat. Add the spelt flakes and sugar, and cook the flakes, stirring constantly, for about 3 minutes, or until light brown.

2. Remove the skillet from the heat, and stir in the walnuts and wheat germ.

3. Place equal portions of the mixture in 4 individual serving bowls. Top each bowl with one fourth of the peaches, 1 cup of the kefir, and 1 tablespoon of the yogurt, and serve.

*Kefir, a creamy fermented drink much like yogurt, can be found prepared or in powdered form in health foods stores. When using the powder, stir 2 tablespoons of kefir grains into 4 cups of milk, and allow the mixture to stand overnight at room temperature. When the milk coagulates, it is ready to use.

Cream of Spelt Bulgur

Yield: 4 servings

2 cups low-fat milk (or substitute)

1 cup spelt bulgur

2 tablespoons honey

2 tablespoons dark raisins or chopped dried mixed fruit

TOPPING

1 teaspoon ground cinnamon

1/4 cup turbinado sugar

Cream of Spelt Bulgur is a tasty change from hot oatmeal, and is ideal for schoolchildren on cold winter days.

1. Place the topping ingredients in a small bowl, and mix. Set aside.

2. Place the milk in a 2-quart saucepan, and bring to a boil over medium-high heat, stirring constantly to avoid burning.

3. Remove the pan from heat, and stir in the bulgur, honey, and raisins.

4. Return the pan to the stove, and cook for 4 minutes over medium-low heat, stirring constantly, until the mixture reaches the desired consistency. (If the mixture becomes too thick, add a little more milk.)

5. Place equal portions of the bulgur in 4 individual serving bowls, sprinkle with the topping, and serve.

Serving Suggestion

• For a creamier cereal, top the cooked bulgur with a few tablespoons of milk.

Sesame‑Seed Flapjacks

The chuck wagons that fed lumberjacks in the old West turned out stacks of griddlecakes for the jacks, and the cooks would flip (flap) the cakes on the griddle. And so the name flapjack came into usage.

1. Place the yeast and water in a 1-quart bowl, and allow to stand for 5 minutes at room temperature.

2. Place all the remaining ingredients except the oil in a 2-quart bowl, and mix.

3. Pour the yeast mixture into the flour mixture, and mix well.

4. Grease a 10-inch skillet with 1 tablespoon of the oil, and heat it over medium-high heat. When the oil is hot but not smoking, reduce the heat to medium. Drop the batter onto the pan, using 2 tablespoons for each flapjack. Make sure the flapjacks do not run into each other. (The pan should hold about 6 flapjacks.) When bubbles form on the surface of the flapjacks, turn them with a spatula and brown the other side.

5. Remove the cooked flapjacks from the pan, and keep them warm in the oven until all the flapjacks are cooked. Before starting each new batch, add oil as necessary and allow it to heat before spooning in more batter.

6. Serve hot with the topping of your choice.

Yield: 20 pancakes

1 package dry active yeast

1¼ cups warm water

1 cup whole-grain spelt flour

2 tablespoons blackstrap molasses

⅓ cup ground sesame seeds

¼ cup instant low-fat dry milk

Dash herb seasoning salt

3 tablespoons canola oil

Serving Suggestions

• Top the hot flapjacks with nonfat sour cream or fruit compote.

• Lightly spread canola margarine over the flapjacks and stack them in groups of 3 or 4. Then drizzle maple syrup or honey over the top.

Variation

• For a lighter flapjack, fold a stiffly beaten egg white into the mixture before cooking.

Helpful Hints

• To speed your morning preparation, make the flapjack mixture the night before, cover, and store in the refrigerator until breakfast time.

• Prepare the flapjacks ahead of time, and freeze them in an airtight container. Then thaw and heat the cakes in a conventional, microwave, or toaster oven.

Johnnycakes

Yield: 24 small pancakes

2 cups stone-ground white cornmeal

1 cup white spelt flour

1 tablespoon turbinado sugar (or other sweetener)

1 tablespoon nonaluminum baking powder

½ teaspoon baking soda

Dash sea salt

3½ cups low-fat buttermilk

2 eggs, beaten (or substitute)

¼ cup canola oil

Two different stories have been told to explain the name of these little cakes. One claims that Johnnycakes originated with the Shawnee Indians, and were known to early settlers as Shawnee cakes. The other story claims they were called journey cakes, because travelers in earlier times found them easy to prepare during their long trips. Whichever is true, these light cakes are sure to be a family favorite.

1. Place the cornmeal, flour, sugar, baking powder, baking soda, and salt in a 3-quart bowl, and mix thoroughly. Set aside.

2. Place the buttermilk and eggs in a 2-quart bowl, and mix.

3. Slowly stir the liquid ingredients into the dry ingredients.

4. Grease a 10-inch skillet with 1 tablespoon of the oil, and heat it over medium-high heat. When the oil is hot but not smoking, reduce the heat to medium. Drop scant ¼ cups of the batter onto the pan, and cook until bubbles form on the surface. Turn the cakes with a spatula and brown the other sides.

5. Remove the Johnnycakes from the pan, and keep them warm in the oven until all the cakes are cooked. Before starting each new batch, add oil as necessary and allow it to heat before pouring in more batter.

6. Serve hot with pure maple syrup or the topping of your choice.

Apple-and-Spelt Bread Crisp

Yield: 4 servings

2 tablespoons canola margarine

6 slices spelt bread, cut into ½-inch cubes

2 tablespoons turbinado sugar (or other sweetener)

Dash ground cinnamon

2 apples, peeled, cored, quartered, and sliced thin

This sweet apple dish is a good way to start the day. It is popular with children and wonderfully quick to make.

1. Place the margarine in a 10-inch skillet, and melt over medium-high heat. Add the bread, sugar, and a sprinkling of cinnamon, and cook, stirring frequently, until the bread cubes are crisp.

2. Add the apple slices to the skillet, and continue to cook, mixing thoroughly and turning regularly, until the apples are soft.

3. Transfer the mixture to a serving platter, and sprinkle with additional sugar. Serve hot.

Giant Dutch Pannekoek

A pannekoek—simply a pancake, called by its Dutch name—is very versatile and may wear many hats in culinary creations.

Yield: 6 servings

2 eggs (or substitute)

½ cup whole-grain spelt flour

½ cup low-fat milk (or substitute)

¾ teaspoon herb seasoning salt, divided

1 tablespoon canola margarine

2 tablespoons canola oil

2 medium carrots, peeled and sliced into thin rounds

1 small zucchini, sliced into thin rounds

½ cup sliced pimiento-stuffed green olives

2 teaspoons chopped fresh dill, or ½ teaspoon dried dill

2 teaspoons chopped fresh summer savory, or ½ teaspoon dried summer savory

½ cup grated Gouda cheese, divided

Dill sprigs (garnish)

1. Preheat the oven to 450°F. Heat a heavy 10-inch ovenproof skillet on the lowest oven shelf until the skillet is very hot.

2. Place the eggs, flour, milk, and ¼ teaspoon of the herb seasoning in a 2-quart bowl, and mix. Beat the mixture with a wire whisk for about 3 minutes, or until smooth.

3. Remove the skillet from the oven, and add the margarine. As the margarine melts, tilt the skillet so that it beomes evenly coated with the margarine. Immediately pour in the batter.

4. Place the skillet on the lowest shelf of the oven and bake for 10 minutes. Then reduce the heat to 350°F, and bake for another 10 minutes, or until golden brown. Remove the skillet from the oven and set aside.

5. In another 10-inch skillet, add the canola oil, and place over medium heat. Add the carrots and zucchini, and sauté for about 5 minutes, or until the vegetables are soft.

6. Add the olives, dill, savory, and remaining ½ teaspoon of herb seasoning to the sautéed vegetables. Reduce the heat to low, and stir in half of the cheese. Cook, stirring constantly, for about 2 minutes, or until the cheese melts and coats the vegetables.

7. Set the oven to broil. Spread the vegetable-cheese mixture over the pancake, top with the remaining cheese, and broil for about 2 minutes, or until golden brown.

8. Cut the pancake into 6 wedges, garnish with the dill sprigs, and serve hot.

Serving Suggestions

• Serve the freshly baked pancake as a side dish to accompany an entrée of chicken or fish.

• For a light evening meal, serve the pancake with a green salad and muffins.

• Omit the vegetables and cheese, and top the pancake with chopped fruit or preserves for a delicious dessert.

Old-World Buttermilk Waffles

Yield: 6 waffles

2 cups whole-grain or white spelt flour

2 teaspoons nonaluminum baking powder

Dash sea salt

½ cup melted canola margarine

¼ cup turbinado sugar (or other sweetener)

3 eggs, separated

2 cups low-fat buttermilk

Settlers from Belgium, the Netherlands, and Luxembourg introduced waffles to America, and today it is the custom for descendants of these ethnic groups to give a bride a waffle iron engraved with with her new name and the date of her wedding.

1. Place the flour, baking powder, and salt in a 3-quart bowl, and sift together. Set aside.

2. Place the margarine, sugar, and egg yolks in a 2-quart bowl, and blend with a wire whisk or fork. Add the buttermilk, and continue to blend until the ingredients are thoroughly combined.

3. Pour the liquid mixture into the dry mixture, and mix with a whisk only until the batter is smooth.

4. Beat the egg whites until they are stiff. Spread the whites over the batter, and gently fold them into the batter.

5. Following the manufacturer's instructions, lightly grease your waffle iron. Pour an appropriate amount of batter into the iron, and bake at a moderately hot setting until the iron has stopped steaming and the waffle is crisp and light- to medium-brown. Keep the cooked waffles warm in the oven until all the waffles are done.

6. Serve hot with the topping of your choice.

Serving Suggestions

- Top the waffles with warm applesauce.
- Drizzle maple syrup or another flavored syrup over the waffles.

Variations

- To make Cheese Waffles, follow the basic recipe, but after folding in the beaten egg whites, fold ½ cup of grated Cheddar cheese into the batter.

- To make Carob Drop Waffles, follow the basic recipe, but sprinkle a handful of carob chips over the batter before closing the waffle iron.

- To make Poppy Seed Waffles, follow the basic recipe, but add ¼ cup of poppy seeds to the dry ingredients.

- To make Gingerbread Waffles, follow the basic recipe, but add 1 teaspoon of allspice to the dry ingredients, and mix 2 tablespoons of blackstrap molasses into the liquid ingredients.

• To make Orange Spice Waffles, follow the basic recipe, but add to the dry ingredients 1 tablespoon of freshly grated orange peel, a dash of nutmeg, and a dash of cinnamon. Substitute orange juice for the buttermilk in the liquid ingredients.

• To make Crispy Hazelnut Waffles, follow the basic recipe, but add 1 cup of finely ground hazelnuts to the batter, and mix thoroughly.

• To make Fruited Waffles, follow the basic recipe, but thoroughly mix 1 cup of fresh berries or diced fruit and a tablespoon of vanilla sugar into the final mixture.

Chocolate Spelt Waffles

This Vita-Spelt prize winner came to us from John O. Johnson of Tulsa, Oklahoma. If you don't wish to use chocolate in your waffles, feel free to use carob instead.

Yield: 4 waffles

1¼ cups whole-grain spelt flour

1 tablespoon nonaluminum baking powder

½ teaspoon sea salt

½ cup softened canola margarine

1 cup turbinado sugar (or other sweetener)

2 eggs (or substitute)

2 squares baking chocolate, melted

1 teaspoon vanilla extract

1¼ cups low-fat milk (or substitute)

½ cup chopped black walnuts

1. Place the flour, baking powder, and salt in a 2-quart bowl, and sift together. Set aside.

2. Place the margarine and sugar in a 2-quart bowl, and cream together. Add the eggs to the margarine mixture, and mix thoroughly. Add the melted chocolate and vanilla, and mix once more. Beat in the milk with an electric mixer.

3. Gently fold the flour mixture into the margarine mixture. Add the walnuts, and mix the batter thoroughly.

4. Following the manufacturer's instructions, lightly grease your waffle iron. Pour an appropriate amount of batter into the iron, and bake at a moderately hot setting until the iron has stopped steaming and the waffle is crisp and light- to medium-brown. Keep the cooked waffles warm in the oven until all the waffles are done.

5. Serve hot with the topping of your choice.

Serving Suggestions

• Top the hot waffles with whipped cream.

• Spread cold waffles with softened ice cream to make ice cream sandwiches.

Cheese Blintzes

Yield: 10 blintzes

⅔ cup Vita-Spelt Pancake/Muffin
Mix (or equivalent product)

2 egg whites

⅔ cup low-fat milk (or substitute)

⅓ cup spring water

¼ cup canola oil

FILLING

1½ cups low-fat small-curd
cottage cheese, drained of
excess liquid

1 tablespoon maple syrup

½ teaspoon orange extract

¼ cup golden raisins

½ cup chopped canned
Mandarin oranges, drained

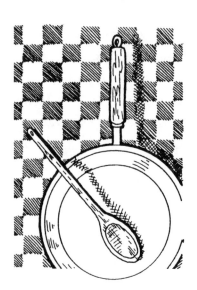

Blintzes, which originated with Jewish cooking, are a form of thin, rolled pancake that can be stuffed with a variety of fillings. But for the Jewish festival of Shavuot, they are usually stuffed with a dairy product such as cheese.

1. Place the pancake mix in a 2-quart bowl. Make a deep well in the mix, and set aside.

2. Place the egg whites, milk, and water in a 1-quart bowl, and quickly combine, using a wire whisk.

3. Pour the egg mixture into the well in the pancake mix, and quickly mix together, again using a wire whisk.

4. Pour about 1 tablespoon of canola oil into an 8-inch skillet, and heat over medium-high heat. Drop 2 to 3 tablespoons of batter into the skillet, and reduce the heat to medium. Tip the skillet to allow the batter to spread over the bottom of the pan. When the bottom of the blintz is brown, turn it with a spatula, and brown the other side.

5. Transfer the cooked blintz to a preheated serving platter, and cover with a clean kitchen towel to keep warm. Before cooking each new blintz, add oil as necessary and allow it to heat before spooning in the batter.

6. In a 2-quart bowl, combine all the filling ingredients. Spread 1 heaping tablespoon of the filling on each blintz, working from the middle outwards to within 1 inch of the edge. Roll each blintz into a log, and serve hot with the topping of your choice.

Serving Suggestion

• Sprinkle each blintz with a little turbinado sugar, or top with a few spoonfuls of flavored nonfat yogurt.

Red Currant Blintzes

When red currants are in season, treat your family to this delightful breakfast dish. These blintzes are spread with red currant preserves before being rolled and topped with a yogurt-honey dressing containing fresh red currants.

1. Place the flour, salt, and baking powder in a 3-quart bowl, and sift together. Make a deep well in the flour mixture, and set aside.

2. Place the eggs, milk, water, and vanilla in a 2-quart bowl, and quickly combine using a wire whisk.

3. Pour the liquid ingredients into the well in the flour mixture, and quickly mix, again using a wire whisk.

4. Pour about 1 tablespoon of the canola oil into an 8-inch skillet, and heat over medium-high heat. Drop 2 to 3 tablespoons of batter onto the skillet, and reduce the heat to medium. Tip the skillet to allow the batter to spread over the bottom of the pan. When the bottom of the blintz is brown, turn it with a spatula, and brown the other side.

5. Transfer the cooked blintz to a preheated serving platter, and cover with a clean kitchen towel to keep warm. Before cooking each new blintz, add oil as necessary and allow it to heat before spooning in the batter.

6. To make the topping, place the fresh currants in a 1-quart bowl, and mash gently with a fork. Add the honey and yogurt, and mix thoroughly.

7. Spread 1 tablespoon of the red currant preserves on each blintz, working from the middle outwards to within 1 inch of the edge. Roll each blintz into a log, and spoon a heaping tablespoon of the topping over each one. Serve hot.

Variations

• Instead of using currant preserves, fill the blintzes with a half-and-half mixture of low-fat cottage cheese and red currant jam.

• For a fast and easy topping, simply sprinkle the blintzes with a little turbinado sugar and cinnamon.

• For a change of pace, use fresh raspberries, cherries, or gooseberries instead of the currants.

Yield: 10 blintzes

⅔ cups whole-grain spelt flour

¼ teaspoon sea salt

1 teaspoon nonaluminum baking powder

2 eggs (or substitute)

⅔ cup low-fat milk (or substitute)

⅓ cup spring water

Few drops vanilla extract

¼ cup canola oil

FILLING

½ cup plus 2 tablespoons red currant preserves

TOPPING

½ cup fresh red currants

2 tablespoons honey

¼ cup plain nonfat yogurt

Herbed Brunch Scones

Yield: 16 wedges

1½ cups whole-grain spelt flour

½ cup yellow cornmeal

¼ cup grated Parmesan cheese

½ teaspoon sea salt

1 tablespoon baking powder

¼ teaspoon freshly ground black pepper

½ cup plain nonfat yogurt

⅓ cup canola oil

2 teaspoons fresh lemon juice

1 egg (or substitute)

½ teaspoon minced fresh garlic

2 tablespoons minced scallions

1 tablespoon chopped fresh basil, or 1 teaspoon dried basil

1 teaspoon chopped fresh oregano, or ½ teaspoon dried oregano

This Vita-Spelt prize-winning recipe was created by Elaine Michura of Chicago, Illinois. Elaine says, "This recipe is fast and tasty, and the scones look great in a cloth-lined basket."

1. Preheat the oven to 375°F.

2. Place the flour, cornmeal, cheese, salt, baking powder, and pepper in a 3-quart bowl, and mix. Set aside.

3. Place the remaining ingredients in a 1-quart bowl, and mix.

4. Add the yogurt mixture to the flour mixture, and thoroughly blend with a fork until a soft dough forms.

5. Place the dough on a lightly floured surface, and knead lightly until the mixture is smooth and elastic. Divide the dough in half, and form each half into a ball. Working with one ball of dough at a time, use a lightly floured rolling pin to roll each ball into a ½-inch-thick circle.

6. Place the dough circles on an ungreased 15-x-11-inch cookie sheet, and, using a knife, lightly score each circle into 8 equal wedges. Bake the dough for 15 to 20 minutes, or until lightly browned.

7. Transfer the scones to a wire rack, cool, and serve with the topping of your choice.

Hazelnut Granola

Yield: 6 to 8 cups

1 cup rolled oats

1 cup toasted spelt flakes

1 cup chopped hazelnuts

½ cup whole-grain spelt flour

⅛ teaspoon ground allspice

Pinch sea salt

½ cup maple syrup

⅓ cup canola oil

1 teaspoon vanilla extract

1 package (6 ounces) chopped dried fruit mix

By making your own granola, rather than buying it in the store, you can be sure of the ingredients, and can even tailor the cereal to suit your tastes by using different fruits and adjusting the flavoring.

1. Preheat the oven to 350°F. Lightly coat a 15-x-11-inch baking sheet with nonstick cooking spray, and set aside.

2. Place all the ingredients except the dried fruit in a 3-quart bowl, and stir until the wet and dry ingredients are well mixed.

3. Spread the mixture on the prepared baking sheet, and bake for about 25 minutes, or until the granola is dark brown but not burned. Use a spatula to turn the granola several times during baking.

4. Remove the baking sheet from the oven, and allow the granola to cool completely at room temperature. Add the fruit, and mix thoroughly.

5. Store the granola at room temperature in zip-type plastic bags or airtight plastic containers until ready to use.

Serving Suggestions

• Top with low-fat milk or a milk substitute before serving.

• Give this delicious granola as a gift, packaged either in a ribbon-tied glass container or a colorful decorated gift box.

• To make a candy treat, simply add peanut butter, mixing thoroughly. Then shape the mixture into round balls, and roll the balls in coconut flakes. Store the coconut-granola balls in an airtight container in the refrigerator.

Vanilla French Toast

This oven-baked toast is very easy to prepare and may be served with a variety of toppings. It is perfect for a lazy Sunday morning breakfast or brunch.

1. Preheat the oven to 400°F.

2. Place the melted margarine in a 9-x-13-inch baking pan. Add the rice syrup and mix thoroughly.

3. Place the cinnamon and sugar in a 1-quart bowl, and mix. Sprinkle the mixture over the margarine and syrup.

4. Place the eggs, juice, vanilla sugar, and salt in a 2-quart bowl, and mix. Dip the bread slices into the egg mixture, thoroughly coating the bread without letting it get soggy. Arrange the slices close together in the prepared pan.

5. Bake for about 12 minutes, without turning, or until the toast has a nice crust. Serve hot with the topping of your choice.

Yield: 6 slices

¼ cup melted canola margarine

2 tablespoons rice syrup

½ teaspoon ground cinnamon

2 tablespoons turbinado sugar (or other sweetener)

3 eggs (or substitute)

½ cup apple juice

1 tablespoon vanilla sugar

Dash sea salt

6 slices spelt bread, sliced about 1 inch thick

Serving Suggestions

• Create a completely new flavor by combining a little vanilla sugar with applesauce, and topping each piece of toast with a heaping tablespoon of the mixture.

• Prepare hot cinnamon syrup by heating ¾ cup of malted barley syrup, 2 tablespoons of water, and ½ teaspoon of cinnamon in a 2-quart saucepan. Drizzle the syrup over the hot toast.

English Spelt Muffins

Yield: 8 to 10 muffins

1 package (¼ ounce) dry active yeast

½ cup warm water

½ cup plain nonfat yogurt

1 teaspoon apple cider vinegar

¼ teaspoon sea salt

½ teaspoon baking soda

½ cup boiling water

3 cups whole-grain spelt flour, divided

¼ cup fine white cornmeal

Because of the combination of vinegar and yogurt, these muffins have a pleasant, slightly sour taste. The taste improves with increased rising time, so when time permits, prepare the dough the evening before and allow it to rise all night. That way, you'll be able to make delicious fresh muffins at breakfast time.

1. Place the yeast and warm water in a deep 1-quart bowl and mix, allowing the yeast to dissolve. Set aside for 5 to 10 minutes.

2. Place the yogurt, vinegar, salt, baking soda, and boiling water in a 3-quart bowl, and mix. Stir in the yeast mixture and 2 cups of the flour. Cover the bowl with a towel, and transfer it to a warm place to allow the dough to double in size. (This will take from 1 to 2 hours, depending on the quality of the yeast and the degree of warmth.)

3. After the dough has doubled, remove it from the bowl and place it on a lightly floured board. Add the remaining flour and knead thoroughly, using more flour as needed until the dough is no longer sticky.

4. Shape the dough into a ball, and place it in a lightly greased 3-quart bowl. Cover with a towel, transfer to a warm place, and allow the dough to rise for an additional 30 minutes.

5. After the dough has risen, punch it down and return it to the floured surface. Using a floured rolling pin, roll the dough into a ½-inch-thick sheet. Using a large cookie cutter or a large drinking glass, cut the dough into circles.

6. Lightly flour a 15-x-11-inch cookie sheet. Dust both sides of the dough-circles with cornmeal, and place them on the prepared sheet. Cover with a towel, and allow the dough to rise for 45 minutes to an hour, or overnight if desired.

7. Lightly coat a heavy 10-inch iron skillet with nonstick cooking spray. Place half of the muffins in the skillet, and cook over medium-high heat for about 10 minutes, or until well browned, turning them once during cooking. Repeat with the remaining muffins.

8. Cool the muffins and split them horizontally using two forks back to back. Toast and serve immediately with the topping of your choice, or refrigerate them in an airtight container for up to 5 days.

Black-Pepper Cheese and Asparagus Quiche

Quiches, with their savory custard fillings, are popular for both brunch and lunch. Usually, though, it's a little difficult to neatly remove wedges of the quiche from the pie pan in which it was baked. This quiche, as well as the one on page 30, is baked in a springform pan with a removable collar, making it far easier to cut and serve.

1. Preheat the oven to 375°F. Lightly coat a 9-inch springform pan with nonstick cooking spray, and set aside.

2. Place all the crust ingredients in a 2-quart mixing bowl and, using a hand mixer, beat until the mixture is well blended. Form the dough into a ball, and place it in the middle of the prepared pan. Press the dough against the pan, forming a crust on the bottom of the pan and about $1\frac{1}{2}$ inches up the sides.

3. Place all the filling ingredients in a 3-quart bowl, and beat with a wire whisk until the eggs and milk are thoroughly blended. Pour the mixture into the crust, and bake for about 45 minutes, or until the egg mixture is firm, and a wooden toothpick inserted in the quiche comes out clean.

4. Allow the quiche to cool at room temperature for 5 minutes. Unclasp the springform collar, and serve the quiche immediately, or cool before serving.

Variation

• Instead of the asparagus, use chopped leek, chopped spinach leaves, freshly steamed green peas, chopped celery, or sliced mushrooms.

Yield: 4 servings

QUICHE CRUST

$\frac{1}{2}$ cup white spelt flour

$\frac{1}{2}$ cup whole-grain spelt flour

$\frac{1}{4}$ cup Vita-Spelt Pancake/Muffin Mix

Dash sea salt

$\frac{1}{4}$ cup canola margarine

$\frac{1}{4}$ cup plus 2 tablespoons water

FILLING

5 eggs (or substitute)

1 cup low-fat milk (or substitute)

2 tablespoons black-pepper cheese (available from grocery store gourmet departments)

6 asparagus stalks, cut into 2-inch pieces

Crunchy Brunchies

Yield: 24 biscuits

1½ cups whole-grain or white spelt flour

½ cup grits

1 tablespoon plus 1 teaspoon nonaluminum baking powder

1 teaspoon sea salt

¼ cup canola margarine

¾ cup grated low-fat Cheddar cheese

½ cup chopped scallions

½ cup low-fat milk (or substitute)

Elizabeth Rainey, the creator of this prize-winning recipe, says, "My biscuits are not only delicious for breakfast, but they freeze really well, and thus can be served with any meal."

1. Preheat the oven to 425°F. Sprinkle an ungreased 16-x-11-inch baking sheet with 1 tablespoon of grits, and set aside.

2. Place the flour, grits, baking powder, and salt in a 3-quart bowl, and mix. Cut the margarine into the flour mixture using a pastry blender or a large fork. Then use a wooden spoon to thoroughly mix the dough.

3. Fold the cheese and scallions into the dough. Add the milk a little at a time, and knead very gently until the dough forms a soft ball.

4. Place the dough on a lightly floured wooden board. Using a lightly floured rolling pin, roll the dough into a 8-x-9-inch rectangle. Use a sharp knife to cut the dough into 24 3-x-1-inch biscuits.

5. Place the biscuits about 1 inch apart on the prepared baking sheet, and bake for 10 to 12 minutes, or until golden brown.

6. Transfer the biscuits to a serving plate, and serve warm with the topping of your choice.

Serving Suggestion

- For a delicious treat, top warm Crunchy Brunchies with honey.

Pennsylvania Spelt-Potato Biscuits

Yield: 12 biscuits

1½ cups white spelt flour

1 tablespoon plus 1½ teaspoons nonaluminum baking powder

Dash sea salt

1 large potato, cooked, peeled, and mashed

¼ cup canola margarine

¼ cup turbinado sugar (or other sweetener)

The Pennsylvania Dutch—in reality, the Pennsylvania Germans—still use many recipes that reflect their ancestral background, which ranges from the Rhine Valley, to the Palatinate section of Germany, to the German-speaking part of Switzerland. This recipe is a version of a Pennsylvania Dutch dish that combines potatoes with flour to make a hearty, versatile dough that is then shaped into biscuits and baked.

1. Preheat the oven to 425°F. Lightly coat a 16-x-11-inch baking sheet with nonstick cooking spray, and set aside.

2. Place the flour, baking powder, and salt in a 2-quart bowl, and sift together. Set aside.

3. Place the potato, margarine, and sugar in a 1-quart bowl, and mix.

4. Cut the potato mixture into the flour mixture using a pastry blender. Mix until the dough is well blended.

5. Place the dough on a lightly floured wooden board, and knead for 1 to 2 minutes, or until the dough is of a pastelike consistency. Using a lightly floured rolling pin, roll the dough into a ½-inch-thick sheet. Using a 2-inch biscuit cutter, cut the dough into 12 biscuits.

6. Place the biscuits about 1 inch apart on the prepared baking sheet, and bake for 12 minutes, or until lightly browned.

7. Transfer the biscuits to a serving plate, and serve warm with the topping of your choice.

Variations

• To make Sweet Potato Biscuits, replace the regular mashed potato with the same amount of mashed sweet potato.

• For variety, cut the dough in half and bake one half as is, making 6 biscuits. Combine the remaining dough with ¼ cup of grated sharp Cheddar cheese, and roll it into a log. Cut the log into 1-inch slices, and bake for about 12 minutes, or until lightly browned.

Helpful Hints

• To speed your final preparation, mix the dough in advance and freeze until needed. To ensure that the dough stays fresh, wrap it first in plastic wrap and then in aluminum foil.

Oven-Baked Tomato and Chive Omelet

In this recipe, the spelt flakes must be well soaked prior to cooking. An overnight soaking will allow you to prepare the breakfast omelet quickly in the morning.

1. Place the eggs, spelt flakes, milk, and chives in a 2-quart bowl, and mix thoroughly with a wire whisk. Cover and place in the refrigerator for at least 2 hours. If possible, refrigerate overnight.

2. Preheat the oven to 350°F.

3. Remove the egg mixture from the refrigerator, add the herb seasoning, and mix.

Yield: 2 servings

4 beaten eggs (or substitute)

¼ cup toasted spelt flakes

¼ cup low-fat milk (or substitute)

1 tablespoon chopped fresh chives

¼ teaspoon herb seasoning salt

1 tablespoon canola margarine

1 large tomato, thinly sliced

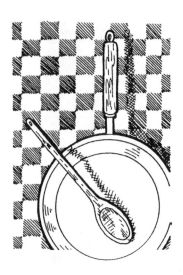

4. Place the margarine in a 10-inch ovenproof skillet, and place over medium-high heat until the margarine is hot. Add the omelet mixture, turn the heat to low, and cook for about 5 minutes. From time to time, lift the edges of the omelet with a spatula to allow the mixture to run to the bottom of the skillet. The surface of the omelet should still be runny.

5. Remove the skillet from the heat, and arrange the tomato slices on top. Place the skillet in the oven, and bake for 5 minutes, or just until the egg mixture is firm. Serve hot.

Serving Suggestion

• Sprinkle freshly grated Parmesan cheese over the tomatoes just before serving.

Variation

• Substitute fresh parsley or dill for the chives.

Sweet Onion and Tofu Quiche

Yield: 4 servings

1 prepared Quiche Crust (page 27)

FILLING

1 tablespoon canola oil

1 medium yellow onion, thinly sliced

½ teaspoon herb seasoning salt

2 tablespoons turbinado sugar

2 tablespoons water

1½ cups mashed tofu

1 cup egg substitute, or 4 eggs

1 tablespoon chopped fresh dill, or 1½ teaspoons dried dill

1 tablespoon chopped fresh chives

Dash paprika

¼ cup low-fat milk (or substitute)

The tofu in this quiche gives it the appearance of a custard pie, and the sugared and browned onions give it a very special flavor.

1. Preheat the oven to 375°F.

2. Place the oil in a 10-inch skillet over medium-heat. Add the onions, and sprinkle the herb seasoning and sugar over the onions. Sauté for about 15 minutes, or until the onions are soft and golden. During the last 5 minutes of cooking, add the 2 tablespoons of water and cover the skillet with a lid. Stir occasionally. Remove the onions from the heat and drain off any excess liquid.

3. Place the tofu in a 2-quart bowl, and add the egg substitute, dill, chives, paprika, and milk. Using a wire whisk, blend all ingredients until the mixture is creamy. Stir the onions into the mixture.

4. Pour the mixture into the crust, and bake for about 40 minutes, or until the egg mixture is firm, and a wooden toothpick inserted in the quiche comes out clean.

5. Allow the quiche to cool at room temperature for 5 minutes. Unclasp the springform collar, and serve the quiche immediately, or cool before serving.

Easy Mushroom Soufflé

The French claim that a soufflé waits for no one, but this delicious egg dish—filled with mushrooms, onions, and bell peppers—can be made the day before it is eaten, and even if one of your guests is not on time, the soufflé will not fall.

1. Lightly spray a deep 15-x-10-inch glass baking dish with nonstick cooking spray. Set aside.

2. Place the margarine in a 10-inch skillet, and melt over medium-high heat. Add the mushrooms, and sauté for about 5 minutes, or until lightly browned.

3. Arrange a third of the bread cubes over the bottom of the prepared baking dish. Top with the cooked mushrooms and the onions, celery, peppers, mayonnaise, and herb seasoning. Sprinkle with the pepper, and cover with another third of the bread cubes.

4. Place the eggs and milk in a 1-quart bowl, and mix. Pour the mixture over the layered ingredients. Cover the dish with aluminum foil, and refrigerate for several hours or overnight.

5. Preheat the oven to 300°F. Evenly spread the soup over the layered ingredients, and top with the remaining bread cubes. Bake uncovered for 50 minutes. Sprinkle the grated cheese over the top, and bake for an additional 10 minutes, or until lightly browned. Serve hot.

Serving Suggestion

• For a beautiful presentation, cut the soufflé into squares and serve over a bed of lettuce, surrounded by freshly cut vegetables such as broccoli, cauliflower, or cherry tomatoes.

Yield: 6 servings

2 tablespoons canola margarine

1 pound mushrooms, coarsely chopped

8 slices spelt bread, crusts removed, buttered, and cut into 1-inch cubes

½ cup chopped yellow onion

½ cup chopped celery

¼ cup chopped green bell pepper

¼ cup chopped red bell pepper

½ cup low-fat mayonnaise (or substitute)

1 teaspoon herb seasoning salt

¼ teaspoon freshly ground white pepper

2 eggs, lightly beaten (or substitute)

1½ cups low-fat milk (or substitute)

1 can undiluted low-fat cream of mushroom soup

½ cup grated mild Cheddar cheese

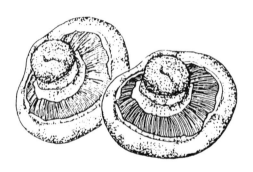
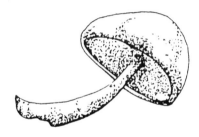

Muesli Breakfast Bars

Yield: 8 bars

1 tablespoon canola margarine

$\frac{1}{2}$ cup toasted spelt flakes

1 tablespoon turbinado sugar (or other sweetener)

$\frac{1}{4}$ teaspoon ground allspice

1 cup whole-grain spelt flour

$\frac{1}{4}$ cup warmed vegetable milk* or low-fat milk

1 level tablespoon dry active yeast

$\frac{1}{4}$ teaspoon sea salt

2 tablespoons yogurt, any flavor

2 tablespoons honey

$\frac{1}{2}$ cup chopped prunes (5 to 6 large prunes)

$\frac{1}{3}$ cup finely ground nuts

$\frac{1}{4}$ cup coarsely chopped hulled sunflower seeds

MILK WASH

2 tablespoons vegetable milk* or low-fat milk

Pinch ground allspice

TOPPING

1 tablespoon ground nuts

1 tablespoon chopped sunflower seeds

*Made from dehydrated vegetables, vegetable milk powder is available from health foods stores under the name Vegelicious. To prepare the milk, you mix the white powder with water.

These bars are perfect for healthful, satisfying breakfasts and nutritious snacks.

1. Place the margarine in an 8-inch skillet, and melt over medium heat. Add the spelt flakes, sugar, and allspice, and cook until lightly browned.

2. Transfer the flakes to a wooden board, and use a rolling pin to crush them into medium-fine granules. Reserve 1 tablespoon of the crushed flakes for the topping. Set aside.

3. Place the flour in a 2-quart bowl, and make a well in the center of the flour.

4. Place the warmed milk in a 1-quart bowl, and add the yeast, salt, yogurt, and honey. Use a fork to thoroughly mix. Pour the mixture into the well in the flour and, using a wooden spoon, quickly work the mixture into a soft ball. Cover the bowl with a clean kitchen towel, and place it in a warm draft-free place for 1 hour.

5. Preheat the oven to 350°F. Spray a 9-x-13-inch baking sheet with nonstick cooking spray, and set aside.

6. Place the prunes and nuts in a 1-quart bowl, and use a fork to separate the pieces. Add this mixture and the sunflower seeds to the dough, and mix well. Set aside.

7. To make the milk wash, place the 2 tablespoons of milk in a 1-quart bowl. Add the allspice, and use a fork to mix well. Set aside.

8. To make the topping, place the topping ingredients and the tablespoon of reserved spelt flakes in a 1-quart bowl, and mix well. Set aside.

9. Divide the dough into 8 equal pieces, and form each piece into a 4-x-1-inch bar. Brush the tops and sides of each bar with the milk mixture. Then sprinkle the wet surfaces with the topping mixture.

10. Place the bars on the prepared baking sheet, and bake for 20 minutes, or until golden brown.

11. Transfer the bars to a rack, and cool completely before serving.

Chicken-Waldorf Salad Cups

This innovative dish is ideal for brunch.

Yield: 8 servings

1. Place all of the salad ingredients except the parsley in a 2-quart bowl. Mix well, cover, and store in the refrigerator until the crêpe cups are prepared.

2. Preheat the oven to 350°F.

3. Place 8 inverted ovenproof custard cups on a 16-x-11-inch baking sheet. Drape and shape 1 crêpe over each inverted cup. Bake for about 25 minutes, or until the crêpes are crisp.

4. Transfer the crêpe cups to individual serving plates. Fill the cups with equal amounts of the chicken salad, sprinkle with the parsley, and serve.

8 prepared Basic Spelt Crêpes (page 148)

CHICKEN-WALDORF SALAD

3 cups cubed cooked chicken breast

½ cup halved seedless grapes

¼ cup coarsely chopped celery

¼ cup minced scallions

¼ cup chopped pecans

½ cup plain nonfat yogurt

¼ cup nonfat mayonnaise (or mayonnaise substitute)

Dash curry powder

Dash dry mustard

2 tablespoons chopped fresh parsley (garnish)

Seafood Eggs Benedict

Basic Spelt Béchamel Sauce adds a gourmet touch to this easy-to-assemble brunch dish.

Yield: 4 servings

1. Cut 1 muffin half into four equal wedges, and arrange in a wheel pattern on a small plate. Place 1 asparagus spear and 1 shrimp on each quarter. Repeat for each muffin half, until 4 individual plates have been prepared. Set aside.

2. Place the prepared sauce in a double boiler, and heat until warm. Add the lemon juice and lemon pepper, and stir. Set aside.

3. To poach the eggs, fill a large shallow pan with enough water to cover the eggs, and bring to a boil over high heat. One at a time, break each egg into a saucer. Create a small whirlpool by swirling the water with a spoon, and drop the egg into the whirlpool. Repeat with the remaining eggs. Reduce the heat until the water reaches a gentle simmer, and cook for 2 to 3 minutes, or until the whites are firm.

2 prepared English Spelt Muffins (page 26), halved

16 freshly steamed asparagus spears

16 cooked shrimp

1 recipe prepared Basic Spelt Béchamel Sauce (page 102)

Juice of ½ lemon

1 tablespoon lemon pepper

4 eggs

4. Place 1 poached egg in the center of each wheel-style arrangement. Spoon 2 to 3 tablespoons of the warm sauce on top of each egg, and serve immediately.

Serving Suggestion

• Serve with a fruit salad topped with chopped nuts.

Variation

• For a change of pace, use fresh crab meat instead of shrimp.

Overnight Spinach Breakfast Casserole

Yield: 6 servings

4 slices toasted spelt bread, cut into $\frac{1}{2}$-inch cubes

2 cups washed and finely chopped fresh spinach leaves

1$\frac{1}{2}$ cups Zesty Ranch Cheese (a combination of grated Monterey Jack and Cheddar cheeses found in most grocery stores)

6 eggs (or substitute)

2 cups low-fat milk (or substitute)

$\frac{1}{2}$ teaspoon dry mustard

Sea salt and white pepper to taste

Young spinach leaves are smaller, more fine-textured, and considerably tastier than large ones. Use the smaller leaves in this dish for a truly special breakfast.

1. Generously coat a 9-x-13-inch glass casserole dish with nonstick cooking spray. Arrange the bread cubes over the bottom of the dish. Spread the spinach over the bread, and sprinkle with the cheese.

2. Place the eggs, milk, and spices in a 3-quart bowl, and beat thoroughly with a wire whisk. Pour the egg mixture over the casserole-dish mixture. Cover the dish with aluminum foil, and refrigerate overnight.

3. Preheat the oven to 350°F. Remove the cover from the dish, and bake for 45 minutes, or just until the egg mixture is firm. Serve hot.

Serving Suggestion

• For a light dinner, serve this casserole as an entrée, accompanied by a green salad.

Variation

• When asparagus are in season, substitute steamed asparagus stalks for the spinach leaves.

3

The Soup and Stew Pot

Savory soups and stews are among the most versatile dishes I know. And when made with spelt, these already healthful dishes become all the more nutritious and tempting.

Soups are, perhaps, the biggest boon to menu planners. They can be the stimulating start of a meal, or, when sufficiently robust and nourishing, they can almost be a meal in themselves. In this chapter, you will find recipes for both types of soup. Parslied Lemon Bulgur Soup, for instance, is a light soup that's perfect to serve before the main course. Turkey Wing Soup With Angel Hair Pasta, on the other hand, is more substantial, and makes a deliciously filling entrée.

Soups are also wonderful dishes for people with busy lifestyles. Most soups can be prepared whenever you have the time, and then refrigerated or even frozen until needed. In fact, you can enhance the flavor of many soups by making them in advance, refrigerating them for up to twenty-four hours, and reheating just before serving.

Although there is a widely held belief that homemade soups cannot be prepared without a meaty

bone in the pot, this chapter's Veggie Stock recipe proves otherwise. And this stock will crop up often in the book, not just in the preparation of soups. Rich in the good things that nature provides, this stock is an excellent substitute for the old bouillon-cube standby. When making your Veggie Stock, whenever possible, use leftover pot liquor—water from vegetables or spelt pasta preparation—instead of water. As an alternative to using homemade stock, use a commercial low-fat, low-sodium vegetable stock. Good ones can be found in most health foods stores.

Although many soups are perfect without any garnish or accompaniments, soup toppings such as croutons can dress up a plain soup or make a light soup more filling. In fact, there are few soups that will not benefit from a topping that is both nourishing and delicious, like the spelt toppings presented in this chapter. Seasoned Spelt Croutons are ideal for consommés; Cheesy Straw Twists or Cracker Balls, for creamed soups; and Oven-Roasted Chili Flakes, for bisques and chowders. Experiment with spelt toppings until you find the ones that best complement your favorite soups.

Of course, even the most robust soup is no match for a stew when you are in the mood for a hearty stick-to-the-ribs meal. Dishes such as Eggplant, Pepper, and Rotini Stew, and White Bean Chili With Elbows, will satisfy the biggest of appetites when accompanied by a green salad and spelt bread or muffins.

Like soups, stews can be made at your leisure and refrigerated or frozen for later use. And like soups, a stew made with fresh vegetables and spelt is as nutritious as it is flavorful and filling.

This chapter offers a variety of soups and stews—delicious dishes that are brimming with the goodness of spelt. I hope that they will encourage you to make soups and stews part of your menu planning.

SOUP STOCKS

Veggie Stock

I created this stock over fifteen years ago, and since then, I have used it successfully in a host of recipes. Feel free to use leftover potato and turnip peelings instead of cut-up potatoes and turnips. You may also use leftover parsley, dill, basil, or rosemary stems instead of the leaves.

1. Combine all of the ingredients in a 5-quart kettle, and bring to a boil over high heat. Reduce the heat to medium-low, cover, and simmer for 2 hours.

2. Remove the pot from the heat, and strain the stock by pouring it through a cheesecloth-lined colander or a large strainer. Discard the solids. Transfer the stock to containers with tight-fitting lids or to ice cube trays, and refrigerate or freeze until needed.

Yield: 2 quarts

8 cups water

4 cups diced, unpeeled, well-scrubbed potatoes and turnips

2 cups chopped carrot greens

2 cups chopped celery stalks and leaves

2 large onions, chopped

4–5 scallion tops, chopped

1 clove garlic, minced

4 whole peppercorns

1 bay leaf

½ cup chopped fresh garden herbs such as parsley, dill, and basil

Chicken Stock

I created this stock to use up chicken parts that are normally discarded, and it has proved to be an excellent standby whenever something more savory than Veggie Stock is needed. This stock is different from most canned stocks in that it is low in sodium and nearly fat-free.

1. Combine all ingredients in a 5-quart kettle, and bring to a boil over high heat. Reduce the heat to medium-low, cover, and simmer for 3 hours.

2. Remove and discard the chicken pieces and vegetables, and cool the stock to room temperature. Place the covered pot in the refrigerator, and chill for 4 hours, or until the fat congeals on the surface of the soup. Skim off and discard the fat.

3. Place the pot over high heat, and cook the stock nearly to the boiling point. Remove the pot from the heat, and strain the stock by pouring it through a cheesecloth-lined colander or a large strainer. Transfer the stock to containers with tight-fitting lids or to ice cube trays, and refrigerate or freeze until needed.

Yield: 2 quarts

8 cups water

3 pounds skinless chicken parts, including bones

2 cups chopped carrot greens

2 cups chopped celery stalks and leaves

2 large onions, chopped

1 turnip, peeled and grated

1 clove garlic, minced

4 whole peppercorns

½ cup chopped fresh parsley and thyme

½-inch piece fresh ginger (optional)

SOUPS

Minestrone

Yield: 6 servings

1 tablespoon canola oil

1 medium yellow onion, chopped

1 clove garlic, minced

2 carrots, peeled and thinly sliced

2 stalks celery, sliced

1 can (28 ounces) Italian stewed
tomatoes

4 cups Veggie Stock (page 37)

2 tablespoons chopped fresh
parsley

2 teaspoons dried basil, or 1
tablespoon plus 1 teaspoon
chopped fresh basil

1 teaspoon dried oregano, or 2
teaspoons chopped fresh
oregano

1 teaspoon herb seasoning salt

¼ teaspoon ground fennel seeds

Pinch freshly ground white pepper

1 can (15 ounces) red kidney
beans, drained

1 cup coarsely shredded fennel

1 medium zucchini, thinly sliced

1 cup spelt small shell pasta

¼ cup grated Parmesan cheese
(garnish)

Minestrone had its humble beginnings in Italy during the Middle Ages. Then, the monks of a monastery near Rome prepared a large kettle of this soup daily to nourish the tired and hungry pilgrims making their way to the holy city. Now, this hearty vegetable soup is a favorite throughout the Western world.

1. Place the oil in a 3-quart kettle over medium heat. Add the onions, garlic, carrots, and celery, and cook, stirring frequently, for about 5 minutes, or until the onions are tender.

2. Add the tomatoes, stock, parsley, basil, oregano, herb seasoning, fennel seeds, and pepper to the pot. Increase the heat to high, and bring the mixture to a boil. Reduce the heat to medium-low, cover, and simmer for 30 minutes, stirring occasionally.

3. Add the kidney beans and fennel, and simmer for 10 minutes. Add the zucchini and pasta, and cook for an additional 10 minutes, or until the pasta is tender.

4. Transfer the soup to 6 soup bowls. Top each serving with a tablespoon of cheese, and serve immediately.

Cabbage and Spelt Soup

Cabbage and spelt kernels make this soup thick and hearty, while the sage gives it a mouth-watering aroma and taste.

Yield: 4 servings

1. Place the margarine in a 3-quart kettle, and melt over medium heat. Add the bacon substitute and onions, and cook, stirring frequently, until the onions are soft.

2. Add the cabbage, salt, pepper, and sage to the kettle, and stir until the cabbage is lightly browned. Add the flour and continue to stir, allowing the flour to coat the cabbage.

3. Add the stock to the kettle. Increase the heat to high and bring to a boil, stirring occasionally. Add the spelt kernels, and reduce the heat to low. Cover the pot, and simmer for 15 minutes.

4. Transfer the soup to 4 large soup bowls, and top each with a tablespoon of grated cheese. Serve immediately.

2 tablespoons canola margarine

1/4 cup no-cholesterol bacon substitute

2 tablespoons minced yellow onion

4 cups thinly sliced green cabbage

1/4 teaspoon sea salt

1/4 teaspoon freshly ground black pepper

1/2 teaspoon dried sage, or 1 teaspoon chopped fresh sage

1 tablespoon white or whole-grain spelt flour

6 cups Chicken Stock (page 37) or Veggie Stock (page 37)

1/2 cup cooked spelt kernels (page 3)

1/4 cup grated Swiss cheese

Parslied Lemon Bulgur Soup

This light, refreshing soup takes only about seven minutes to prepare. The piquant tartness of the lemon enlivens the different flavors, giving this soup its special taste.

Yield: 4 servings

1. Place the water and chicken stock granules in a 2-quart saucepan, and bring to a boil over high heat. Reduce the heat to medium, and stir in the ground bulgur and herb seasoning. Simmer uncovered for 3 minutes, stirring frequently.

2. If desired, place the egg yolk in a large cup, and beat in 2 tablespoons of the hot broth. Using a wire whisk, slowly stir the egg yolk mixture into the soup.

3. Remove the pot from the heat, and stir in the lemon juice and parsley. Transfer the soup to 4 soup bowls, and serve immediately.

4 cups water

1 tablespoon low-fat, low-sodium chicken stock granules

1/2 cup spelt bulgur, ground (page 4)

1/4 teaspoon herb seasoning salt

1 egg yolk, optional (do not use egg substitute)

1/4 cup fresh lemon juice

2 tablespoons chopped fresh parsley

Chick 'n' Pasta Soup

Yield: 8 servings

2 cans (13¾ ounces each) low-sodium chicken broth

3 cups water

1 cup chopped onion

1 cup thinly sliced carrot

1 chicken breast, skinned, boned, and diced

1 teaspoon cumin

1 teaspoon dried coriander

1 cup spelt small shell pasta

1 cup canned whole kernel corn

3 tablespoons lime juice

1 cup diced seeded tomatoes

2 tablespoons chopped fresh cilantro

1 small avocado, peeled and diced

½ cup crushed tortilla chips

½ cup shredded Monterey Jack cheese

This prize-winning recipe came to us from Gloria Bradley of Naperville, Illinois. Gloria says, "This soup is loaded with color and great flavor."

1. Place the broth, water, onions, and carrots in a 3-quart kettle, and bring to a boil over high heat. Reduce the heat to medium-low, cover, and simmer for 15 minutes.

2. Sprinkle the chicken with the cumin and coriander, and add the chicken and pasta shells to the pot. Cover and simmer for about 15 minutes, or until the pasta is tender.

3. Add the corn, lime juice, tomatoes, cilantro, and avocado to the pot, and simmer just until the soup is heated through—no more than a few minutes. Place 1 tablespoon each of tortilla chips and cheese in each of 8 soup bowls, and ladle the soup over the chips and cheese. Serve immediately.

Consommé With Crêpes Julienne

Yield: 4 servings

4 prepared Basic Spelt Crêpes (page 148)

8 cups Veggie Stock (page 37) or Chicken Stock (page 37)

2 tablespoons chopped fresh parsley

This soup can be made in minutes, because all that is needed is hot chicken or vegetable broth and leftover crêpes, which you julienne—cut into long, thin strips.

1. Tightly roll up each crêpe and, using a sharp knife, cut it into julienne strips. Divide the strips among 4 large soup bowls.

2. Place the stock in a 3-quart kettle, and bring to a boil over high heat. Divide the soup among the bowls, pouring the hot soup over the crêpes. Sprinkle each serving with parsley, stir once, and serve immediately.

Spelt Flour and Cheese Soup

Most Americans are unfamiliar with flour and bread soups. These soups, however, are well-loved in many European countries, where the goodness of cheese and whole-grain flour are combined with delicious results.

1. Place the margarine in a 2-quart saucepan, and melt over medium heat. Add the flour, and cook, stirring constantly with a wooden spoon, for about 3 minutes, or until the flour browns.

2. Add the water or stock to the saucepan, and beat the mixture with a wire whisk until smooth. Reduce the heat to low, and add the basil, salt, and pepper. Allow the mixture to simmer uncovered for 30 minutes, stirring occasionally. *Do not boil.*

3. Remove the pot from the heat, and stir the grated cheese into the soup. Transfer the soup to 4 soup bowls, and serve immediately.

Yield: 4 servings

¼ cup canola margarine

½ cup whole-grain spelt flour

5 cups water, Veggie Stock (page 37), or Chicken Stock (page 37)

½ teaspoon dried basil, or 1 teaspoon chopped fresh basil

Sea salt to taste

Freshly ground white pepper to taste

¼ cup grated Parmesan cheese

Variation:

• To make Spelt Flour and Potato Soup, increase the liquid to 6 cups, substitute 2 finely grated potatoes for the cheese, and substitute marjoram for the basil. Sprinkle each serving with chopped parsley.

Toasted Spelt and Vegetable Soup

The unique aroma of toasted spelt flakes is imparted to this vegetable soup.

1. Place the margarine in a 3-quart kettle, and melt over medium heat. Add the onions and spelt flakes, and cook, stirring constantly, until the flakes have browned.

2. Add the carrots, zucchini, and water to the pot. Increase the heat to high, and bring to a boil. Reduce the heat to low, and add the salt, pepper, bouillon cubes, and nutmeg. Cook uncovered for 30 minutes.

3. Transfer the soup to 6 soup bowls. Sprinkle each serving with a little parsley, and serve immediately.

Yield: 6 servings

2 tablespoons canola margarine

1 white onion, finely chopped

1 cup toasted spelt flakes

2 cups grated carrot

2 cups grated zucchini

6 cups water

½ teaspoon sea salt

⅛ teaspoon freshly ground white pepper

2 vegetable bouillon cubes

Pinch ground nutmeg

1 tablespoon chopped fresh parsley

Tomato and Spelt Kernel Soup

Yield: 4 servings

2 tablespoons plus 2 teaspoons canola margarine, divided

1 cup cooked spelt kernels (page 3)

1 teaspoon herb seasoning salt

3 tablespoons canola oil

1 medium white onion, finely chopped

2 stalks celery with leaves, finely chopped

1 tablespoon dried oregano, or 2 tablespoons chopped fresh oregano

1 tablespoon dried basil, or 2 tablespoons chopped fresh basil

1 teaspoon celery seeds

3 cups chopped tomatoes

2 cups water

1 vegetable bouillon cube

½ teaspoon sea salt

⅛ teaspoon freshly ground white pepper

1 cup low-fat milk (or substitute)

2 tablespoons chopped fresh parsley (garnish)

¼ cup grated Parmesan cheese (garnish)

Browned spelt kernels have a savory flavor that blends with the other ingredients, giving this tomato soup an unusually intriguing flavor.

1. Place 2 tablespoons of the margarine in an 8-inch skillet, and melt over medium heat. Add the spelt kernels, and cook, stirring constantly, until the kernels are brown.

2. Sprinkle the herb seasoning over the kernels, and cook for an additional 5 minutes, stirring occasionally. (The kernels will puff slightly, but must not be allowed to burn.) Transfer the kernels to a paper towel to drain and cool.

3. Place the canola oil in a 3-quart kettle. Add the onion and celery, and sauté over medium heat until the vegetables are light brown. Add the oregano, basil, celery seeds, and tomatoes, and reduce the heat to low. Simmer uncovered for 15 minutes, stirring occasionally.

4. Transfer the contents of the kettle to a blender or food processor, in batches if necessary, and process on "purée" until the mixture is smooth and creamy. Return the mixture to the kettle, and add the water and bouillon cube. Increase the heat to high, and bring the mixture to a boil, stirring often. Reduce the heat to low, and allow the mixture to simmer uncovered for 15 minutes, stirring occasionally.

5. Add the reserved kernels and the salt and pepper to the pot, and simmer for 10 minutes. Meanwhile, place the milk and the remaining 2 teaspoons of margarine in a 1-quart saucepan and cook over medium heat, stirring constantly to avoid burning the milk. Cook just until the milk is heated through. *Do not boil.*

6. Turn off the heat under both pots, and stir the milk mixture into the tomato soup mixture. Transfer the soup to 4 soup bowls. Sprinkle each serving with a little parsley and, if desired, 1 tablespoon of cheese. Serve immediately.

Variation

• Use leftover cooked spelt pasta, such as small shells or elbows, instead of the browned spelt kernels.

Gazpacho Con Elote

If you have ever traveled through the West, you are probably familiar with gazpacho. This cold vegetable soup is a culinary gift from Spain, and most Spanish restaurants claim to have the best original recipe. Few, however, serve the soup con elote—with corn. This unusual gazpacho is both colorful and refreshingly different in taste. Serve with toasted spelt bread for a real treat.

1. Combine the tomatoes, green pepper, cucumbers, onion, spelt kernels, and corn kernels in a 3-quart bowl. Set aside.

2. Place the garlic, olive oil, vinegar, wine, basil, and celery seeds in a jar with a tight-fitting lid, and shake well. Drizzle the garlic mixture over the chopped vegetables. Add the herb seasoning and pepper, and mix well. (If the soup seems a little too thick, adjust the consistency with a little cool water.)

3. Cover the soup, and chill for at least 2 hours or overnight. Transfer the soup to 4 bowls, and top each serving with a tablespoon of sour cream and a sprinkling of fresh chives. Serve immediately.

Yield: 4 servings

8 medium tomatoes, peeled, seeded, and chopped

1 large green bell pepper, seeded and chopped

2 small cucumbers, peeled, seeded, and chopped

1 medium yellow onion, chopped

½ cup cooked spelt kernels (page 3)

Kernels from 2 stalks of lightly steamed sweet corn

1 clove garlic, crushed

¼ cup plus 1 tablespoon olive oil

¼ cup apple cider vinegar

¼ cup red wine

1 tablespoon dried basil, or 2 tablespoons chopped fresh basil

1 tablespoon celery seeds

Herb seasoning salt to taste

Freshly ground black pepper to taste

¼ cup nonfat sour cream (garnish)

2 tablespoons chopped fresh chives (garnish)

Turkey Wing Soup With Angel Hair Pasta

Yield: 6 servings

1 turkey wing, cut into 3 sections

1 medium yellow onion, chopped

1 clove garlic, minced

6 cups water

4 carrots, peeled and chopped

2 vegetable bouillon cubes

1 bay leaf

½ teaspoon dried thyme, or 1 teaspoon chopped fresh thyme

½ teaspoon dried rosemary, or 1 teaspoon chopped fresh rosemary

½ teaspoon herb seasoning salt

Pinch freshly ground white pepper

1 cup frozen green peas

4 ounces spelt angel hair pasta

Rich with puréed vegetables and the goodness of turkey, this is a hearty and flavorful soup.

1. Generously spray a nonstick 5-quart kettle with nonstick cooking spray, and place over medium heat. Add the turkey sections, onions, and garlic, and sauté until the onions and turkey are lightly browned, about 5 minutes.

2. Add the water, carrots, bouillon cubes, bay leaf, thyme, rosemary, herb seasoning, and pepper to the pot. Increase the heat to high, and bring the mixture to a boil. Reduce the heat to medium-low, cover, and simmer for 3 hours, stirring occasionally.

3. Remove and discard the bay leaf and turkey sections. Transfer the contents of the kettle to a blender or food processor, in batches if necessary, and process on "purée" until the mixture is smooth and creamy. Return the mixture to the kettle.

4. Turn the heat to medium-high, and add the peas and pasta. Cook for about 5 minutes, or just until the peas and pasta are tender. Transfer the soup to 6 soup bowls, and serve immediately.

STEWS

White Bean Chili With Elbows

Chili con carne is a versatile dish that is popular throughout the United States. In fact, chili is so well loved that nearly everyone claims to have the best or most authentic recipe. This meatless stew, made with spelt elbow pasta and white lima beans, puts a new and healthful spin on the spicy southwestern dish.

1. Place the beans in a 6-cup bowl. Add 4 cups of cold water, cover, and allow to soak overnight at room temperature.

2. Drain the beans, and transfer them to a 2-quart saucepan. Add water until the liquid level is 2 inches above the beans. Add the salt, a few drops of canola oil, and the garlic clove. Cover and cook over medium heat for about 1 hour and 30 minutes, or until the beans are tender. Remove the pot from the heat, and remove and discard the garlic. Set the pot aside.

3. Place the margarine in a 3-quart kettle, and melt over medium heat. Add the onions, and sauté until transparent.

4. Add the flour and chili seasoning to the onions, and stir for a few seconds to mix. Pour the liquid from the beans over the mixture, allowing the beans to remain in the pot. Stir vigorously until the chili mixture is of a thick, smooth consistency.

5. Add the water, tomato sauce, herb seasoning, and pepper to the onion mixture, and bring to a boil. Add the pasta, and continue to boil for 5 minutes, stirring frequently.

6. Reduce the heat to low, and add the beans. Simmer uncovered for about 15 minutes, or until the beans are tender. Transfer the chili to 4 deep plates, and serve immediately.

Serving Suggestion

• For a beautiful presentation, try topping the chili with a heaping tablespoon of guacamole. The bright green of the avocado will contrast strikingly with the white beans, brown pasta, and light-red base of the stew.

Yield: 4 servings

1 cup dried white lima beans, rinsed

1 teaspoon sea salt

Canola oil

1 clove garlic

2 tablespoons canola margarine

1 large white onion, finely minced

2 tablespoons whole-grain spelt flour

1½–2 tablespoons prepared chili seasoning mix

2 cups water

2 cups tomato sauce

½ teaspoon herb seasoning salt

Pinch freshly ground white pepper

1 cup spelt elbow pasta

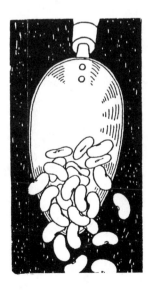

Corn and Okra Stew With Riebles

Yield: 4 servings

8 cups cold water

4 chicken wings

1 teaspoon herb seasoning salt

1 large scallion, chopped

½ teaspoon dried thyme, or 1 teaspoon chopped fresh thyme

2¼ cups fresh or frozen whole kernel corn

2¼ cups chopped fresh or frozen okra

2 tablespoons chopped fresh parsley (garnish)

RIEBLES

1 cup white or whole-grain spelt flour

1 egg (or substitute)

Dash ground nutmeg

Dash herb seasoning salt

Riebles are tiny flour dumplings, and were introduced to us by the Amish people when they settled in Pennsylvania. Each only about the size of a fingernail, the riebles in this recipe are made with spelt flour instead of the usual white flour.

1. To make the riebles dough, place the flour in a 1-quart bowl, and break the egg over the flour. Sprinkle the nutmeg and herb seasoning over the egg. Then, using a fork and starting in the middle, quickly blend the ingredients until they form a lumpy mixture. Using your hands, lightly knead the mixture into a dough, and shape the dough into a smooth round ball.

2. To form the riebles, lightly flour a wooden board, and place a hand-held vegetable or cheese grater that has large holes over the board. Move the dough ball up and down against the grater, allowing the riebles to fall through the holes and onto the board. If the dough becomes too soft to grate, sprinkle both the dough and your hands with flour. Allow the riebles to dry on the board for 2 hours.

3. While the riebles are drying, place the water and chicken wings in a 3-quart kettle, and bring to a boil over high heat. Reduce the heat to medium-low, and add the herb seasoning, scallion, and thyme. Cover and simmer for one hour.

4. Remove the chicken pieces from the stock. If desired, remove the chicken meat from the bones, cut it into strips, and return it to the pot.

5. Increase the heat to high, and bring the stock to a boil. While stirring, slowly add the dried riebles, corn, and okra. Reduce the heat to medium-low, cover, and simmer for 10 minutes.

6. Transfer the stew to 4 deep plates. Sprinkle each serving with a little parsley, and serve immediately.

Eggplant, Pepper, and Rotini Stew

Eggplant holds a prominent place in both Western and Eastern cooking, and is cultivated in a variety of shapes and colors. The popularity of this vegetable is well deserved, as the mild flavor of the eggplant blends well with most seasonings.

Yield: 4 servings

1. Place the oil in a 5-quart kettle over medium heat. Add the onions, garlic, and red pepper, and sauté for about 1 minute. Add the eggplant and basil, and cook, stirring constantly, for about 5 minutes, or until the eggplant browns.

2. Add the stock, herb seasoning, and pepper to the pot. Increase the heat to high, and bring the mixture to a boil. Reduce the heat to low, cover, and allow the mixture to simmer for 25 minutes, stirring occasionally.

3. Increase the heat to medium-high, and add the pasta. Cook for about 8 minutes, or just until the pasta is tender.

4. Reduce the heat to low, and stir the roux cubes into the eggplant mixture to thicken the stew. Transfer the stew to 4 soup bowls, and serve immediately.

2 tablespoons canola oil

1 small onion, chopped

1 clove garlic, finely chopped

1 cup chopped red bell pepper

4 cups cubed unpeeled eggplant

1 tablespoon dried sweet basil, or 2 tablespoons chopped fresh sweet basil

4 cups Chicken Stock (page 37) or Veggie Stock (page 37)

½ teaspoon herb seasoning salt

Pinch freshly ground white pepper

2 cups spelt rotini pasta

2 Spelt Roux cubes (page 100)

Serving Suggestion

• Top each serving of stew with grated Parmesan or Romano cheese, and accompany with Spelt Buns (page 68) or Harvest Spelt Bread (page 67).

Collard, Black-Eyed Pea, and Dumpling Stew

Yield: 4 servings

6 cups water

2 vegetable bouillon cubes

1 cup dried black-eyed peas, rinsed

¼ teaspoon sea salt

¼ teaspoon canola oil (optional)

8 tender collard leaves, with tough stems removed, chopped

1 scallion, chopped

DUMPLINGS

½ cup white spelt flour

½ cup white cornmeal

1 tablespoon nonaluminum baking powder

¼ teaspoon herb seasoning salt

¼ cup canola margarine

1 egg (or substitute)

¼ cup low-fat milk (or substitute)

This stew blends collards, black-eyed peas, and cornmeal—three Southern favorites that create a rich and hearty flavor. In fact, this dish is so satisfying and nutritious that no accompaniments are needed.

1. Place the water and bouillon cubes in a 5-quart kettle, and bring the the mixture to a boil over high heat. Add the peas, salt, and oil. (The oil minimizes foaming while the peas are cooking.) Reduce the heat to medium-low, cover, and simmer for 30 minutes, stirring occasionally.

2. Add the collard greens and scallion to the pot, and simmer for an additional 15 minutes.

3. While the stew is simmering, place the flour, cornmeal, baking powder, and herb seasoning in a 2-quart bowl. Cut the margarine in using a fork or pastry blender. Using both hands, knead the dough until it becomes crumbly. Set aside.

4. Place the egg and milk in a 1-quart bowl, and beat lightly with a fork. Add the egg mixture to the flour mixture, and stir until you have a pasty dough.

5. Turn the dough onto a lightly floured board, and knead until the dough is pliable and no longer feels crumbly. Shape the dough into a 12-inch log, and use a sharp knife to cut the log into 1-inch pieces.

6. Place the dough pieces in a vegetable steamer set over boiling water. Cover the pot, and steam the dumplings over high heat for about 15 minutes, or until the dumplings are cooked through.

7. Add the dumplings to the stew. Transfer the stew to 4 soup bowls, and serve immediately.

Serving Suggestion

• Ladle the stew into large, deep bowls, and arrange several dumplings in the center of each serving. Top the dumplings with a dollop of nonfat sour cream, sprinkle with chopped parsley, and serve.

SOUP TOPPINGS

Seasoned Spelt Croutons

Bread made from Vita-Spelt Whole Grain Bread Mix gives these croutons a nutty, full-bodied flavor. But any leftover spelt bread or buns will yield delicious croutons.

1. Preheat the oven to 200°F. Combine the margarine, garlic, herb seasoning, paprika, parsley, basil, and thyme in a 1-quart bowl, and cream the mixture thoroughly using the back of a soup spoon. Stir in the cheese.

2. Spread one side of each bread slice with the margarine mixture. Then, placing the spread sides of the bread together, make 5 stacks of bread, 2 slices to a stack. Using a sharp knife, cut the stacks into ¼-inch-wide strips. Cut each strip into ¼-inch pieces.

3. Place the oil in a 10-inch ovenproof skillet over medium heat. Add the bread cubes, and cook, stirring constantly, for 2 to 3 minutes, or until the croutons are lightly browned. Place the skillet in the oven, and bake for 12 to 15 minutes, or until the croutons are crisp and completely dried out, but not burned.

4. Spread the croutons on a paper towel, and cool to room temperature. Serve immediately, or store in an airtight container in the refrigerator for up to 7 days.

Yield: 4 cups

¼ cup canola margarine

1 small clove garlic, minced

¼ teaspoon herb seasoning salt

¼ teaspoon paprika

1 teaspoon dried parsley, or 2 teaspoons chopped fresh parsley

¼ teaspoon dried basil, or ½ teaspoon chopped fresh basil

Pinch ground thyme

¼ cup finely grated Parmesan cheese

10 slices spelt bread, crusts removed

2 tablespoons sunflower oil

Oven-Roasted Chili Flakes

These flakes add a spicy crunch to soups and stews.

1. Preheat the oven to 350°F.

2. Place the spelt flakes and chili powder in a 1-quart bowl, and mix well. Add the oil, and mix again to coat.

3. Spread the mixture evenly over a 15-x-11-inch baking sheet, and bake, turning the flakes every 5 minutes, for 15 minutes, or until the flakes are crisp. Use immediately, or cool to room temperature and store in an airtight container in the refrigerator for up to 7 days.

Yield: 1 cup

1 cup toasted spelt flakes

1 teaspoon chili powder

2 tablespoons canola oil

Cracker Balls

Yield: 36 to 40 balls

¾ cup whole-grain spelt flour

1 heaping tablespoon potato starch

½ cup water

2 tablespoons canola margarine

Dash sea salt

¼ teaspoon herb seasoning salt

3 egg yolks, beaten

¼ teaspoon nonaluminum baking powder

Nutritious Cracker Balls are delightful in both clear and creamy soups. The versatile Cracker Ball dough can also be used to make small dumplings.

1. Preheat the oven to 350°F. Spray a 16-x-14-inch cookie sheet with nonstick cooking spray, and sprinkle with spelt flour, finely ground spelt flakes, or spelt bread crumbs. Set aside.

2. Combine the flour and potato starch in a 1-quart bowl. Set aside.

3. Place the water, margarine, salt, and herb seasoning in a 1-quart saucepan, and bring to a boil over medium-high heat. Remove the pan from the heat, and pour the sifted mixture into the saucepan all at once. Working fast, use a wooden spoon to stir the mixture together until a round, smooth ball of dough is formed.

4. Place the saucepan over medium heat, and continue stirring for barely 60 seconds, when a thin skin should form on the bottom of the pan. Immediately transfer the dough to a deep 1-quart bowl.

5. Add the egg yolks to the dough one at a time, stirring the dough hard until it becomes shiny but still soft. When the dough is almost cool, add the baking powder and mix well.

6. Using a teaspoon, cut a small amount of dough about the size of a thumb nail, and place it on the prepared cookie sheet. Repeat with the remaining dough, spacing the pieces 1 inch apart.

7. Bake the dough for 7 to 10 minutes, or until the balls begin to brown. Do not open the oven until they have puffed and browned on top, or they will collapse. Cool to room temperature, and use immediately or store in an airtight container in the refrigerator for up to 7 days.

Variations

• For a more professional appearance, place the dough in a pastry bag with a decorative nozzle, and pipe the dough onto a cookie sheet to create different shapes.

• To make soup dumplings, mix 1 tablespoon of finely chopped parsley into the dough, and drop tablespoons of the dough into boiling broth. Reduce the heat to medium-low, and simmer uncovered for 10 minutes.

• Use a pastry bag to make spiral shapes with a 1½-inch-wide base. After they have baked and puffed, cut each puff in half, and fill the bottom with a savory mixture such as Blue Cheese and Avocado Spread (page 94). Replace the top, and serve.

Cheesy Straw Twists

These twists are ideal accompaniments to creamy soups. Although best when freshly baked, the twists may be made ahead and stored in the refrigerator until needed.

1. Preheat the oven to 350°F. Combine the flour, salt, and baking soda in a 2-quart bowl. Cut the margarine into the flour mixture with a pastry blender or fork until the mixture resembles coarse meal. Add the cheese, and blend the mixture with a fork until well mixed.

2. Stir the dough with a fork as you add the water 1 tablespoon at a time. Continue to stir until the mixture no longer sticks to the sides of the bowl. Turn the mixture onto a floured board, and gently knead into a soft dough.

3. Using your hands, roll a heaping tablespoon of dough into a 6-inch rope. Cut the rope in half, and twist the two pieces together, forming a twisted stick. Place the twist on an 17-x-14-inch baking sheet. Repeat with the remaining dough, spacing the straws 2 inches apart in 3 rows.

4. Place the egg and milk in a 1-quart bowl, and beat lightly with a fork. Using a pastry brush, lightly coat each straw with the egg glaze. Sprinkle each straw with a small amount of caraway seeds.

5. Bake the straws for 15 to 20 minutes, or until the twists are browned. Transfer the straws to a wire rack, and cool to room temperature. Serve immediately, or store in an airtight container in the refrigerator for up to 7 days.

Yield: 18 to 20 pieces

2 cups whole-grain or white spelt flour

¼ teaspoon sea salt

¼ teaspoon baking soda

¼ cup canola margarine

1 cup finely grated sharp Cheddar cheese

⅓ cup water

1 egg (or substitute)

¼ cup low-fat milk (or substitute)

2 tablespoons finely chopped caraway seeds

4

The Salad Bowl

The salad is not by any means a twentieth century phenomenon. Salads were first eaten during the time of the Roman Empire in the form of herbs and other greens. Salt was the only dressing used in those days. In fact, the word *salad* comes from the Latin word *sal*, meaning "salt."

Today, salads include virtually every type of food, as reflected by the recipes in this chapter. Wilted Spinach Salad With Chili Flakes uses fresh greens as its base, Fresh Green Bean Bulgur Salad includes vegetables, Sweet and Sour Spelt Salad boasts two types of fruit, and Chef's Salad With Spelt Croutons is made robust by the addition of cheese and chicken. Of course, each of these salads is enhanced by spelt, whether in the form of spelt bread, spelt pasta, spelt sprouts, spelt bulgur, spelt kernels, or spelt flakes. These spelt products add new flavor to the salads, and make them more satisfying and nutritious as well.

Whenever a recipe calls for spelt sprouts, you can grow the sprouts yourself in a matter of days. A few tablespoons of spelt kernels will produce a handy crop of green shoots when sprouted in a jar or, even better, a shallow dish. Just line the dish with a folded paper towel. Then sprinkle the kernels over the towel, and add just enough water to soak the paper. Wet the towel each day until the sprouts are ready to eat. Usually, you can expect to harvest the sprouts in three to five days. When you use spelt sprouts, do so sparingly because their flavor is strong. Just a little goes a long way.

A few of the recipes in this chapter use spelt pasta in the form of elbows or spaghetti. Pasta is a wonderful base for salads, and often makes the dish substantial enough to serve as a light entrée. When cooking pasta for a salad, you might want to add a quarter-teaspoon of vegetable oil to the cooking water to prevent the pasta pieces from sticking to each other and to the pot. Cook the pasta until just al dente—firm to the tooth—and drain it well. Then rinse it under cool running water to remove any excess starch, and drain again.

When planning a menu that includes a salad, bear in mind that if the salad is not the main dish, it should complement, rather than compete with, your entrée and any accompanying dishes. You might want to match a tart salad with a heavy entrée, for instance, or use a slaw when serving sandwiches and other casual fare. Elaborate aspics, such as the Spelt Kernel Waldorf, are perfect for buffets, where they are shown off to best advantage. And composed salads, such as Moroccan Pasta Salad, make wonderful luncheon dishes.

When preparing your salads, be sure to use the freshest ingredients possible—crisp lettuce, firm ripe tomatoes, and bright crunchy carrots, for instance. This alone will boost vitamin content, enhance presentation, and maximize taste. Also consider eye appeal when cutting up ingredients. You might want to slice bell peppers into rings, perhaps, or score cucumbers with the tines of a fork before slicing them. Keep your use of

herbs, onions, and other strongly flavored ingredients in rein to prevent them from taking over your salad. Finally, match your dressing to the piquancy of the ingredients. Bitter greens, for instance, need stronger dressings, while delicate butterhead lettuce requires a lighter dressing.

Whether a tempting appetizer, a between-courses palate cleanser, a colorful side dish, or a light entrée, the salad adds a pleasing dimension to dining. Certainly, in this age of fitness and healthier eating, the versatile salad is a welcome dish—especially when high-nutrient spelt is one of the ingredients. This chapter will hopefully be just the start of your experimentation with salads. With the many salad ingredients available and a little creativity, you can make the healthful salad an important and delicious part of many memorable meals.

Chef's Salad With Spelt Croutons

Legend has it that the first chef's salad was prepared at the turn of the century by Chef L. Diat of New York's Ritz-Carlton. Diat's salad was unique for the flavor imparted by smoked meats. This chef's salad is unique for the flavor imparted by spelt croutons, which have a distinctive nutty taste as well as a delightful crunch.

1. To make the croutons, place the margarine in a 10-inch skillet, and melt over medium heat. Add the bread cubes, and allow them to brown, stirring frequently and turning once or twice with a spatula. Transfer the croutons to a paper towel to drain and cool.

2. To prepare the dressing, place all of the dressing ingredients in a blender or food processor, and process on "blend" until the parsley is finely chopped. Set aside.

3. Make a bed of the lettuce and cabbage on each of 4 large, deep plates. Divide the pepper and onion rings among the plates, and spread over the lettuce. Sprinkle with the cucumbers and beans. Evenly space 4 tomato halves around the rim of each plate, and heap the cheese and, if desired, the chicken in the center.

4. Spoon 2 to 3 tablespoons of dressing over each serving, and garnish with the croutons. Serve, placing the remaining dressing in a bowl so that guests can add more if desired.

Yield: 4 servings

1 head leaf lettuce, washed and torn into bite-sized pieces

¼ cup finely shredded green cabbage

¼ cup finely shredded red cabbage

½ red bell pepper, sliced into thin rings

½ green bell pepper, sliced into thin rings

½ white onion, sliced into thin rings

½ medium cucumber, peeled and diced

¼ cup canned kidney beans, rinsed

¼ cup finely diced cooked green beans

8 cherry tomatoes, halved

½ cup diced low-fat Swiss cheese

½ cup diced cooked chicken (optional)

DRESSING

½ cup canola oil

2 tablespoons apple cider vinegar

Juice of 1 lemon

1 teaspoon turbinado sugar (or other sweetener)

¼ cup chopped fresh parsley

¼ teaspoon dried basil, or ½ teaspoon chopped fresh basil

½ teaspoon sea salt

Dash freshly ground white pepper

CROUTONS

2 tablespoons canola margarine

4 slices spelt bread, crusts removed, cubed

Spelt-Buckwheat Coleslaw

Yield: 4 servings

2½-ounces spelt buckwheat spaghetti

2 cups finely shredded green cabbage

¼ teaspoon caraway seeds

1 cup boiling water

1 medium carrot, peeled and grated

2 tablespoons chopped fresh chives

¼ teaspoon herb seasoning salt

⅛ teaspoon freshly ground white pepper

2 tablespoons fresh lemon juice

2 tablespoons plain nonfat yogurt

2 tablespoons nonfat mayonnaise

This colorful slaw combines dark noodles with green cabbage and orange carrots.

1. Cook the buckwheat spaghetti until al dente according to package directions. Drain well, rinse under cool running water, and drain again. Set aside.

2. Place the cabbage in a 2-quart heatproof bowl, and sprinkle with the caraway seeds. Pour the boiling water over the cabbage, and allow to sit for 5 minutes.

3. Pour the cabbage mixture into a colander, and drain thoroughly. Return the cabbage to the bowl, add the cooked noodles, and toss to mix. Add the carrot, chives, salt, pepper, lemon juice, yogurt, and mayonnaise, mixing well after each addition.

4. Cover the bowl, and chill for at least 2 hours before serving.

Chinese Cabbage and Caraway Salad

Yield: 4 servings

¼ cup plus 2 tablespoons canola oil, divided

¼ cup minced white onion

½ teaspoon caraway seeds

½ teaspoon turbinado sugar (or other sweetener)

4 cups chopped Chinese cabbage

1 teaspoon sea salt

¼ teaspoon freshly ground white pepper

2–3 tablespoons apple cider vinegar

1 tablespoon freshly chopped spelt sprouts (page 53)

Chinese cabbage is growing in popularity in this country, with bok choy, pak choy, bok choy sum, and Napa cabbage available in many grocery stores. Chinese cabbage may have tight heads or flowery ones, but should never have ragged or bruised leaves. For this recipe, you may use any type of Chinese cabbage. Freshly chopped spelt sprouts give the dressing a sharp wild-grass taste, and only about a tablespoon is needed.

1. Place 2 tablespoons of the oil in a 10-inch skillet over medium heat. Add the onions, caraway seeds, and sugar, and sauté until the onions are golden.

2. Place the cabbage in a 2-quart bowl, and pour the onion mixture over the cabbage. Add the salt, pepper, vinegar, remaining ¼ cup of oil, and sprouts, and mix well.

3. Cover the bowl, and allow the flavors to blend at room temperature for 1 hour, adjusting the seasoning as necessary. (Apple cider vinegar brands vary in strength.) Serve at room temperature.

Moroccan Pasta Salad

This delightfully different salad was created by prize winner Gail Dean of St. Augustine, Florida. Gail says, "Treat yourselves and experience a taste of Mediterranean cuisine."

1. Cook the pasta until al dente according to package directions. Drain well, rinse under cool running water, and drain again. Set aside.

2. To prepare the dressing, place all of the dressing ingredients in a 1-quart bowl, and mix thoroughly with a wire whisk. Set aside.

3. Transfer the pasta to a 3-quart bowl, and add the raisins, scallions, peppers, and parsley. Toss to mix. Add the salad dressing, and stir gently to mix. Cover the bowl, and chill for at least 1 hour or until cold.

4. Place 1 spinach or lettuce leaf on each of 4 dinner plates. Arrange 4 orange segments on each plate, equally spacing them around the edges of the plate. Mound one fourth of the pasta in the center of each plate, leaving part of the orange segments visible. Garnish each mound of pasta with pine nuts and mint leaves, and serve.

Yield: 4 servings

5 ounces spelt small shell or elbow pasta

½ cup golden raisins

½ cup chopped scallions

¼ cup chopped red bell pepper

¼ cup chopped green bell pepper

¼ cup chopped yellow bell pepper

¼ cup chopped fresh parsley

4 large spinach or romaine lettuce leaves

16 orange segments

2 tablespoons pine nuts (garnish)

Whole mint leaves (garnish)

DRESSING

1 cup plain low-fat or nonfat yogurt

1 tablespoon plus 1½ teaspoons orange juice

2 teaspoons grated fresh orange peel

1 teaspoon minced fresh mint leaves

½ teaspoon ground cinnamon

½ teaspoon sea salt

½ teaspoon freshly ground black pepper

½ teaspoon turbinado sugar (or other sweetener)

¼ teaspoon ground cumin

¼ teaspoon garlic powder

Marinated Pasta and Vegetables

Yield: 4 servings

1 cup spelt elbow pasta

1 small head broccoli, cut into bite-sized pieces

5 cauliflower florets

¼ cup chopped red onion

2 tablespoons chopped fresh parsley

⅓ cup chopped pimiento

⅓ cup grated low-fat Parmesan cheese

MARINADE

½ cup canola oil

½ cup red wine vinegar

½ cup ketchup

½ teaspoon paprika

½ teaspoon dry mustard

½ teaspoon dried oregano

Prize winner Josie Clapper of Meeker, Colorado, created this special salad. Josie says, "This salad is best when it is marinated for at least two hours." Josie also advises that any tasty vegetable combination will work beautifully in this recipe.

1. Cook the pasta until al dente according to package directions. Drain well, rinse under cool running water, and drain again. Set aside.

2. To make the marinade, place all of the marinade ingredients in a 1-quart bowl, and blend well. Set aside.

3. Place the broccoli, cauliflower, onion, parsley, pimiento, and cheese in a 3-quart bowl, and toss to mix. Add the marinade, and toss well. Fold in the pasta, and toss well.

4. Cover the bowl, and chill for at least 2 hours before serving.

Spelt Kernel Waldorf

Yield: 4 servings

½ cup white wine

1 package unflavored gelatin

1½ cups boiling water

1 cup cooked spelt kernels (page 3)

½ cup halved seedless green grapes

½ cup chopped celery

½ cup diced peeled apple

¼ cup chopped walnuts or pecans

5–6 small bunches grapes (garnish)

Waldorf Salad was named after New York's Waldorf-Astoria hotel, where it was first served. In Spelt Kernel Waldorf, you will find hidden in the aspic all of the ingredients for a traditional Waldorf Salad, plus healthful spelt kernels.

1. Place the wine in a heatproof 1-quart bowl, and sprinkle the gelatin over the top. Allow the mixture to sit for 1 minute. Add the boiling water, stir, and allow the mixture to sit for 10 minutes.

2. Add all of the remaining ingredients, except for the garnish, to the wine mixture, and mix well. Pour the mixture into a 1-quart decorative mold. Cover and chill for 4 hours, or until the gelatin is firm.

3. To unmold the salad, place the inverted mold in the center of a platter. Soak a kitchen towel in hot water, and carefully wring it out so that it is damp, but not wet. Wrap the towel around the mold, and lift the mold just clear of the platter. The molded salad will fall out as soon as the heat penetrates the sides of the mold. Garnish the mold with the grape clusters, and serve immediately.

Sweet and Sour Spelt Salad

The ingredients in this recipe are not only colorful, but have been chosen to enhance and complement one another's flavors.

1. Place the spelt kernels in a 1-quart bowl, and add enough water to cover. Cover the bowl, and allow to soak overnight at room temperature.

2. Drain the kernels in a colander, and rinse under cool running water. Transfer the kernels to a 1-quart saucepan, and add the honey and cinnamon. Cover the kernels with water, and bring to a boil over high heat. Reduce the heat to low, cover, and simmer for 45 minutes, or until the kernels are soft, stirring frequently and adding more water if necessary.

3. Remove the kernels from the heat, transfer to a colander, and drain well. Transfer the drained kernels to a 2-quart bowl, and allow to cool completely.

4. Add the raisins, pineapple, carrots, scallions, ginger, allspice, vinegar, and pineapple juice to the cooled kernels. Toss the mixture to blend, and serve.

Yield: 4 servings

½ cup spelt kernels
1 tablespoon honey
¼ teaspoon ground cinnamon
¼ cup dark raisins
½ cup diced canned pineapple, drained
1 cup peeled and grated carrots
1 tablespoon finely chopped scallions
⅛ teaspoon ground ginger
Pinch allspice
1 tablespoon apple cider vinegar
¼ cup pineapple juice

Fresh Green Bean Bulgur Salad

The Middle Eastern dish tabouli, a salad made with bulgur wheat, has enjoyed a surge of popularity in the last decade or so because of its whole-grain goodness. Spelt bulgur is even higher in nutrients, and in this salad is coupled with green beans, making this dish a healthful and delicious choice.

1. Place the green beans in a steamer, and cook over simmering water for about 3 minutes, or just until tender. Set aside to cool.

2. Place the bulgur in a heatproof 2-quart bowl, and pour the boiling water over the bulgur. Set aside for 5 minutes.

3. Add the green beans, scallions, lemon juice and peel, oil, and parsley to the bulgur, and mix well. Cover the bowl, and chill for at least 2 hours.

4. To serve, arrange lettuce leaves around the edge of a serving platter, and spoon the salad into the center. Surround the salad with cherry tomatoes, Greek olives, and chunks of feta cheese, and serve.

Yield: 4 servings

2 cups fresh green beans cut into ¼-inch slices
1 cup spelt bulgur
1½ cups boiling water
2 scallions, chopped
¼ cup plus 2 tablespoons fresh lemon juice
1 teaspoon grated fresh lemon peel
2 tablespoons canola oil
2 tablespoons chopped fresh parsley
10 lettuce leaves (garnish)
8 cherry tomatoes (garnish)
12 Greek olives (garnish)
8 chunks (1-inch each) feta cheese (garnish)

Spelt Walnut Summer Salad

Yield: 6 servings

1 cup spelt kernels

2 tablespoons canola margarine

3 cups water

1½ cups chopped walnuts

½ green bell pepper, cut into 1-inch slivers

1 carrot, peeled and shredded

2 stalks celery, chopped

DRESSING

3 tablespoons walnut oil

¼ cup rice wine vinegar

¼ cup minced fresh parsley

1 tablespoon turbinado sugar (or other sweetener)

½ teaspoon sea salt

Jean Meyer of Gahanna, Ohio, created this prize-winning recipe. Jean says that when stored in a refrigerated airtight container, this crunchy salad will keep for five to seven days.

1. Preheat the oven to 350°F. Place the spelt kernels, margarine, and water in a 2-quart saucepan. Cover, and bring to a boil over high heat. Reduce the heat to low, and allow the kernels to simmer for 1 hour.

2. While the spelt is cooking, half fill a 1-quart saucepan with water, and bring to a boil over high heat. Add the walnuts, and boil for 2 minutes. Drain the nuts in a colander, and spread them on paper towels to dry.

3. Arrange the dry walnuts on a 17-x-14-inch cookie sheet, and toast them in the preheated oven for 20 to 30 minutes, turning them several times. When done, the walnuts should be a deep golden brown. Remove the nuts from the oven, and set aside to cool.

4. To make the dressing, combine all of the dressing ingredients in a 1-quart bowl. Set aside.

5. Drain the cooked kernels in a colander, rinse under cool running water, and drain again. Transfer the kernels to a 3-quart bowl. Add the green pepper, carrot, celery, and dressing, and toss until the ingredients are well coated. Fold in the reserved walnuts.

6. Cover the bowl, and chill for at least 2 hours before serving.

Spelt Kernel and Feta Cheese Salad

The prize-winning recipe for this distinctly Greek salad comes to us from Linda P. Harkless of Cleveland, Ohio.

Yield: 6 servings

1 cup spelt kernels

2½ cups water

1 cup chopped fresh parsley

4 scallions, finely chopped

4 cloves garlic, minced

2 teaspoons chopped fresh mint

¼ cup crumbled feta cheese

¼ cup chopped black olives

2 tablespoons currants

3 tablespoons fresh lemon juice

3 tablespoons olive oil

Sea salt and black pepper to taste

2 cups shredded lettuce (garnish)

8 cherry tomatoes (garnish)

1. Place the spelt kernels in a blender or food processor, and process at low speed for a few seconds, or until the kernels have broken into pieces. The consistency should be that of medium bulgur.

2. Place the water in a 2-quart saucepan, and bring to a boil over high heat. Add the spelt, and boil for a few seconds. Reduce the heat to low, cover, and simmer for 1 hour, or until the water is completely absorbed, taking care not to scorch the spelt. Remove the pan from the heat, and allow the kernels to cool to room temperature.

3. Transfer the spelt to a 3-quart bowl, and add the parsley, scallions, garlic, mint, feta cheese, olives, currants, lemon juice, and oil. Mix well, adding salt and pepper to taste. Cover the bowl, and chill for at least 2 hours.

4. To serve, line a serving platter with the lettuce, and mound the salad in the center of the dish. Garnish with the tomatoes, and serve.

Cucumber Salad With Spelt Topping

In this recipe, cool, refreshing cucumber is complemented by crunchy toasted spelt flakes.

Yield: 4 servings

1 large cucumber, peeled and thinly sliced

1 tablespoon sea salt

1 tablespoon canola margarine

2 tablespoons toasted spelt flakes

1 small white onion, sliced into thin rings

DRESSING

¼ cup low-fat buttermilk

1 tablespoon canola oil

4–6 drops tamari soy sauce

1 tablespoon chopped fresh chives

¼ teaspoon celery seeds

Dash sea salt

1. Place the cucumber in a 2-quart bowl, and sprinkle with the salt. Mix well, and set aside for 5 to 10 minutes. (This will help remove excess water from the cucumber.)

2. Place the margarine in a 10-inch skillet, and melt over medium heat. Add the spelt flakes, and sauté until lightly browned, stirring constantly. Remove the skillet from the heat, and allow the flakes to cool.

3. Drain the cucumber in a colander, and use both hands to squeeze any excess liquid from the slices. Return the cucumber to the bowl, and add the onion rings. Mix well.

4. Place all of the dressing ingredients in a 1-quart bowl, and blend well with a wire whisk. Pour the dressing over the cucumber, and mix well. Cover the bowl, and set aside for 15 minutes to allow the flavors to blend.

5. Transfer the salad to 4 bowls, top with the spelt flakes, and serve.

Wilted Spinach Salad With Chili Flakes

Yield: 4 servings

3 tightly packed cups chopped spinach

¼ teaspoon sea salt

⅛ teaspoon freshly ground white pepper

2 hard boiled eggs, chopped (optional)

2 tablespoons Oven-Roasted Chili Flakes (page 49)

DRESSING

3 tablespoons canola oil

2 shallots, cut into fine rings

1 tablespoon no-cholesterol bacon substitute

1 teaspoon turbinado sugar (or other sweetener)

2 tablespoons apple cider vinegar

For this salad, fresh spinach is wilted with a hot oil-and-vinegar dressing. For added taste, the salad is sprinkled with Oven-Roasted Chili Flakes—crunchy chili-flavored flakes of spelt.

1. Place the spinach in a medium-sized serving bowl, and sprinkle with the salt and pepper. Set aside.

2. To make the dressing, place the oil in a 10-inch skillet over medium-high heat. Add the shallots and bacon substitute, and sauté for about 2 minutes, or until the shallots are soft. Reduce the heat to low, add the sugar, and cook for an additional 30 seconds, stirring constantly.

3. Remove the skillet from the heat. Add the vinegar and mix well.

4. Pour the hot dressing over the prepared spinach, and gently mix. Adjust the seasoning, adding more vinegar, salt, or pepper if necessary. Top with the eggs, if desired, sprinkle with the Chili Flakes, and serve immediately.

5

The Bread Box

Few if any foods are as comforting and fundamentally satisfying as freshly baked bread. Indeed, from time immemorial, bread, in one form or another, has been the mainstay of civilization.

The forms that bread can take are legion in terms of both shape and ingredients, and are seemingly limited only by the imagination. However, all breads generally fall into one of two categories: yeast breads and quick breads. This chapter contains recipes for both types of breads, and includes breads baked in loaf form, as buns, and as muffins.

If you are an experienced bread baker, you can probably jump right in and begin baking delicious spelt breads without further ado. If you are new to this area of cookery, though, the information provided below will help ensure success.

MAKING YEAST BREADS

Yeast breads, as the name implies, rely on yeast for their rising power. These breads can be made from any flour, although some flours are better than others for this purpose. Wheat flour rises highest, for instance, while rye flour needs to be combined with wheat to achieve an appealing texture. Owing to its low gluten content, spelt does not rise quite as high as wheat flour. However, it does produce rich, wholesome, satisfying loaves of firm-textured breads with crunchy crusts. And, of course, the unique flavor of spelt bread sets it apart from other breads.

While flours may vary in their characteristics, the truly fickle player in the bread drama is yeast. But even this temperamental ingredient will be your friend if you treat it properly during mixing, kneading, rising, and baking.

I prefer dry active yeast to compressed yeast, not only because it has a longer shelf life, but also because its consistency makes it easy to use. Of course, certain ingredients must be present in a recipe to coax the yeast into doing its job. For instance, small amounts of salt and sugar are needed to activate the yeast. Most important, though, is the liquid that is initially mixed with the yeast. This liquid—usually water—must be warm, but not hot, if the dough is to rise. If the liquid is too cold, the yeast will be lazy; if too hot, the yeast will die. The best temperature for the liquid—and, in fact, for all yeast bread ingredients—is about 105°F.

In the case of most yeast breads, proper kneading of the dough is essential to the production of a fine, even-textured loaf. Knead your dough on a clean, dry surface that has been sprinkled with flour. Using floured hands, first flatten the mound of dough. Then fold the dough in half by folding the upper part of the dough—the portion farthest from you—over the lower part. With the heels of your hands, press the dough down and away from you. Then give the dough a quarter turn and repeat the folding, pressing, and turning process until the dough becomes elastic and smooth. This should take from three to five minutes, depending on the type and quantity of the dough.

Rising is yet another important part of the bread-making process. If you have made yeast breads in the past, you may have noticed that bread baking is almost always successful in the summer, but is more failure-prone in the winter, when even a centrally heated home may be cool and drafty. This is because, as discussed earlier, yeast needs warmth to rise. One easy way to provide yeast with the warmth it needs is to place the rising dough in an electric or gas oven that has been preheated to a temperature of not more than 105°F. Use an oven thermometer to make sure that the correct temperature has been reached. Then turn the oven off, place the dough in the oven, and close the oven door. Usually, the dough is allowed to rise until it doubles in size, a process that can take from one and a half to two hours. Test the dough to see if it has sufficiently risen by pressing it with two fingers. If the indentations remain, the dough has doubled in size.

Of course, the last step in the making of a perfect loaf is the baking. With most breads, you will know that the bread is ready when it is golden brown and has shrunk slightly from the sides of the pan. Allow the loaf to cool slightly in the pan. Then remove it from the pan, and tap it with your knuckle. The loaf should sound hollow.

Cool the fresh-baked loaf by placing it on a wire rack in a draft-free area. Once the loaf is completely cool, it may be sliced and served. If preferred, wrap the loaf in waxed paper or aluminum foil, or enclose it in a plastic bag. Just make sure that the bread is cool when you wrap it. If still warm, the wrapped bread is likely to mold quickly.

If you keep your bread in a bread box, be sure to ventilate and clean the box every three weeks by scalding it with boiling water. This will deter mold growth. Stale bread can be refreshed by placing it in an ovenproof dish that has been rinsed with cold water. Place the still-damp dish and the bread in a cold oven, turn the heat to 250°F, and heat for ten to fifteen minutes.

An easy time-saving alternative when making yeast breads is the Vita-Spelt line of prepared bread mixes. Available with either whole-grain or white spelt flour, these virtually foolproof mixes contain all of the ingredients necessary to produce a delicious loaf of homemade bread. All you need do is add water and follow package directions. These mixes are also highly adaptable. For instance, you may add saffron threads to the water to make saffron bread; add various herbs to the dough for fragrant herb bread; or top the loaf with sesame or sunflower seeds. Several of the yeast bread recipes presented in this chapter use Vita-Spelt bread mixes to decrease preparation time and ensure good results.

Whether you choose to make your yeast breads with a mix or with your own ingredients, careful measuring, mixing, kneading, and baking will yield delicious baked goods. In this chapter, you will find a range of yeast bread recipes, many of which have won prizes. Some, like No-Need-to-Knead Pumpernickel Bread and Easy Yeast Bread, will even allow you to make home-baked bread from scratch *without* spending an inordinate amount of time in the kitchen. All are sure to be winners with family and friends.

MAKING QUICK BREADS AND MUFFINS

Quick breads and muffins are generally faster to make than yeast breads. This is because, rather than relying on yeast as a leavening agent, these baked goods use either baking powder or baking soda or, in some cases, both powder and soda. Therefore, they do not require kneading and rising. In addition, because yeast is not involved, results are generally more consistent, especially when a novice baker is at work.

When making quick breads and muffins, avoid overmixing the batter, as this often results in a product that is coarsely grained and tunneled. When combining wet and dry ingredients, unless the recipe states otherwise, it is usually necessary to mix just until the dry ingredients are moistened. When heavy ingredients such as peanut butter are involved, though, you should mix more thoroughly. Depending on the density of the ingredients, ten to twenty strokes are all that is usually needed.

Always be sure to use the stated baking temperature when following a muffin or quick bread recipe. This is especially important when baking muffins, as an overly hot oven will cause the muffins to sink into themselves. If you like your muffins very moist, try adding batter to all the wells in the pan except one, and fill the remaining well with water. Use the toothpick test to determine when the muffins are done. A toothpick inserted in the center of the muffin should come out clean when the muffins are ready to be removed from the oven.

After removing a muffin tin from the oven, run a knife around the edge of each cup to loosen the muffins.

Then turn each muffin sideways in its well, and allow the muffins to cool in the tin for about five minutes. Invert the tin, and transfer the muffins to a wire rack to cool. To reheat, wrap the muffins loosely in aluminum foil to prevent them from drying out, and place them briefly in a 250°F oven.

Quick breads, like muffins, are done when a toothpick inserted in the center of a loaf comes out clean. Once the loaf has been removed from the oven, allow it to remain in the pan for about 10 minutes. Then invert the tin, transfer the loaf to a wire rack, and cool the loaf completely before slicing and serving. To reheat a loaf, wrap it in aluminum foil and place it briefly in a 250°F oven.

As shown by the recipes that follow, both quick breads and muffins can be either sweet or savory, and so are a real boon to menu planning. Simple Spelt Cornbread, for instance, is ideal at breakfast time or as a between-meals snack; Cottage Cheese and Dillweed Muffins are a perfect accompaniment to soups and salads; and Lemon Spice Quick Bread makes a wonderful light dessert. And with spelt as a key ingredient, breads and muffins alike are sure to provide you and your family with the energy you need all day long.

YEAST BREADS

Onion Flat-Bread

Yield: One 10½-inch round loaf

2–2¼ cups Vita-Spelt Whole Grain Bread Mix (or equivalent product), divided

⅓ cup warm low-fat milk (or substitute)

1 egg, beaten (or substitute)

TOPPING

2 tablespoons canola margarine

2 large yellow onions, sliced into thin rings

½ teaspoon caraway seeds

1 teaspoon turbinado sugar (or other sweetener)

2 eggs, beaten (or substitute)

¼ cup nonfat sour cream

2 tablespoons toasted spelt flakes

Pinch sea salt

Pinch freshly ground white pepper

Pinch ground paprika

Onions have been a popular food for thousands of years. In addition to having a unique taste, these edible bulbs have long been thought to possess curative powers. Here, the healthful, pungent onion lends its flavor to a flat-bread, making the loaf a perfect complement to hearty fare.

1. Place 1¾ cups of the bread mix, the milk, and the egg in a 2-quart bowl, and mix until a soft dough is formed. Cover the bowl with a clean kitchen towel, and let rise in a warm place for 1 hour.

2. While the dough is rising, place the margarine in a 10-inch skillet, and melt over medium heat. Add the onions, caraway seeds, and sugar, and sauté, stirring frequently, for 4 to 6 minutes, or until the onions are golden brown. Remove the skillet from the heat, and set aside to cool.

3. Combine the eggs, sour cream, spelt flakes, salt, pepper, and paprika in a 2-quart bowl. Add the cooled onions, and gently mix. Set aside.

4. Preheat the oven to 400°F. Coat a 10½-inch springform pan with nonstick cooking spray, and lightly sprinkle with spelt bread crumbs. Set aside.

5. Turn the dough onto a lightly floured board, and add ¼ cup of the remaining bread mix. Knead the mixture for about 5 minutes, or until the dough becomes pliable, adding additional bread mix if required.

6. Using a floured rolling pin, roll the dough into a 12½-inch-diameter circle, and place it in the prepared pan. Using 2 fingers, press the dough 1 inch up the sides of the pan. Spread the cooled onion mixture evenly over the dough, and cover the pan with a clean kitchen towel. Let rise in a warm place for an additional 30 minutes.

7. Bake for 20 minutes at 400°F. Increase the oven temperature to 425°F, and continue baking for 5 to 10 minutes, or until the onions are browned and the dough rim looks crisp.

8. Unclasp the springform collar, and allow the bread to cool for about 10 minutes before cutting into wedges and serving.

Harvest Spelt Bread

Marilyn Mulgrew of Rochester, New York, created this prize-winning recipe. Marilyn says, "This is the perfect bread for any occasion. It has a savory flavor that complements almost any meal."

1. Place the water in a 1-quart bowl, and sprinkle with the yeast. Stir once or twice, and set aside for 5 to 10 minutes.

2. Combine the milk, margarine, maple syrup, and beaten egg in a 2-quart bowl. Set aside.

3. Combine the whole-grain flour, spices, and salt in a 3-quart bowl. Stir in the yeast mixture, the milk mixture, and the pumpkin, and mix thoroughly. Add the white flour, a little at a time, until a dough is formed.

4. Turn the dough onto a lightly floured board, and knead for 3 to 4 minutes, or until the dough is slightly elastic. Cover with a clean kitchen towel, and let rise on the board in a warm place for 1 to 2 hours, or until the dough has doubled in size.

5. Punch down the dough, and divide it in half. Shape each half into a loaf, either round or oblong, and cover. Let the loaves rise in a warm place for 1 to 2 hours, or until doubled in size.

6. Preheat the oven to 350°F, and lightly coat a 17-x-11-inch baking sheet with nonstick cooking spray. Place the loaves on the baking sheet, spacing them about 3 inches apart, and bake for 45 minutes, or until the loaves sound hollow when tapped. Allow the loaves to cool on the sheet for 10 minutes. Transfer the loaves to a wire rack, and cool completely before slicing and serving.

Yield: Two 1½-pound loaves

½ cup warm water

2 packages (¼ ounce each) dry active yeast

1 cup warm low-fat milk (or substitute)

2 tablespoons melted canola margarine

½ cup maple syrup

1 egg, beaten (or substitute)

3 cups whole-grain spelt flour

1 teaspoon ground cinnamon

1 teaspoon ground allspice

½ teaspoon sea salt

1 can (1 pound) pumpkin

3 cups white spelt flour

Spelt Buns

Yield: 20 buns

3½ cups warm water, divided

2 packages (¼ ounce each) dry active yeast

3 eggs (optional)

½ teaspoon baking soda

1 teaspoon sea salt

⅓ cup liquid lecithin*

⅓ cup canola oil

⅓ cup honey

11 cups whole-grain spelt flour

Nonstick cooking spray

*Lecithin, a nutritious by-product of soybean oil refining, can be found in most health foods stores.

Prize winner Mary Watkins of Manning, North Dakota, created this recipe. Mary says that the key to making these buns super-delicious lies in spraying them with nonstick cooking spray just before baking.

1. Place ½ cup of the water in a 1-quart bowl, and sprinkle with the yeast. Stir once or twice, and set aside for 5 to 10 minutes.

2. Combine the remaining 3 cups of water, the eggs, if desired, and the baking soda, salt, lecithin, oil, and honey in a 3-quart bowl. Add 4 cups of the flour, and mix thoroughly. Set aside for 15 minutes.

3. Add the yeast mixture to the flour mixture, and mix thoroughly. Add enough of the remaining flour to make a stiff dough.

4. Turn the dough onto a lightly floured board, and knead for 10 minutes, or until the dough is smooth and elastic. Cover the dough with a clean kitchen towel, and let rise on the board in a warm place for 1 to 1½ hours, or until the dough has doubled in size.

5. Punch down the dough, and divide it into 20 equal-sized pieces. Arrange the pieces on the board, spacing them 1 inch apart, and allow the dough to rest for 10 minutes.

6. Lightly coat two 17-x-11-inch cookie sheets with nonstick cooking spray. Using floured hands, shape the dough into buns, and place the buns on the prepared cookie sheets, spacing them about 2 inches apart. Cover the buns with clean kitchen towels, and let rise for 45 minutes to 1 hour, or until the buns have doubled in size.

7. Preheat the oven to 425°F. Spray the buns lightly with nonstick cooking spray, and bake for about 15 minutes, or until golden brown. Allow the buns to cool on the cookie sheets for 5 minutes. Transfer the buns to a wire rack, and cool completely before serving.

Lemon Lite Bagels

Bagels, a gift from Jewish cuisine, are delightful at any meal, but are especially popular at breakfast and brunch time. This bagel recipe is easier than most because it uses a time-saving spelt bread mix.

1. Combine the warm water and 1 tablespoon of the honey in a deep 1-quart bowl. Add the milk and lemon juice, and mix.

2. Place 1¾ cups of the bread mix in a 2-quart bowl, and slowly add the honey mixture to the bread mix, thoroughly blending to form a soft dough.

3. Cover the dough with a clean kitchen towel, and let rise in a warm place for 1 hour. Punch down the dough, cover once more, and allow to rise for 1 additional hour.

4. Turn the dough onto a lightly floured board. Clean the bowl, coat it lightly with nonstick cooking spray, and set aside.

5. Add the remaining ½ cup of bread mix to the dough a little at a time, kneading the dough until it no longer feels sticky. Continue to knead for about 5 minutes, or until the dough feels elastic.

6. Shape the dough into a round ball, and place it in the coated bowl. Cover the dough with the kitchen towel, and let rise in a warm place for 1 to 2 hours, or until the dough has doubled in size.

7. Preheat the oven to 375°F. Coat a 17-x-11-inch cookie sheet with nonstick cooking spray, and set aside.

8. Turn the risen dough onto a lightly floured board. Using your hands, roll the dough into a 10-inch-long log, and cut the log into 8 equal pieces with a sharp knife. Roll each piece of dough into a rope that is 1 inch thick and 6 inches long. Shape each rope into a ring, pinching the ends firmly together so they will not separate during baking.

9. Bring a 3-quart saucepan of water to a boil over high heat, and add the 2 remaining tablespoons of honey. Drop the dough rings into the boiling water 1 at a time, until all of the rings are in the water. Reduce the heat to medium, and boil the bagels for 3 to 5 minutes, or until they rise to the surface. Remove the bagels from the water with a slotted spoon, and transfer them to the prepared cookie sheet.

10. Make the egg glaze by mixing the glaze ingredients together in a small bowl. Using a pastry brush, brush the glaze over the top and sides of the bagels. Place the bagels on the middle rack of the oven, and bake for 25 to 30 minutes, or until deep brown in color.

Yield: 8 bagels

½ cup warm water

3 tablespoons honey, divided

1 tablespoon low-fat milk (or substitute)

2 tablespoons fresh lemon juice

2¼ cups Vita-Spelt Whole Grain Bread Mix (or equivalent product), divided

1 tablespoon grated fresh lemon peel

EGG GLAZE

1 egg yolk, beaten

1 tablespoon water

1 tablespoon honey

11. Transfer the bagels to a serving platter, and serve warm or at room temperature.

Variation

• After applying the egg glaze, sprinkle the bagels with poppy or sesame seeds.

Easy Yeast Bread

Yield: 1 round loaf

1½ cups whole-grain spelt flour

2 packages (¼ ounce each) dry active yeast

¼ teaspoon sea salt

1 cup plain nonfat yogurt

½ cup club soda

¼ cup honey

2 tablespoons canola margarine

1 egg, beaten (or substitute)

1⅓ cups whole-grain spelt flour

Deborah L. Arieda of Stanwood, Washington, developed this prize-winning recipe. Deborah says, "This bread is great served warm or cold. Within two hours from the start, you can spoon your favorite spread onto this rich, sourdough-flavored bread."

1. Combine the 1½ cups of flour, the yeast, and the salt in a 3-quart bowl. Mix lightly and set aside.

2. Combine the yogurt, club soda, honey, and margarine in a 2-quart saucepan. Place over medium heat, and cook until the mixture is warm, but not too hot to touch with your fingers. *Do not boil.*

3. Add the yogurt mixture to the flour mixture, and stir to combine. Add the egg, and mix the ingredients with an electric mixer set at low speed until the dry ingredients are moistened. Increase the mixer to medium speed, and beat for 3 additional minutes. Add the remaining 1⅓ cups of flour, and mix thoroughly.

4. Coat a 1½-quart casserole dish with nonstick cooking spray, and pour the batter into the dish. Cover with a clean kitchen towel, and let rise in a warm place for 1 to 1½ hours, or until the dough has reached the top of the dish.

5. Preheat the oven to 375°F. Bake the loaf for 35 to 40 minutes, or until golden in color. Allow the bread to cool in the dish for 5 minutes. Remove the loaf from the dish, and transfer to a wire rack. Serve warm or at room temperature.

Raisin Bread

It pays to put the time and effort into baking this bread, as the finished loaves freeze beautifully. Just slice the bread before freezing, and remove a slice or two whenever you want a delicious breakfast bread or nutritious snack. Toast the frozen slices in your toaster, and enjoy!

Yield: Four 1-pound loaves

1 box (15 ounces) dark raisins

1 cup apple juice

2 packages (¼ ounce each) dry active yeast

½ cup warm water

¾ cup plus 2 tablespoons canola margarine, at room temperature

1 cup turbinado sugar (or other sweetener)

1 teaspoon sea salt

2 teaspoons grated fresh lemon peel

2 teaspoons almond extract

5 cups low-fat milk (or substitute)

5 cups sifted white spelt flour

5 cups unsifted whole-grain spelt flour

4 eggs, well beaten (or substitute)

1. Place the raisins and apple juice in a 2-quart bowl. Cover the bowl with plastic wrap, and allow to soak at room temperature overnight. The next day, drain and discard the excess apple juice, reserving the raisins.

2. Place the yeast and warm water in a 1-quart glass bowl. Stir once or twice, and set aside for 5 to 10 minutes.

3. Place the margarine, sugar, salt, lemon peel, and almond extract in a 3-quart bowl, and cream together. Set aside.

4. Place the milk in a 2-quart saucepan, and cook over high heat just until bubbles form around the edges of the milk. Do not boil.

5. Pour the scalded milk over the reserved raisins. Add the raisin mixture to the margarine mixture, and stir until the margarine is completely melted.

6. Place the white spelt flour and the whole-grain spelt flour in a 3-quart bowl, and mix well. When the margarine mixture has cooled to lukewarm, add 2 cups of the flour mixture to the margarine mixture, and beat with an electric mixer for about 2 minutes.

7. Add the yeast mixture to the dough, and blend. Stir in half of the remaining flour, ½ cup at a time, beating with the mixer for a few seconds after each addition. Add the beaten eggs, pouring in ½ cup at a time, to make a soft dough.

8. Turn the dough onto a lightly floured surface, and knead for about 3 minutes, adding more flour if the dough is too sticky. Grease a 5-quart bowl, form the dough into a large smooth ball, and place in the bowl. Cover the bowl with a clean kitchen towel, and let rise in a warm place for about 2 hours, or until the dough has doubled in size.

9. Punch the dough down. Then lift the dough from the bowl, and set it aside. Grease the bowl again, using your hands. Run your greased hands over the ball of dough, and return it to the bowl. Cover the dough with greased waxed paper and a towel. (At this point, if desired, you may store the dough in the refrigerator for up to 7 days.)

10. Spray four 1-pound loaf pans with nonstick cooking spray, and lightly flour each pan. Divide the dough into 4 equal pieces. Form each piece into a loaf, and place each loaf in a pan, making sure that the ends

of the pans are well filled to promote even rising. Cover the pans with clean kitchen towels, and let rise in a warm place for about 2 hours, or until the loaves have doubled in size.

11. Preheat the oven to 375°F. Bake the loaves for 50 minutes, or until they sound hollow when tapped. Let the loaves cool slightly before removing them from the pans. Transfer the loaves to a wire rack, and cool completely before serving or freezing.

No-Need-to-Knead Pumpernickel

Yield: One 2-pound loaf

3½ cups whole-grain spelt flour

1½ cups rye flour

⅔ cup warm water

1 package (¼ ounce) dry active yeast

2 tablespoons honey

2 tablespoons molasses

⅔ cup warm water

1 teaspoon sea salt

⅓ cup oat bran

1⅓ cups warm water

1 tablespoon sesame seeds

This prize-winning recipe was created by Virginia Hoyt of Centralia, Washington. Virginia says, "This bread is a positive improvement over whole-wheat. . . . It is quick and easy to make and has an exceptionally delicious taste."

1. Preheat the oven to 250°F. Combine the spelt and rye flours in a 3-quart ovenproof bowl. Place the bowl in the oven for 20 minutes.

2. Place ⅔ cup of warm water in a 1-quart bowl, and sprinkle with the yeast. Add the honey, and stir to mix thoroughly. Set aside for 5 to 10 minutes.

3. Combine the molasses and ⅔ cup of warm water in a 1-quart bowl. Add the yeast mixture to the molasses mixture, and blend. Slowly stir this mixture into the warmed flour. Add the salt, oat bran, and 1⅓ cups of warm water, and mix thoroughly.

4. Coat a 2-pound loaf pan with nonstick cooking spray, and pour the batter into the pan. Wet a spatula with cold water, and use it to smooth the top of the batter. Sprinkle the sesame seeds over the batter, cover with a clean kitchen towel, and let rise in a warm place for 1 to 2 hours, or until the dough has risen to the top of the pan.

5. Preheat the oven to 400°F, and bake for 35 minutes, or until the loaf sounds hollow when tapped. Allow the loaf to cool in the pan for 10 minutes. Remove the loaf from the pan, and transfer to a wire rack. Cool completely before slicing and serving.

Native American Indian Bread

This bread, which is also known as squaw bread, tastes slightly sweet and has a beautiful glossy crust.

1. Place ¼ cup of the warm water in a 1-quart bowl, and stir in the yeast and sugar. Set aside for 5 to 10 minutes.

2. Place the buttermilk in a 2-quart saucepan, and cook over medium heat until warm. Stir in the margarine, the remaining ¾ cup of warm water, and the molasses and salt.

3. Pour the buttermilk mixture into a 3-quart bowl, and add the yeast mixture, the whole-grain spelt flour, the rye flour, and half of the white spelt flour. Using a whisk, beat the mixture until smooth. Cover the bowl with a clean kitchen towel, and let rise in a warm place for 30 minutes.

4. Mix the remaining white flour into the dough a half cup at a time, until the dough pulls away from the side of the bowl without sticking. Turn the dough onto a lightly floured board and knead for 5 minutes, or until the dough is smooth and elastic, adding more flour as necessary.

5. Clean the 3-quart bowl, and generously coat it with nonstick cooking spray. Return the dough to the bowl, and cover with the towel. Let rise in a warm place for about 2 hours, or until the dough has doubled in size.

6. Punch down the dough, and turn it onto the floured board. Knead for 3 minutes, or until the dough is no longer sticky. Divide the dough in half, and shape each piece into a smooth round ball.

7. Coat two 8-inch round baking pans with nonstick cooking spray, and sprinkle generously with cornmeal. Place 1 of the dough balls in each pan, cover with a towel, and let rise in a warm place for 1 hour.

8. Preheat the oven to 375°F. Make the egg glaze by placing the glaze ingredients in a 1-quart bowl, and beating with a fork until well mixed. Using a pastry brush, brush each loaf with a little glaze. Using a sharp knife, cut a cross in the top of each loaf.

9. Bake for 40 minutes, or until nicely browned. Allow the loaves to cool slightly before removing them from the pans. Transfer the loaves to wire racks, and cool completely before slicing and serving.

Yield: Two 1-pound loaves

1 cup warm water, divided

1 package (¼ ounce) dry active yeast

2 tablespoons turbinado sugar (or other sweetener)

1 cup low-fat buttermilk

¼ cup canola margarine

½ cup blackstrap molasses

1 tablespoon sea salt

1 cup whole-grain spelt flour

1 cup rye flour

3–3½ cups white spelt flour

EGG GLAZE

1 egg white

2 tablespoons low-fat milk

QUICK BREADS

Lemon Spice Quick Bread

Yield: One 1-pound loaf

1 cup Vita-Spelt Pancake/Muffin Mix or 1 cup whole-grain spelt flour

¾ cup barley flour

½ cup brown rice flour

1 tablespoon nonaluminum baking powder

¼ cup canola margarine

1 teaspoon grated fresh lemon rind

½ cup rice syrup

½ teaspoon vanilla extract

Pinch ground cinnamon

Pinch ground cloves

2 eggs, separated

1 cup water

2 tablespoons fresh lemon juice

This recipe was created by Philip Snow of Hendersonville, North Carolina. Philip says, "This favorite recipe of mine is relatively simple to prepare." Just as important, Philip's prize-winning loaf is simply delicious.

1. Preheat the oven to 350°F. Lightly coat a 1-pound loaf pan with nonstick cooking spray, and set aside.

2. Sift the pancake mix or spelt flour and the barley flour, rice flour, and baking powder into a 2-quart bowl. Set aside.

3. Place the margarine in another 2-quart bowl, and, using a fork, cream it until soft and smooth. Add the lemon rind, rice syrup, vanilla, cinnamon, and cloves, and mix thoroughly. Add the egg yolks, and again mix well.

4. Combine the water and lemon juice in a 3-quart bowl. Begin beating the lemon mixture with a wooden spoon. Continue to beat as you alternately add small amounts of the flour and margarine mixtures, beginning and ending with the flour.

5. Place the egg whites in a 1-quart bowl, and beat with an electric mixer until they form stiff peaks. Gently fold the whites into the batter.

6. Spoon the batter into the prepared pan, and bake for 45 to 60 minutes, or until a toothpick inserted in the center of the loaf comes out clean. Allow the bread to cool in the pan for 10 minutes. Remove the loaf from the pan, and transfer to a wire rack. Cool completely before slicing and serving.

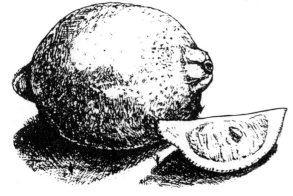

Simple Spelt Cornbread

This prize-winning recipe comes from Kay Hill of Mineral Wells, West Virginia. Kay says, "This recipe was especially created for my gluten-intolerant daughter, but the whole family loves it."

Yield: One round loaf

1 cup whole-grain spelt flour

1 cup yellow cornmeal

½ cup turbinado sugar (or other sweetener)

1 teaspoon baking soda

2 teaspoons nonaluminum baking powder

½ teaspoon sea salt

1 cup low-fat milk (or substitute)

2 eggs (or substitute)

2 tablespoons canola oil

1. Preheat the oven to 425°F. Generously spray an 8- or 9-inch cast-iron skillet with nonstick cooking spray, and set aside.

2. Combine the flour, cornmeal, sugar, baking soda, baking powder, and salt in a 3-quart bowl. Beat continuously with a wooden spoon while adding the milk, eggs, and oil.

3. Pour the mixture into the prepared skillet, and bake for 30 minutes, or until golden brown.

4. Let the bread cool slightly before removing it from the skillet. Cut into wedges and serve warm.

Variation

• To make Corn Muffins, simply coat 12 muffin cups with cooking spray, and divide the batter among the cups. Bake at 400°F for 20 minutes, or until a toothpick inserted in the center of a muffin comes out clean.

Sesame Tahini Sprout Bread

This prize-winning recipe was developed by Lauren Kruse of Colts Neck, New Jersey. The recipe's unusual ingredients combine to make a delicious bread.

Yield: One 1-pound loaf

¼ cup sesame seeds

¼ cup tahini

¼ pound medium tofu

¼ cup plus 2 tablespoons apple juice concentrate, divided

1½ cups packed fresh alfalfa sprouts or other sprouts

2 cups whole-grain spelt flour

3 tablespoons nonaluminum baking powder

¼ teaspoon sea salt

¾ cup water

1. Preheat the oven to 350°F. Arrange the sesame seeds on a cookie sheet, and roast them until they turn dark and give off a nutty aroma. Set aside.

2. Reduce the oven temperature to 325° F. Lightly coat a 1-pound loaf pan with nonstick cooking spray, and set aside.

3. Place the tahini, tofu, and 2 tablespoons of the apple juice concentrate in a blender, and process on "purée" until smooth. Add the sprouts, and continue to blend until the sprouts are chopped and thoroughly combined.

4. Combine the flour, baking powder, salt, and toasted sesame seeds in a 3-quart bowl. Add the tahini mixture to the flour mixture, and stir just until the mixture is crumbly. Add the remaining ¼ cup of apple juice concentrate and the water, and mix just until the dry ingredients are moistened. Do not overmix.

5. Spoon the batter into the prepared pan, and bake for 50 minutes to 1 hour, or until a toothpick inserted in the center of the loaf comes out clean. Allow the bread to cool in the pan for 10 minutes. Remove the loaf from the pan, and transfer to a wire rack. Cool completely before slicing and serving.

Spelt Whole-Grain Bread

Yield: One 2-pound loaf

3 cups plus 2 tablespoons whole-grain spelt flour, divided

2 tablespoons honey

2 cups warm water

½ teaspoon dry active yeast

2 cups rye flour

1 cup rolled oats

1 tablespoon plus 1 teaspoon nonaluminum baking powder

2 teaspoons baking soda

2 teaspoons sea salt

2 eggs (or substitute)

2 tablespoons sesame seeds

This prize-winning recipe was created by Kathleen Hoyt of Wilsonville, Oregon. Kathleen says that even people who claim to like only supermarket white bread love this whole-grain loaf. Kathleen's bread is unusual because while a quick bread, it also contains yeast, which in this case is used as a flavoring.

1. Preheat the oven to 325°F. Coat a 2-pound loaf pan with nonstick cooking spray, and sprinkle it with 2 tablespoons of the spelt flour. Set aside.

2. Combine the honey and water in a 2-quart bowl, and sprinkle the yeast over the mixture. Set aside for 5 to 10 minutes.

3. In a 3-quart bowl, combine the remaining 3 cups of spelt flour with the rye flour, oats, baking powder, baking soda, and salt.

4. Beat the eggs into the honey mixture. Slowly add the honey mixture to the flour mixture, and mix just until the dry ingredients are well moistened.

5. Place the dough in the prepared pan. Sprinkle the loaf with the sesame seeds, pressing the seeds into the dough with the back of a large spoon.

6. Bake for 1 hour and 5 minutes, or until a toothpick inserted in the center of the loaf comes out clean. Allow the bread to cool in the pan for 10 minutes. Remove the loaf from the pan, and transfer to a wire rack. Cool completely before slicing and serving.

Melissa's Banana Bread

This recipe comes from Melissa Billings of Springfield, Oregon, who created it for her three allergy-sensitive children. I'm sure that you'll love this moist banana bread as much as Melissa's kids do.

1. Preheat the oven to 375°F. Coat a 1-pound loaf pan with nonstick cooking spray, and set aside.

2. Place the bananas and lemon juice in a 1-quart bowl, and mash with a fork until smooth. Set aside.

3. Place the margarine and honey in a 3-quart bowl, and cream with a fork until smooth. Add the banana mixture to the margarine mixture, and mix thoroughly.

4. Combine the flour, rice bran, baking powder, baking soda, salt, cardamom, and cinnamon in a 2-quart bowl. Add the flour mixture to the margarine mixture, and stir just until the dry ingredients are moistened. Fold in the walnuts.

5. Spoon the batter into the prepared pan, and bake for 35 to 45 minutes, or until a toothpick inserted in the center of the loaf comes out clean. Allow the bread to cool in the pan for 10 minutes. Remove the loaf from the pan, and transfer to a wire rack. Cool completely before slicing and serving.

Yield: One 1-pound loaf

3 very ripe bananas

Juice of 1 lemon

½ cup canola margarine

½ cup honey

1¾ cups white spelt flour

¼ cup rice bran

1½ teaspoons nonaluminum baking powder

½ teaspoon baking soda

½ teaspoon sea salt

½ teaspoon ground cardamom

1 teaspoon ground cinnamon

½ cup chopped walnuts

Serving Suggestion

• For a satisfying dessert, top slices of this sweet bread with fresh fruit.

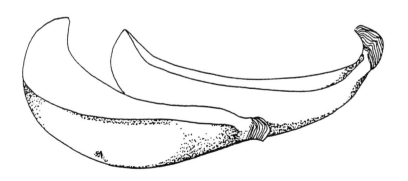

MUFFINS

Cranberry Buttermilk Muffins

Yield: 12 muffins

1¼ cups coarsely chopped cranberries

¼ cup honey

¼ teaspoon orange extract

¾ cup white spelt flour

¾ cup rye flour

½ cup yellow cornmeal

¼ cup oat bran

2 teaspoons nonaluminum baking powder

¼ cup turbinado sugar (or other sweetener)

¼ teaspoon sea salt

Dash allspice

2 eggs, beaten (or substitute)

1 egg white, beaten

1½ cups low-fat buttermilk

¼ cup canola oil

Oat bran gives these muffins a pleasingly coarse texture, while fresh cranberries and buttermilk impart a tart flavor.

1. Preheat the oven to 400°F. Coat 12 muffin wells with nonstick cooking spray or line them with paper cups. Set aside.

2. Combine the cranberries, honey, and orange extract in a 1-quart bowl. Set aside.

3. Sift the spelt and rye flours into a 3-quart bowl. Add the cornmeal, oat bran, baking powder, sugar, salt, and allspice, and stir to blend. Set aside.

4. Place the whole eggs, egg white, buttermilk, and oil in a 2-quart bowl, and beat lightly. Add the egg mixture and the cranberry mixture to the flour mixture, and stir just until the dry ingredients are moistened.

5. Fill the prepared muffin wells a little more than ½ full with the batter. Bake for 20 to 25 minutes, or until the muffins are lightly browned and a toothpick inserted in the center of a muffin comes out clean. Turn the muffins sideways in the wells, and allow them to cool in the tins for about 5 minutes. Remove the muffins from the tins and transfer to a wire rack. Serve warm or at room temperature.

Carbo Cakes

Margaret Wittenberg of Buda, Texas, created this prize-winning recipe. Margaret says, "My ultra-marathon cyclist husband can't get enough of these healthy snacks."

Yield: 12 muffins

1 cup finely grated carrots

½ cup finely diced apples

¾ cup apple juice

1 egg, beaten (or substitute)

2 tablespoons plus 1½ teaspoons canola oil

1½ teaspoons vanilla extract

1¾ cups whole-grain spelt flour

¼ teaspoon sea salt

½ teaspoon baking soda

1 teaspoon nonaluminum baking powder

½ teaspoon ground cinnamon

⅓ cup dark raisins

⅓ cup chopped walnuts

1. Preheat the oven to 400°F. Coat 12 muffin wells with nonstick cooking spray or line them with paper cups. Set aside.

2. Combine the carrots, apples, apple juice, egg, oil, and vanilla in a 2-quart bowl. Set aside.

3. Combine the flour, salt, baking soda, baking powder, cinnamon, raisins, and walnuts in a 3-quart bowl. Add the carrot mixture to the flour mixture, and blend just until the dry ingredients are moistened.

4. Fill the prepared muffin wells ½ full with the batter. Bake for 20 minutes, or until a toothpick inserted in the center of a muffin comes out clean. Turn the muffins sideways in the wells, and allow them to cool in the tins for about 5 minutes. Remove the muffins from the tins and transfer to a wire rack. Cool completely before serving.

Peanut Butter and Jelly Muffins

This prize-winning recipe comes from Gloria Bradley of Naperville, Illinois. Gloria says that these healthful muffins appeal to kids of all ages.

Yield: 12 muffins

¾ cup chunky peanut butter

⅓ cup honey

½ cup egg substitute

1 cup skim milk (or substitute)

2 cups Vita-Spelt Pancake/Muffin Mix (or equivalent product)

¼ cup fruit spread or jam (any flavor)

1. Preheat the oven to 400°F. Coat 12 muffin wells with nonstick cooking spray or line them with paper cups. Set aside.

2. Place the peanut butter and honey in a 2-quart bowl, and stir until thoroughly blended. Add the egg substitute and milk, and stir to blend. Add the spelt mix, and stir just until the mix is moistened.

3. Fill the prepared muffin wells ½ full with the batter. Indent the center of each muffin with a teaspoon, and spoon 1 teaspoon of the fruit spread or jam into each indentation.

4. Bake for 16 to 18 minutes, or until a toothpick inserted in the center of a muffin comes out clean. Turn the muffins sideways in the wells, and allow them to cool in the tins for about 5 minutes. Remove the muffins from the tins and transfer to a wire rack. Cool completely before serving.

Coconut and Bulgur Muffins

Yield: 12 muffins

¼ cup egg substitute

2 egg whites

1 cup low-fat milk

¼ teaspoon coconut extract

2 tablespoons melted canola margarine

¼ cup plus 2 tablespoons turbinado sugar (or other sweetener)

1 cup spelt bulgur

1 cup boiling water

½ cup shredded coconut

1 cup white spelt flour

2½ teaspoons nonaluminum baking powder

These muffins are easy to make and a joy to eat for breakfast, lunch, snacks, or dinner.

1. Preheat the oven to 400°F. Coat 12 muffin wells with nonstick cooking spray or line them with paper cups. Set aside.

2. Place the egg substitute, egg whites, milk, coconut extract, margarine, and sugar in a 1-quart bowl, and beat with a fork until well blended. Set aside.

3. Place the bulgur in a 1-quart bowl. Add the boiling water, stir, and set aside for 5 minutes. Add the coconut, and stir to blend. Set aside.

4. Sift the flour and baking powder into a 2-quart bowl. Add the bulgur mixture, and stir. Add the egg mixture, and stir just until the dry ingredients are moistened.

5. Fill the prepared muffin wells ¾ full with the batter. Bake for 35 minutes, or until a toothpick inserted in the center of a muffin comes out clean. Turn the muffins sideways in the wells, and allow the muffins to cool in the tins for about 5 minutes. Remove the muffins from the tins and transfer to a wire rack. Cool completely before serving.

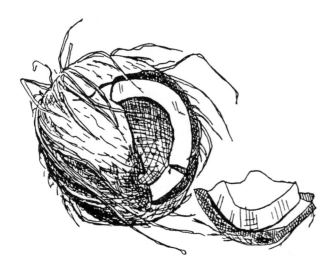

Cottage Cheese and Dillweed Muffins

Dried dill and fresh onions give these savory muffins a special flavor. Serve them with soups and salads.

Yield: 6 large muffins

1. Preheat the oven to 375°F. Coat 6 muffin wells with nonstick cooking spray or line them with paper cups. Set aside.

2. Combine the milk, egg, oil, and maple syrup in a 1-quart bowl. Set aside.

3. Combine the cornmeal, flour, and baking powder in a 2-quart bowl. Add the milk mixture to the flour mixture, and stir just until the dry ingredients are moistened.

4. Combine the cottage cheese, onion, and dill in a 1-quart bowl. Pour the cheese mixture over the batter, and stir just until the cheese is evenly distributed throughout the batter.

5. Fill the prepared muffin wells ¾ full with the batter, and bake for 20 minutes. Reduce the oven temperature to 300°F, and bake for an additional 15 minutes, or until a toothpick inserted in the center of a muffin comes out clean. Turn the muffins sideways in the wells, and allow them to cool in the tin for about 5 minutes. Remove the muffins from the tin and transfer to a wire rack. Cool completely before serving.

¼ cup low-fat milk (or substitute)

1 egg (or substitute)

1 tablespoon canola oil

1 tablespoon maple syrup

½ cup cornmeal

½ cup whole-grain spelt flour

1 tablespoon nonaluminum baking powder

¾ cup dry curd cottage cheese

1 tablespoon finely minced onion

1 teaspoon dried dill

6

The Sandwich Platter

When hunger prevented John Montagu, the Fourth Earl of Sandwich, from devoting his full mind to the gaming table, he would order his servants to bring him food enclosed in bread so that he could eat and play at the same time. And so the sandwich was born.

Two hundred years later, there can be little doubt that this British invention is among America's most popular foods. Why has this simple culinary idea been embraced so wholeheartedly? One reason is that sandwiches are highly versatile. Depending on the occasion and on personal taste, sandwiches may be hot or cold, sweet or savory, open-faced or closed, made on a dainty bun or on the largest of rolls or loaves. Most sandwiches are also highly portable, making them perfect picnic and lunch box fare. And, as the Earl of Sandwich knew, sandwiches are easy and fast to eat, making them a favorite with both active children and on-the-go adults.

Of course, as well loved as sandwiches are, they become even more tantalizing—and certainly more nutritious—when spelt is among the ingredients. With its firm texture and unique taste, spelt breads and buns turn even an ordinary sandwich into a culinary treat. And when spelt is also a filling ingredient, the goodness of this wholesome grain is doubled.

This chapter presents a variety of sandwich and sandwich-filling recipes—enough to satisfy a wide range of appetites and tastes. If you are looking for a healthful alternative to the usual hamburger, for instance, try Parslied Peanut and Spelt Patties, Spelt Burgers, or Spicy Turkey-Bulgur Burgers. Served on spelt buns, these burgers are flavorful enough to satisfy any burger enthusiast.

When a quick snack or light sandwich is the order of the day, Granola-Striped Grahams—delightfully sweet sandwiches made with spelt graham crackers—fit the bill. Grilled Cheese and Savory Onion Toast is another satisfying but not-too-filling sandwich idea. Or try Open-Faced Tea Sandwiches. Topped by a variety of spreads, these finger sandwiches are as perfect at after-school snack time as they are at afternoon tea.

When heartier fare is called for, Beandogs Baked in Spelt-Puff Pastry make ideal lunch or dinner entrées. Serve with hot soup or a crisp salad, and your meal is complete.

Of course, spelt sandwiches are as welcome at parties as they are at everyday meals. Three-Pepper Pizza Crescents, for instance, make delicious appetizers, while Buffet-Style Sandwich Loaf is a tempting and decorative addition to any holiday buffet.

While the recipes in this chapter provide enough sandwich ideas for many meals and snacks, it is my hope that they will also inspire you to add spelt to your own favorite sandwich recipes. Try peanut butter and jelly on Easy Yeast Bread. (To make the sandwich even more nutritious, use homemade or health-foods-store nut butter.) Make your next cheese sandwich with No-Need-to-Knead Pumpernickel. Add cooked spelt kernels to your own burger mixture, or stir spelt sprouts into your kids' favorite sandwich spread. You will find that adding spelt is an easy way to boost nutrition, enhance flavor, and provide a change of pace that family and friends are sure to love.

SANDWICHES

Beandogs Baked in Spelt-Puff Pastry

To create these vegetarian-style hot dogs, dough is wrapped around a "frankfurter" shaped from Bean and Spelt Kernel Spread.

1. To make the pastry, sift the flour and salt into a 2-quart bowl. Cut in the margarine with a pastry blender or knife, and use your fingers to work the dough until it has a crumbly consistency. Stir in the yogurt, and mix until the dough forms a ball.

2. Place the dough on a lightly floured board, and knead gently for a few minutes, or until smooth and pliable. Cover the dough with a clean kitchen towel, and set aside for 30 minutes.

3. Preheat the oven to 350°F. Line a 13-x-9-inch baking sheet with nonstick parchment cooking paper, and set aside.

4. Roll the dough out into a 16-x-8-inch rectangle. Use a sharp knife to cut the sheet into four 8-x-4-inch rectangles.

5. Using wet hands, take 3 tablespoons of the spread and roll into a 6-inch log. Repeat with the remaining spread until you have 4 beandogs.

6. Place 1 beandog in the middle of each dough rectangle. Wrap the dough around each beandog, and seal the edges by brushing a little water on the seams and pinching them together with your fingers. Tuck the dough under the roll at each end, so that the filling will not run out of the pastry.

7. Place the beandogs seam side down on the prepared baking sheet, and brush the tops and sides with half of the mayonnaise. Bake for 20 minutes. Turn the beandogs over, and brush the tops and sides with the remaining mayonnaise. Bake for an additional 20 minutes, or until the pastry is lightly browned. Serve immediately.

Serving Suggestions

• Give the baked beandogs added flavor and eye appeal by running squiggly lines of ketchup and mustard along the top before serving.

• Place a few tablespoons of hot-dog relish beside each beandog for dipping.

Yield: 4 beandogs

¾ cup Bean and Spelt Kernel Spread (page 95)

1 tablespoon nonfat mayonnaise

PUFF PASTRY

1¼ cups sifted white spelt flour

¼ teaspoon sea salt

2 tablespoons canola margarine

⅓ cup plain nonfat yogurt

Parslied Peanut and Spelt Patties

Yield: 4 servings

1 cup cooked spelt kernels (page 3)

½ cup shelled peanuts

1 egg (or substitute)

2 tablespoons chopped fresh parsley

¼ teaspoon tamari soy sauce

¼ teaspoon herb seasoning salt

¼ teaspoon freshly ground white pepper

4 Spelt Buns (page 68)

¼ cup low-fat mayonnaise (or substitute)

4 lettuce leaves

4 slices tomato

¼ cup pickle slices

Most savory dishes benefit from the mild flavor of parsley, an herb that is flavorful enough to stand alone, and also mixes well with most other herbs. Flat-leaf Italian parsley is more piquant than the curly-leaf American variety, but whichever you purchase, this herb is at its best when rich green in color, with no traces of yellow.

1. Place the spelt kernels and peanuts in a food processor, and, using a fine cutting circle, process on "grind." (Alternatively, use a hand grinder or a blender. But be aware that because the kernels have been cooked, they can become mushy and clog the blender.)

2. Place the ground mixture in a 2-quart bowl, and add the egg, parsley, tamari, herb seasoning, and pepper. Mix thoroughly.

3. Using wet hands, form the mixture into 4 patties. Coat a nonstick 10-inch skillet with nonstick cooking spray, and cook the patties over medium heat for 5 to 7 minutes on each side, or until browned and crisp. Transfer the patties to paper towels, and allow to drain.

4. Cut each Spelt Bun in half. Spread the bottom half of each bun with mayonnaise, and top with a leaf of lettuce. Follow with a drained patty, a slice of tomato, and a few pickle slices. Replace the top of the bun, and serve immediately.

Variation

• Just before the patties are finished cooking, top each with a slice of low-fat cheese, and allow it to melt slightly before serving.

Spelt Burgers

This prize-winning recipe was created by Martin Oswald of San Francisco, California. For those of us who love hamburgers but avoid them for health reasons, Martin's recipe provides a wonderful alternative.

1. Preheat the oven to 350°F.

2. Place the spelt kernels in a blender, and process at medium speed for 2 minutes, or until the kernels are half the size of a grain of rice. Set aside.

3. Place the margarine in a 3-quart saucepan, and melt over medium heat. Add the onion, celery, carrots, and garlic, and cook, stirring often, until the vegetables are tender but firm. Add the stock and the ground kernels, and mix well. Increase the heat to high, and bring the mixture to a boil.

4. Pour the vegetable mixture into a 2-quart casserole dish, and cover with aluminum foil. Bake for 20 minutes, or until the mixture is sticky and has the consistency of cooked white rice.

5. Cool the mixture to room temperature. Add ketchup and mustard to taste, and stir to mix.

6. Using wet hands, form the mixture into 4 patties. If the mixture does not hold together well, add the egg and mix well before forming the patties. Place the oil in a nonstick 10-inch skillet, and cook the patties over medium heat for 5 to 7 minutes on each side, or until browned and crisp. Transfer the patties to paper towels, and allow to drain.

7. Cut each Spelt Bun in half. Spread the bottom half of each bun with mayonnaise, and top with a leaf of lettuce and a slice of onion. Follow with a drained patty, a slice of tomato, and a few pickle slices. Replace the top of the bun, and serve immediately.

Yield: 4 burgers

1 cup spelt kernels

1 tablespoon canola margarine

¼ cup chopped onion

¼ cup chopped celery

¼ cup chopped carrots

1 clove garlic, minced

2 cups Veggie Stock (page 37)

2 tablespoons ketchup

1 tablespoon mild mustard

1 egg (optional)

¼ cup olive oil

4 Spelt Buns (page 68)

¼ cup low-fat mayonnaise (or substitute)

4 lettuce leaves

4 slices onion

4 slices tomato

¼ cup pickle slices

Spicy Turkey-Bulgur Burgers

Yield: 8 burgers

½ cup spelt bulgur

½ cup boiling water

1½ cups ground turkey breast

¼ cup plus 2 tablespoons egg
  substitute

1 large yellow onion, minced

1½ teaspoons dried marjoram

½ teaspoon sea salt

¼ teaspoon freshly ground white
  pepper

1 tablespoon spicy mustard

8 Spelt Buns (page 68)

½ cup low-fat mayonnaise (or
  substitute)

8 lettuce leaves

8 slices onion

8 slices tomato

½ cup pickle slices

By mixing spelt bulgur with ground turkey breast and spicy mustard, you'll quickly create a spicy burger that's low on fat and high on taste and nutrition.

1. Place the bulgur in a 2-quart heatproof bowl. Add the boiling water, and set the mixture aside for 5 minutes.

2. Add the turkey, egg substitute, onion, marjoram, salt, pepper, and mustard to the bulgur mixture, and mix well.

3. Using floured hands, form the mixture into 8 patties. Coat a nonstick 10-inch skillet with nonstick cooking spray, and cook the patties over medium heat for 7 minutes on each side, or until browned and crisp. Transfer the patties to paper towels, and allow to drain.

4. Cut each spelt bun in half. Spread the bottom half of each bun with mayonnaise, and top with a leaf of lettuce and a slice of onion. Follow with a drained patty, a slice of tomato, and a few pickle slices. Replace the top of the bun, and serve immediately.

Open-Faced Tea Sandwiches

Yield: 12 to 24 tea sandwiches

12 slices No-Need-to-Knead
  Pumpernickel (page 72)

3 cups sandwich spread, any type
  (pages 93–95)

These little open-faced sandwiches are ideal for serving with afternoon tea—a custom first brought to this country by the early English settlers. Children also love these small decoratively shaped sandwiches.

1. Using large cookie cutters, cut each bread slice into 1 or 2 interesting shapes. (If you don't have any cookie cutters, spread the filling over each piece of bread before it is cut, and use a sharp knife to cut it into narrow "finger" shapes.)

2. Spread each shaped piece of bread with the spread of your choice, transfer to a serving platter, and serve.

Crab and Wild-Rice Cakes

Spicy horseradish sauce and spelt buns enhance both the flavor and the nutritional value of these savory crab cakes.

1. Place the margarine in an 8-inch skillet, and melt over medium heat. Add the flour, and stir for about 1 minute, or until the flour is lightly browned. Slowly blend in the yogurt. Remove the skillet from the heat and set aside.

2. Place 1 egg in a 2-quart bowl, and beat lightly with a fork. Gradually stir in the flour mixture. Stir in the lemon juice, pepper, onion, rice, crab meat, and 1 cup of the ground spelt flakes or crumbs. Mix well, cover, and chill for 2 hours.

3. To make the sauce, place the horseradish and yogurt in a 1-quart bowl, and mix well. Cover and refrigerate until needed.

4. Shape the chilled crab meat mixture into 8 flat cakes, using about ¼ cup of the mixture for each cake. Set aside.

5. Place the remaining egg and the milk in a shallow dish, and beat lightly. Spread the remaining cup of ground flakes or crumbs in another shallow dish. Dip both sides of each crab cake first in the milk mixture, and then in the crumbs.

6. Generously coat a nonstick 10-inch skillet with nonstick cooking spray, and cook the crab cakes over medium heat for about 3 minutes on each side, or until golden brown. If the cakes stick during cooking, add more nonstick spray. Transfer the cakes to paper towels, and allow to drain.

7. Cut each spelt bun in half. Spread the bottom half of each bun with the Horseradish Sauce, and top with a leaf of lettuce and a slice of onion. Follow with a drained patty. Replace the top of the bun, and serve immediately.

Yield: 8 cakes

2 tablespoons canola margarine

2 tablespoons whole-grain spelt flour

½ cup plain nonfat yogurt

2 eggs (or substitute), divided

2 tablespoons fresh lemon juice

⅛ teaspoon freshly ground white pepper

2 tablespoons minced red onion

1 cup cooked wild rice

2 cans (6½ ounces each) crab meat, drained and flaked

2 cups finely ground toasted spelt flakes or spelt bread crumbs, divided

¼ cup low-fat milk (or substitute)

8 Spelt Buns (page 68)

8 lettuce leaves

8 slices onion

HORSERADISH SAUCE

¼ cup prepared horseradish

2 tablespoons plain nonfat yogurt

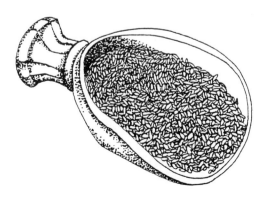

Grilled Cheese and Savory Onion Toast

Yield: 8 sandwiches

1 tablespoon canola oil

2 large yellow onions, thinly sliced

1/8 teaspoon cayenne pepper

1/4 teaspoon ground thyme

1/4 cup apple cider vinegar

1 tablespoon maple syrup

8 slices No-Need-to-Knead Pumpernickel (page 72)

8 slices low-fat Swiss cheese

The word toast stems from the old French word toster, and originally referred only to toasted bread. A second meaning arose from the old practice of floating a snippet of toast in a glass of wine. If the toast remained buoyant, the wine was considered to be of good quality. Eventually, when a glass was raised in a person's honor, it, too, was known as a toast. This tasty toast is an ideal party snack.

1. Preheat the oven to 350°F.

2. Place the oil in a 10-inch skillet over medium heat. Add the onions and sauté, stirring constantly, for about 7 minutes, or until brown.

3. Add the pepper, thyme, vinegar, and syrup to the skillet. Reduce the heat to low, cover, and simmer for 15 minutes.

4. While the onions are simmering, place the bread on a 13-x-9-inch baking sheet, and bake for about 10 minutes on each side, or until the bread is lightly toasted.

5. Remove the onions from the skillet, and drain off any excess liquid. Spread the onions over the bread slices, and top each piece with a slice of cheese.

6. Set the oven to broil, and place the sandwiches under the broiler just until the cheese melts. Serve immediately.

Granola-Striped Graham Sandwiches

Yield: 6 sandwiches

3 tablespoons canola margarine, softened

6 Spelt Honey Graham Crackers (page 186)

1/4 cup plus 2 tablespoons smooth peanut butter

2 large bananas, sliced

2 tablespoons honey

3/4 cup Hazelnut Granola (page 24)

This prize-winning recipe was developed by Eada Phelps of Silverton, Oregon. Eada also created the recipe for Spelt Honey Graham Crackers, which is found in Chapter 11.

1. Spread a thin layer of margarine over each graham cracker. Spread about 1 tablespoon of the peanut butter evenly over the margarine.

2. Arrange 2 diagonal rows of banana slices on top of each cracker. Drizzle the honey between the rows of banana, sprinkle the granola over the honey, and serve.

Three-Pepper Pizza Crescents

These stuffed crescents are made with a spelt yogurt dough and filled with a combination of green, yellow, and red peppers. They are delicious as either snacks or appetizers.

1. To make the pastry, sift the flour and salt into a 2-quart bowl. Cut in the margarine with a pastry blender or knife, and use your fingers to work the dough until it has a crumbly consistency. Stir in the yogurt, and mix until the dough forms a ball.

2. Place the dough on a lightly floured board, and knead gently for a few minutes, or until smooth and pliable. Cover the dough with a clean kitchen towel, and set aside for 30 minutes.

3. Preheat the oven to 400°F. Coat a 17-x-14-inch baking sheet with nonstick cooking spray, and set aside.

4. Generously coat an 8-inch skillet with nonstick cooking spray. Place the skillet over medium heat, add the onion and peppers, and sauté for about 3 minutes, or until the vegetables are soft.

5. Transfer the pepper mixture to a paper towel to drain. Sprinkle the drained mixture with Italian seasoning, and transfer to a 1-quart bowl. Add the tomato sauce and mix well.

6. Place the dough on a floured surface, and divide it into 2 equal balls. Using a rolling pin, roll each piece into a 9-inch circle. Cut each circle into 8 wedges.

7. Place a heaping teaspoonful of the pepper mixture on the wide end of each wedge, and roll up the wedge, beginning at the wide end. Arrange the rolls on the prepared pan, and shape each roll into a crescent by bending the ends inward. Brush the salad dressing over each cresent, and prick the top with a fork.

8. Bake for about 12 minutes, or until the crescents are golden brown. Serve immediately.

Yield: 16 crescents

FILLING

1 tablespoon minced onion

1 tablespoon minced green bell pepper

1 tablespoon minced yellow bell pepper

1 tablespoon minced red bell pepper

1 tablespoon dried Italian seasoning

½ cup tomato sauce

2 tablespoons bottled low-fat Italian dressing

PASTRY

1¼ cups sifted white spelt flour

¼ teaspoon sea salt

2 tablespoons canola margarine

⅓ cup plain nonfat yogurt

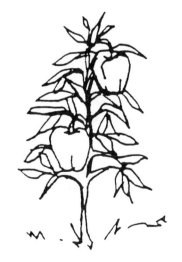

Buffet-Style Sandwich Loaf

Yield: 10 to 12 sandwiches

SALMON FILLING

3 ounces nonfat cream cheese, warmed to room temperature

1/4 cup nonfat sour cream

1/4 cup chopped smoked salmon

2 tablespoons chopped capers

2 tablespoons chopped walnuts

BLUE CHEESE FILLING

3 ounces nonfat cream cheese, warmed to room temperature

2 ounces blue cheese, crumbled

2 tablespoons low-fat buttermilk

1/2 cucumber, seeded and coarsely shredded

1 tablespoon chopped fresh dill

EGG FILLING

4 hard-boiled eggs

1/4 cup nonfat mayonnaise (or substitute)

Pinch sea salt

Pinch freshly ground black pepper

1 teaspoon mustard

1 tablespoon chopped fresh chives

TOPPING

8 ounces nonfat cream cheese, warmed to room temperature

1/4 cup nonfat sour cream

1 scallion, finely sliced

Pinch paprika

1-pound loaf spelt bread

Several large lettuce leaves

1 cup mixed chopped alfalfa and spelt sprouts

12 cherry tomatoes, halved

12 pitted black olives, sliced

Bread made from Vita-Spelt Whole Grain Bread Mix or Vita-Spelt White Bread Mix is ideal for this elegant sandwich loaf, which has three different fillings. The outside is covered with a cream cheese-scallion paste, and the top is colorfully garnished. Because the fillings need to be chilled for one hour to allow the various flavors to blend, they should be prepared first.

1. To make the Salmon Filling, combine all of the ingredients in a 1-quart bowl until blended. Cover and chill for at least 1 hour.

2. To make the Blue Cheese Filling, combine all of the ingredients in a 1-quart bowl until blended. Cover and chill for at least 1 hour.

3. To make the Egg Filling, press the hard-boiled eggs through a sieve, and place the sieved eggs in a 1-quart bowl. Add the remaining ingredients, and combine until blended. Cover and chill for at least 1 hour.

4. To make the topping, combine all of the ingredients in a 1-quart bowl until blended. Set aside.

5. Using a large serrated knife, trim the crusts from the bread. Carefully cut the loaf lengthwise into 4 equal-sized horizontal slices.

6. Line a serving platter with the lettuce leaves. Place 1 of the bread slices on the lettuce, and spread with the Salmon Filling. Top with another bread slice, and spread with the Blue Cheese Filling. Top with a third bread slice, and spread with the Egg Filling. Top with the remaining slice of bread.

7. Using a large knife, spread the topping over the top and all 4 sides of the sandwich stack. Sprinkle the chopped sprouts over the topping, and arrange the tomatoes and olives in a decorative pattern over the sprouts. Serve immediately, slicing each serving as needed.

SANDWICH SPREADS AND FILLINGS

Tofu-Bulgur Sandwich Loaf

The ingredients for these loaves are mixed together in minutes, placed in ramekin dishes, and steamed in a water bath. This is an easy, economical, and healthful way to make your own luncheon "meats."

1. Place the bulgur in a 1-quart heatproof bowl. Mix the boiling water, vinegar, and tamari together in a small bowl, and pour over the bulgur. Set aside for 5 minutes.

2. Squeeze any excess water from the tofu. Place the tofu in a 2-quart bowl, and thoroughly mash it using a potato masher or fork. Mix in the scallions, Wonder-Slim, cheese, pimiento, and bulgur.

3. In a small bowl, quickly stir together the stock and soy flour until the mixture is smooth. Pour the stock mixture over the bulgur mixture, and stir to mix. Set aside.

4. Preheat the oven to 400°F. Fill a 3-inch-deep 3-quart baking dish with 2 inches of water, and set aside.

5. Lightly coat 2 ramekin dishes (3½ inches in diameter and 2 inches deep) with nonstick cooking spray, and pack equal amounts of the bulgur mixture into each dish. Cover each dish with aluminum foil, and place in the water-filled baking dish.

6. Bake for 1 hour and 30 minutes, or until the mixture is firm, checking the water level periodically and adding more water if necessary. Allow the ramekin dishes to cool for about 5 minutes at room temperature. Invert the dishes to remove the loaves, and cool completely. Slice as needed for sandwiches.

Yield: 2 loaves

½ cup spelt bulgur

½ cup boiling water

2 tablespoons apple cider vinegar

¼ teaspoon tamari soy sauce

1 cup crumbled firm tofu

2 scallions, finely chopped

¼ cup WonderSlim* or other fat and egg substitute

¼ cup grated sharp Cheddar cheese

2 tablespoons chopped pimiento

¼ cup Veggie Stock (page 37)

2 tablespoons soy flour

*WonderSlim fat and egg substitute can be found in most health foods stores.

Variation

• For the Mexican-food lover in you, replace the Cheddar cheese with jalapeño pepper cheese.

Chicken and Almond Spread

Yield: 4 cups

2 cups finely diced cooked chicken

1 cup finely diced celery

1 hard-boiled egg, finely diced (optional)

½ cup chopped almonds

Dash sea salt

Dash paprika

2 tablespoons bottled French dressing

¼ cup low-fat mayonnaise (or substitute)

While chicken salad may contain a variety of ingredients, it should taste primarily of chicken. The ingredients in this spread complement the flavor of the chicken, rather than masking it.

1. Combine all of the ingredients in a 1-quart bowl until well mixed.

2. Use immediately, or place in an airtight container and store in the refrigerator for up to 3 days.

Blue Cheese and Avocado Spread

Yield: 2 cups

1 very soft avocado, peeled, pitted, and mashed

8 ounces nonfat cream cheese, warmed to room temperature

1 ounce blue cheese, crumbled

½ cup unsalted hulled sunflower seeds

1 tablespoon fresh lemon juice

While this spread is a rich source of vitamins and minerals, it is also high in calories and fat. Fortunately, a little goes a long way.

1. Place the mashed avocado, cream cheese, and blue cheese in a 2-quart bowl, and blend the mixture with a fork until it forms a smooth paste.

2. Place the sunflower seeds in a blender, and process at medium speed for 2 minutes, or until finely ground. Stir the seeds and the lemon juice into the avocado mixture.

3. Use immediately, or place in an airtight container and store in the refrigerator for no longer than 1 day.

Bean and Spelt Kernel Spread

Besides being a delicious sandwich spread, this is an excellent meat substitute in dishes such as lasagna, stuffed peppers, stuffed cabbage, and stuffed eggplant.

Yield: 4 cups

1. Place the spelt kernels and beans in a food processor, and, using a fine cutting circle, process on "grind." (Alternatively, use a hand grinder or blender. But be aware that because the kernels have been cooked, they can become mushy and clog the blender.) Transfer the ground mixture to a 2-quart bowl.

2. Place the bread in the food processor, and process on "grind." (Processing the bread last helps to clean the machine.) Add the ground bread to the spelt kernel mixture, along with the garlic, majoram, herb seasoning, pepper, and ketchup. Mix well, using a wooden spoon.

3. Use immediately, or place in an airtight container and store in the refrigerator for up to 4 days.

2 cups cooked spelt kernels (page 3)

1 can (15 ounces) red kidney beans, drained, or 2 cups cooked kidney beans

1 slice stale spelt bread

1 clove garlic, minced

1 tablespoon dried marjoram, or 2 tablespoons chopped fresh marjoram

1/4 teaspoon herb seasoning salt

Dash freshly ground white pepper

1/2 cup ketchup

Garlic Spelt Spread

This is a healthful version of the spread used to make smorrebrod, the name still used by Scandinavian-Americans for buttered bread. It can also be used to prepare oven-broiled garlic bread.

Yield: 1 cup

1/4 cup spelt bulgur

1/4 cup boiling water

1 small clove garlic, crushed

1/4 cup plus 2 tablespoons canola margarine, softened

Dash sweet paprika

1. Place the bulgur in a ramekin dish (3½ inches in diameter and 2 inches deep), and pour the boiling water over the bulgur. Set aside for 5 minutes.

2. Add the remaining ingredients to the bulgur, and mix well.

3. Use immediately, or place in an airtight container and store in the refrigerator for up to 3 days.

7

Sauces, Stuffings, and Dressings

For centuries, sauces have been used to enhance the flavor, texture, and appearance of foods. Sauces can add the finishing touch to an already sophisticated dish, or can make a simple plate of steamed vegetables, boiled pasta, or grilled chicken or fish more flavorful and appealing. Stuffings may, of course, perform a similar culinary trick by making a plain entrée more exciting, or may be used to stuff vegetables, poultry, or fish. And dressings can add flavor, moisten and bind salad ingredients, and play a number of other culinary roles.

This chapter presents recipes for a variety of sauces, stuffings, and dressings. Many of these recipes have been made healthy and flavorful with the addition of spelt flour, spelt bread, or another spelt product. Other recipes do not contain spelt, but have been designed to complement such spelt-based foods as pasta.

When following the sauce recipes presented here, you will be delighted to find that with its rich and nutty flavor, spelt flour makes a perfect thickening agent. As you'll learn, spelt's distinctive flavor may be intensified by browning the flour before use. Sauces that use flour as a thickener should turn out perfectly as long as you follow the directions carefully. But if your sauce does become lumpy during cooking, simply pour the mixture into your blender, and blend until smooth. What can you do if your cream sauce isn't thick enough for your taste? By adding my Spelt Roux or Beurre Manié, you can quickly add body to almost any sauce.

A variety of ingredients may be used to make sauces more flavorful, to tailor-make sauces for use with specific dishes, or to adjust the consistency of sauces that are not cream based. Herbs are among the most important sauce seasonings, as they add spark and individuality. When possible, use fresh herbs for their special flavor and color. When only dried herbs are available, keep in mind that they are more concentrated in flavor than fresh, and so should be added in smaller quantities. To further enhance flavor, add such ingredients as chopped onion, celery, garlic, and peppers. When a sauce needs body, add chunky ingredients—chopped tomatoes, zucchini, mushrooms, carrots, and fennel, for instance. Of course, all seasonings should be checked just before serving. At that point, last-minute adjustments can be made by adding a vegetable seasoning salt such as Herbamare; mirin, a sweet, rice-based Japanese cooking wine; tamari soy sauce; or basics such as vinegar or lemon juice.

As you may know, many traditionally made sauces are high in fat and calories. For instance, in its most classic form, Sauce Béchamel contains both butter and whole milk. Fortunately, by using some low-fat ingredients, the sauces presented in this chapter have been made lighter and healthier than traditional ones. I hope that these sauces will not only add to your culinary repertoire, but also encourage you to make lower-fat versions of your own favorite sauces. As a beginning, substitute low-fat milk and cheeses for full-fat dairy products. Or try starting with a liquid base of plain water, vegetable stock, or freshly extracted vegetable juices, such as celery, tomato, or cucumber. You might also want to use these liquids in place of butter or oil when sautéing onion, celery, and other sauce ingredients.

Whether you are whipping up a basic cream sauce to serve atop cooked vegetables or making a savory holiday stuffing, you're sure to find that every dish is improved by the addition of spelt. And when spelt products are used in both the dish itself and the sauce that crowns it, the goodness of spelt is doubled with delicious results.

SAUCE HELPERS

Browned Spelt Flour

Although this recipe specifies the use of 1 cup of flour, it can be used to brown any amount of white or whole-grain flour. Spelt flour browned in this way will give robust sauces a delightfully nutty taste and a rich brown color.

1 cup spelt flour

1. Preheat the oven to 450°F. Spread the flour out on a 16-x-11-inch baking pan until the flour has a depth of about ¼ inch.

2. Place the pan in the oven. When the flour begins to color—after 2 or 3 minutes—begin stirring it every minute or 2 with a wooden spoon. Continue baking and periodically stirring for 5 to 10 minutes, or until the flour is evenly browned.

3. Cool the flour completely before transferring it to an airtight jar. Store in the refrigerator for up to 2 months.

Beurre Manié

Like Spelt Roux, found on page 100, Beurre Manié may be used to thicken sauces, soups, or stews.

¼ cup canola margarine

½ cup whole-grain spelt flour

1. Using a knife, cut the margarine into small pieces and place in a 1-quart bowl. Add the flour, and use your fingertips to work the ingredients into a smooth dough.

2. Transfer the dough to a lightly floured board, and knead for 2 minutes, or until the mixture is shiny and pliable. Coat a sheet of plastic wrap with nonstick cooking spray. Shape the dough into a ball, place in the center of the plastic wrap, and wrap tightly. Store in the refrigerator for up to 10 days.

3. To use the Beurre Manié, add 1 tablespoon of the mixture for each cup of sauce, soup, or stew liquid. Bring the liquid to a boil over medium-high heat. Remove the pan from the heat, add the Beurre Manié, and quickly blend with a whisk until the mixture is smooth. Return the pan to the heat and bring the liquid back to a boil, at which point it will thicken instantly.

Spelt Roux

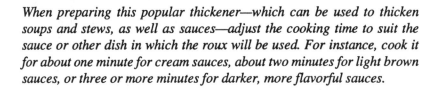

¼ cup canola margarine

½ cup white spelt flour

When preparing this popular thickener—which can be used to thicken soups and stews, as well as sauces—adjust the cooking time to suit the sauce or other dish in which the roux will be used. For instance, cook it for about one minute for cream sauces, about two minutes for light brown sauces, or three or more minutes for darker, more flavorful sauces.

1. Place the margarine in a heavy 1-quart saucepan, and melt over medium heat. Add the flour, and cook, stirring constantly with a wooden spoon, for about 2 minutes, or until the flour and margarine are well mixed and the mixture has browned to the desired color.

2. While the roux is still soft, drop tablespoonfuls of the mixture onto an ungreased baking sheet. Allow to cool at room temperature for 15 minutes. Then place the sheet in the freezer for 30 minutes, or until the spoonfuls of roux are frozen. Transfer the frozen portions of roux to an airtight container or plastic bag, and store in the freezer for up to 3 months.

3. To use Spelt Roux, add 1 portion of frozen roux for each cup of sauce, soup, or stew liquid. Drop the frozen roux into the hot liquid, and stir until the roux has melted.

SAUCES

Zucchini-Cilantro Sauce

Also known as coriander, cilantro, which resembles flat-leaf parsley, is an aromatic, strong-tasting herb that is popular in Mexican and Chinese cooking. In this recipe, the combination of fresh cilantro leaves and zucchini results in a truly refreshing vegetarian sauce that is perfect on any type of pasta.

Yield: 4 cups

2 large ripe tomatoes

2 tablespoons canola oil

2 cups grated zucchini

1 tablespoon plus 1½ teaspoons chopped fresh cilantro

1 clove garlic, crushed

1 tablespoon whole-grain spelt flour

1 teaspoon fresh lemon juice

¼ teaspoon balsamic vinegar

⅛ teaspoon herb seasoning salt

⅛ teaspoon freshly ground white pepper

1. Blanch the tomatoes by placing them in a 3-quart saucepan of boiling water for 1 minute. Remove the tomatoes from the boiling water, and rinse them under cold running water. Using a sharp knife, remove the skins. Cut the tomatoes in half crosswise, and remove the core.

2. Place the tomatoes in a blender or food processor, and process on "purée" for about 2 minutes, or until smooth. Set aside.

3. Place the oil in a 10-inch skillet over medium-high heat. When the oil is hot, add the zucchini, cilantro, garlic, and a sprinkling of flour. Cook, stirring constantly, for about 1 minute, or until the zucchini is wilted.

4. Reduce the heat to low, and stir the puréed tomatoes into the zucchini mixture. Simmer uncovered for about 3 minutes.

5. Add the lemon juice, vinegar, herb seasoning, and pepper to the sauce, and mix well. Use immediately, or cool to room temperature, transfer to an airtight container, and store in the refrigerator for up to 5 days. Reheat in a double boiler, and serve.

Serving Suggestions

• Serve the sauce over any spelt pasta.

• Use as a dipping sauce for Cheesy Straw Twists (page 51).

• Use instead of the suggested sauce when making Zucchini and Tomato Pizza (page 133) or any other spelt-dough pizza.

Basic Spelt Béchamel Sauce

Yield: 3¹/₂ cups

2 cups low-fat milk (or substitute)

1 small bay leaf

¹/₄ cup canola margarine

¹/₃ cup white spelt flour

¹/₂ teaspoon sea salt

¹/₈ teaspoon freshly ground white pepper

Classic Béchamel Sauce is made thick and creamy with sweet butter and whole milk. This lower-fat version, made with canola margarine and bay leaf-flavored low-fat milk, is every bit as satisfying and creamy as the original.

1. Place the milk and bay leaf in a 1-quart saucepan, and cook over medium-high heat, stirring frequently, until the milk comes to a boil. Remove the pan from the heat and set aside.

2. Place the margarine in a 2-quart saucepan, and cook over low heat just until the margarine begins to bubble. Do *not* allow the margarine to turn brown.

3. Add the flour to the melted margarine, and stir constantly for about 2 minutes, or until the mixture forms a thick brown paste.

4. Remove any skin from the boiled milk, and slowly add the milk and the bay leaf to the flour paste, a little at a time, stirring vigorously with a wire whisk until the mixture is smooth.

5. Increase the heat to medium-high, add the salt and pepper, and continue to whisk until the mixture comes to a boil. Reduce the heat to low, and simmer for about 10 minutes, stirring frequently. Remove from the heat and discard the bay leaf.

6. Use the sauce immediately, or cool to room temperature, transfer to an airtight container, and store in the refrigerator for up to 3 days. Reheat in a double boiler, and serve.

Serving Suggestion

• Serve the sauce over spelt dumplings, pasta, or crêpes.

Variations

• To make Anchovy Sauce, add 1 teaspoon of anchovy paste along with the salt and pepper. Because the anchovy paste is so flavorful, use the salt and pepper sparingly.

• To make Cheese Sauce, add 1 cup of grated low-fat Cheddar, Swiss, or Gouda during the last 5 minutes of cooking.

• To make Herb Sauce, add 1 to 2 tablespoons of chopped fresh chives, parsley, fennel, or dill along with the milk.

• To make Lemon Sauce, omit the bay leaf when heating the milk, and add 2 to 3 tablespoons of fresh lemon juice during the last few minutes of cooking time. This sauce is particularly delicious when served over the Lemon Noodles variation of Whole-Grain Spelt Egg Noodles (page 143).

Pesto Sauce

In Italy, a fresh basil sauce is called pesto. This delightfully green sauce is a special treat during the summer and early fall, when basil is in abundance. Pesto is traditionally made with a mortar and pestle—from which it gets its name—but your kitchen blender will make this versatile sauce in a fraction of the time. Always serve this sauce at room temperature.

1. Place all of the ingredients except the cheese in a blender or food processor, and process on "liquefy" for about 5 minutes, or until the sauce is smooth. During processing, periodically stop the blender and use a wooden spoon to scrape the sauce down into the bottom of the blender.

2. If you intend to use the sauce immediately, add the cheese, blend to mix, and serve. If not, transfer the sauce to an airtight container, and store in the refrigerator for up to 2 to 3 weeks. Directly before serving, place the sauce in the blender, add the cheese, and blend to mix. Serve at room temperature.

Serving Suggestion

• Mix the sauce with spelt spaghetti. Garnish with halved cherry tomatoes and freshly grated Parmesan cheese, and serve immediately.

Yield: 1 cup

1 cup packed fresh basil leaves (about 1 bunch), stems removed

½ cup packed fresh parsley, stems removed

⅓ cup packed fresh cilantro, stems removed

½ teaspoon herb seasoning salt

Pinch turbinado sugar (or other sweetener)

1 large clove garlic, crushed

⅓ cup canola oil

½ cup pine nuts

1 tablespoon fresh lemon juice

¼ cup grated low-fat Parmesan cheese

Sweet Paprika Walnut Sauce

Made from sweet red peppers, paprika is a mild seasoning with a hint of sweetness and a color that ranges from red to brown. When added to sauces such as this one, paprika subtly enhances the flavor and imparts a rosy hue.

1. Place the milk in a 3-quart saucepan, and cook over medium-high heat, stirring constantly, for about 4 minutes. Test carefully with your finger. The milk should be quite warm but not hot. (Do *not* allow to boil.)

2. Stir the margarine and cheeses into the warm milk. While whipping slowly and constantly with a wire whisk, slowly add the flour, herb seasoning, and pepper.

3. Bring the mixture to a boil, stirring constantly to prevent burning. When the mixture thickens to the consistency of rich cream, stir in the walnuts and paprika.

Yield: 2½ cups

2 cups low-fat milk (or substitute)

¼ cup canola margarine

¼ cup grated low-fat Swiss cheese

¼ cup grated low-fat Parmesan cheese

¼ cup white spelt flour, whole-grain spelt flour, or Browned Spelt Flour (page 99)

1 teaspoon herb seasoning salt

⅛ teaspoon freshly ground white pepper

¼ cup coarsely chopped walnuts

½ teaspoon paprika

4. Use the sauce immediately, or cool to room temperature, transfer to an airtight container, and store in the refrigerator for up to 3 days. Reheat in a double boiler, and serve.

Serving Suggestion

• Serve with the Spinach Noodles variation of Whole-Grain Spelt Egg Noodles (page 143). The green color of the spinach noodles will be complemented by the rosy sauce. Garnish with chopped parsley.

Apple and Onion Sauce

Yield: 4 cups

¼ cup plus 2 tablespoons fresh or canned tomato juice

1 medium white onion, finely diced

1 medium apple, peeled, cored, and finely diced

1½ teaspoons curry powder

1¼ cups Chicken Stock (page 37) or Veggie Stock (page 37)

1¼ cups low-fat milk (or substitute)

¼ teaspoon sea salt

⅛ teaspoon freshly ground white pepper

2 tablespoons plus 1½ teaspoons Beurre Manié (page 99)

¼ cup white wine

Curry powder gives this versatile sauce a pungent flavor reminiscent of Eastern cuisine.

1. Place ¼ cup of the tomato juice in a nonstick 10-inch skillet over medium heat. When the juice is hot, add the onion and apple, and sprinkle with the curry powder. Stirring constantly, cook for 3 minutes, or until the onion is soft. If the skillet becomes dry, add more tomato juice.

2. Spoon the onion and apple mixture into a 3-quart saucepan, and add the stock, milk, salt, and pepper. Place over medium-low heat, and simmer for 20 minutes, stirring occasionally.

3. Increase the heat to medium-high, and bring the liquid to a boil. Remove the pan from the heat, add the Beurre Manié, and quickly blend with a whisk until the mixture is smooth. Return the pan to the heat, and, continuing to whisk, bring the liquid back to a boil, at which point it will thicken instantly.

4. Remove the pan from the heat, and allow to cool for 2 minutes. Stir in the wine. Use immediately, or cool to room temperature, transfer to an airtight container, and store in the refrigerator for up to 3 days. Reheat in a double boiler, and serve.

Serving Suggestion

• Serve over spelt dumplings, pasta, or crêpes.

Make-Ahead Tomato Sauce

This sauce is a healthful and easy-to-make alternative to store-bought tomato sauce. Prepare it whenever you have the time, and freeze it for later use.

1. Place the oil in a 5-quart kettle over medium heat. Add the onion, and cook, stirring often, until the onion is soft, but not brown. Add the garlic, and continue to cook and stir for 1 minute.

2. Place the tomatoes, celery, green pepper, and carrot in a blender or food processor, and process on "purée" for about 1 minute, or until the tomatoes are well mashed.

3. Add the tomato mixture and all of the remaining ingredients to the onion mixture, and mix well. Reduce the heat to low, and simmer the sauce uncovered for 2 to 3 hours, stirring every 30 minutes.

4. Remove and discard the bay leaf. Taste and adjust the seasoning if necessary, adding tomato paste as required if you desire a thicker sauce. Use immediately, or cool to room temperature and transfer to an airtight container. Store in the refrigerator for up to 5 days, or in the freezer for up to 3 months. Reheat in a double boiler, and serve.

Serving Suggestions

• Serve the sauce over any spelt pasta.

• Use in place of the suggested sauce when making Zucchini and Tomato Pizza (page 133) or any other spelt-dough pizza.

Yield: 12 cups

¼ cup canola oil

1 large white onion, minced

2 cloves garlic, minced

6 cans (1 pound each) whole peeled tomatoes

4 stalks celery, finely chopped

1 small green bell pepper, finely chopped

1 medium carrot, finely grated

1 tablespoon chopped fresh thyme, or 1 teaspoon dried thyme

¼ cup chopped fresh oregano, or 2 tablespoons dried oregano

2 tablespoons chopped fresh basil, or 1 tablespoon dried basil

2 teaspoons turbinado sugar (or other sweetener)

1 large bay leaf

1 tablespoon herb seasoning salt

1 teaspoon freshly ground black pepper

Tomato paste (optional)

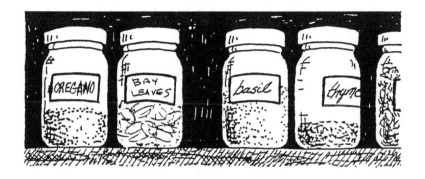

STUFFINGS

Water Chestnut and Bulgur Stuffing

Yield: 4 cups

1 cup spelt bulgur

¼ cup dark raisins

1 cup boiling water

2 tablespoons chopped white onion

1 stalk celery, finely chopped

½ cup diced water chestnuts

¼ teaspoon herb seasoning salt

½ teaspoon ground dried sage

¼ cup WonderSlim* or other fat and egg substitute

*WonderSlim fat and egg substitute can be found in most health foods stores.

While this stuffing can be used in menu planning all year round, it is particularly delicious when teamed up with roast turkey on Thanksgiving.

1. Preheat the oven to 350°F.

2. Place the bulgur and raisins in a 2-quart bowl. Add the boiling water, and set aside for 5 minutes.

3. Add the remaining ingredients to the bulgur mixture, and mix well. Coat a 2-quart casserole dish with nonstick cooking spray. Spoon in the stuffing, and bake for 30 minutes, or until the top is brown. Serve hot.

Variation

• Replace the water chestnuts with regular chestnuts, and use as a stuffing for your turkey. Simply make a gash in the flat side of each of 6 to 10 chestnuts, and place in a saucepan of boiling water. Simmer for 5 minutes. When the nuts are still hot, remove the shells and inner brown skins. Place the shelled chestnuts in boiling water, and cook for 30 minutes, or until tender. Drain, dice, and add to your stuffing mixture.

Fruited Bread Stuffing

Yield: 4 cups

8 slices whole-grain or white spelt bread

2 cups Chicken Stock (page 37)

1 teaspoon chopped fresh thyme, or ½ teaspoon dried thyme, divided

2 tablespoons maple syrup, divided

¼ cup mixed dried fruits

1 egg (or substitute)

¼ teaspoon sea salt

Dash freshly ground black pepper

The beauty of this stuffing is that any variety of dried fruits will give equally delicious results.

1. Preheat the oven to 350°F.

2. Toast the bread slices in a toaster until light brown. Allow the bread to cool. Then tear the slices into 1-inch squares, and place in a 2-quart heatproof bowl.

3. Place the stock in a 2-quart saucepan. Add half of the thyme, 1 tablespoon of the maple syrup, and all of the fruit. Reduce the heat to medium-low, cover, and simmer for 15 minutes to blend the flavors.

4. Pour the stock over the bread pieces. Break the egg over the mixture, and add the remaining thyme and maple syrup, and the salt and pepper. Mix well.

5. Coat a 2-quart casserole dish with nonstick cooking spray. Spoon in the stuffing, and bake for 30 minutes, or until the top is brown. Serve hot.

Variation

• For a tasty prune stuffing, replace the mixed fruits with dried pitted prunes.

Chesapeake Bay Oyster Stuffing

Early nineteenth century American cookbooks made liberal use of oysters, offering recipes for broiled, boiled, deviled, curried, fricasseed, scalloped, pickled, stewed, and steamed oysters. And no wonder! As you'll find when you make this sumptuous stuffing, oysters give dishes a very special taste and texture.

1. Preheat the oven to 350°F.

2. Place the margarine in a 2-quart saucepan, and melt over medium heat. Add the celery and onion, and sauté, stirring often, for about 5 minutes, or until the vegetables are soft.

3. Add the bread to the vegetable mixture, and continue cooking and stirring for 5 minutes, or until the bread cubes are golden brown. Remove the pan from the heat, and stir in the thyme, sage, and celery seeds.

4. Place the oysters in a 3-quart bowl, and sprinkle them with the lemon juice, salt, and pepper. Mix well. Gently fold the seasoned oysters into the bread mixture.

5. Coat a 2-quart casserole dish with nonstick cooking spray. Spoon in the stuffing, and bake for 30 minutes, or until the top is brown. Serve hot.

Yield: 4 cups

¼ cup canola margarine

2 stalks celery, chopped

1 medium onion, chopped

8 slices whole-grain or white spelt bread, cut into ½-inch cubes

1 teaspoon chopped fresh thyme, or ½ teaspoon dried thyme

1 teaspoon chopped fresh sage, or ½ teaspoon dried sage

1 teaspoon celery seeds

2 cups shucked, drained oysters

2 tablespoons fresh lemon juice

½ teaspoon sea salt

½ teaspoon freshly ground white pepper

Serving Suggestions

• Serve alongside chicken or fish, or use as a stuffing for chicken or fish.

• Use as a main dish, accompanying the stuffing with a tossed green salad.

• Double the recipe, and use as a stuffing for turkey.

SALAD DRESSINGS

Tofu Lemonnaise Dressing

Yield: 1 cup

1 cup crumbled firm tofu

2 tablespoons fresh lemon juice

1 tablespoon corn syrup

1 tablespoon apple cider vinegar

2 tablespoons canola oil

$\frac{1}{4}$ teaspoon herb seasoning salt

$\frac{1}{4}$ cup water or Veggie Stock (page 37)

1 tablespoon chopped fresh chives

Made without eggs and with very little oil, this wholesome dressing is a boon for health-conscious cooks.

1. Place all of the ingredients in a blender or food processor, and process on "liquefy" for 1 minute, or until the mixture is smooth and creamy.

2. Use immediately, or transfer to a bottle with a tight-fitting lid and store in the refrigerator for up to 3 days.

Serving Suggestions

- Use as a dressing for spelt pasta or chicken salad.
- Use instead of sour cream to top Twice-Baked Potatoes (page 162).
- Serve as a dipping sauce for Spelt-Crusted Oven Fries (page 159).

Cucumber-Sesame Seed Dressing

Yield: 3 cups

$\frac{1}{4}$ cup sesame seeds

1 cup apple cider vinegar

1 cup water

2 tablespoons fresh lemon juice

$\frac{1}{2}$ medium cucumber, seeded and cut into chunks

1 small white onion, cut into chunks

1 small clove garlic, chopped

$\frac{1}{2}$ teaspoon dried dill, or 2 stems fresh dill

$\frac{1}{4}$ teaspoon herb seasoning salt

$\frac{1}{2}$ teaspoon turbinado sugar (or other sweetener)

Brought to the United States by the first African slaves, sesame seeds were called benne. These seeds were used to flavor desserts, candies, and cookies.

1. Preheat the oven to 350°F. Spread the sesame seeds out on a small baking pan, and bake, stirring frequently, for 10 to 20 minutes, or until the seeds are lightly toasted. Set aside to cool.

2. Place the cooled seeds and the remaining ingredients in a blender or food processor, and process on "purée" for 2 minutes, or until the mixture is smooth and creamy.

3. Use immediately, or transfer to a bottle with a tight-fitting lid and store in the refrigerator for up to 5 days.

Serving Suggestions

- Use as a dressing for spelt pasta salads.
- Add a few tablespoons of the dressing to cooked spelt bulgur to keep it moist when serving as a side dish.

8

Main Dishes

While soups, breads, salads, and side dishes all do their part in making meals satisfying and nutritious, main dishes are certainly the star attractions of most dinners and of many lunches, too. For a long time, entrées almost invariably included meat, poultry, or fish. Now we know that delicious, nutritiously balanced main dishes can easily be made without any of these former staples. But whether you prefer vegetarian fare or still enjoy poultry and fish, this chapter provides a wealth of recipes for taste-tempting entrées, all of which have been made more flavorful and healthy with the use of spelt.

The chapter begins with a wide-ranging collection of chicken and turkey dishes. Chicken Amandine Casserole is a creamy, low-fat dish made crunchy with water chestnuts, almonds, and spelt flakes. Hot and satisfying, this is sure to be a family favorite. Looking for a healthier, tastier version of that reliable standby, meatloaf? In Sweet Marjoram Turkey Loaf, ground turkey is combined with spelt bulgur and seasonings to make a flavorful loaf that is high on taste and nutrition. If you're looking for party or holiday fare, try Tarragon Chicken Wellington—marinated chicken wrapped in pastry for a dish that is "dressy" enough for any occasion. Or perhaps you're in the mood for Mexican food. If so, try Black Bean and Burrito Bake. These and other recipes unite chicken and spelt in dishes that are right for any and every occasion.

Our collection of seafood recipes is just as varied and tempting. Egg Noodles With Shrimp and Broccoli is a party-perfect entrée, redolent with garlic and bursting with the goodness of spelt noodles. For more mundane—but equally delicious—fare, try Salmon-Bulgur Loaf. Artichoke, Squash, and Monkfish Kebabs is a delightfully colorful dish that can be made in the broiler of your oven or on a barbecue grill. Or delight family or friends with Tuna-Tomato Bread Round, an unusual main dish that elevates canned tuna to new heights by blending it with vegetables and baking it on a spelt-bread crust.

The third portion of this chapter presents a dazzling

array of vegetarian dishes. Spelt pasta shows its many faces in a variety of dishes, ranging from Buckwheat Pasta With Eggs and Peppers, to Baked Pasta Olé, to Egg Noodles Indonesian. Spelt kernels make a robust dish in Savory Spelt Kernel Roast. Or team up spelt kernels and toasted spelt flakes to make Spinach-Spelt Balls, which are delicious as is, or may be served over spelt pasta for a meatless Italian feast.

The last portion of this chapter is devoted to vegan fare—dishes made not only without meat, fish, or poultry, but also without cheese, eggs, and other animal products. If you ever thought that vegan meant dull, get ready for a surprise. Spelt flours, pastas, and other products make these dishes as flavorful as they are satisfying. If you love Chinese cooking, treat yourself to Chinese Strudel, a prize-winning recipe that enlivens vegetables with Eastern seasoning, and then encloses

them in a spelt strudel dough. Or try Pumpkin Primavera Pasta, a dish made rich and creamy with silken tofu and tahini. For an easy-to-make mid-week dish, whip up Soy-Curry Casserole, which you can serve as either an entrée or a side dish. No one will miss meat, cheese, or milk when these hearty, flavorful spelt-enriched dishes are on the menu!

Most of the main dishes presented in this chapter need little in the way of accompaniments to make a complete meal. In some cases, all you need add is a salad or a side dish of steamed vegetables. In other cases, a dish of spelt bulgur or pasta will add balance and a pleasant change of taste and texture. Experiment to find the combinations you like best. As long as spelt is part of your meal, you'll know that you're giving your family both the foods they love and the nutrition they need.

CHICKEN AND TURKEY DISHES

Chicken Amandine Casserole

A combination of spelt flakes and almonds makes this casserole a crunchy and delicious variation of basic chicken amandine dishes.

1. Preheat the oven to 375°F.

2. Place all of the casserole ingredients in a 3-quart saucepan, and cook over medium heat for about 10 minutes, or until the mixture is hot and bubbly. Transfer the mixture to an ungreased 3-quart casserole.

3. Combine the topping ingredients in a 2-quart bowl. Spoon the mixture over the chicken mixture, and pat it with your hands until it is firmly packed. Bake for about 30 minutes, or until the topping is nicely browned. Serve immediately.

Variation

• To make Turkey Amandine Casserole, simply substitute cubed cooked turkey for the chicken.

Yield: 4 servings

3 cups cubed cooked chicken

1 can (10¾ ounces) low-fat condensed cream of chicken soup

⅔ cup nonfat mayonnaise (or substitute)

½ cup nonfat sour cream

1 can (4 ounces) sliced mushrooms, drained

1 can (8 ounces) water chestnuts, drained and diced

½ cup chopped celery

½ cup chopped onion

1 teaspoon chopped fresh rosemary, or ½ teaspoon dried rosemary

TOPPING

⅔ cup shredded low-fat Swiss cheese

½ cup slivered almonds

½ cup toasted spelt flakes

3 tablespoons canola margarine, softened

Sweet Marjoram Turkey Loaf

Yield: 4 servings

¹⁄₂ cup spelt bulgur

¹⁄₂ cup boiling water

1¹⁄₂ cups ground turkey breast
(just over 8 ounces)

¹⁄₄ cup plus 2 tablespoons egg
substitute

1 large yellow onion, minced

1¹⁄₂ tablespoons chopped fresh
marjoram, or 1¹⁄₂ teaspoons
dried marjoram

¹⁄₂ teaspoon sea salt

¹⁄₄ teaspoon freshly ground white
pepper

A member of the mint family, marjoram has a sweet, delicate flavor that blends well with many foods, and is especially good in poultry dishes.

1. Preheat the oven to 400°F. Fill a 2-pound loaf pan with 2 inches of water, and set aside. Spray the inside of a 10-x-16-inch Reynolds Oven Bag with nonstick cooking spray, and lightly coat with white spelt flour. Set aside.

2. Place the bulgur in a 2-quart heatproof bowl, and pour the boiling water over the bulgur. Set aside for 5 minutes.

3. Add the remaining ingredients to the bulgur, and mix well. Transfer the mixture to a floured board and, with floured hands, shape the mixture into a loaf.

4. Place the loaf in the prepared bag. Close the bag, sealing it with the supplied nylon tie, and use a sharp knife to cut six ¹⁄₂-inch slits in the top of the bag.

5. Place the bag in the prepared pan, and bake for 1 hour and 15 minutes, checking the water level every 25 minutes and adding more water as necessary. Serve immediately.

Variation

• Use the uncooked mixture to stuff cabbage, chard, collard, or grape leaves, or as a stuffing for bell peppers, eggplant, or squash.

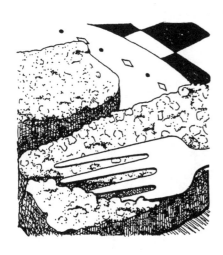

Tarragon Chicken Wellington

Beef Wellington, a classic dish that originated in England, blankets beef in a rich vegetable purée and then encloses it in a rich pastry. This variation uses chicken and spelt dough to make a lighter, healthier dish that is just as flavorful and satisfying as the original.

1. Place all of the marinade ingredients in a small bowl, and stir to blend. Place the chicken in a 1-quart bowl, and add the marinade, turning the chicken in the liquid to coat. Cover, and refrigerate overnight.

2. The next day, place the marinated chicken pieces on a paper towel, and set aside to allow the excess liquid to drain. Reserve the remaining marinade.

3. Place the onion and pepper strips in a small bowl, and stir to mix. Divide the strips into 4 equal portions, and place a portion in the indented side of each chicken breast, where the bone was removed.

4. Cut the noodle dough into 4 equal pieces. Place each piece on a floured board, 1 at a time, and roll it into a 7-x-7-inch square.

5. Place 1 piece of chicken in the center of each square of dough. Fold the left and right edges inward over the chicken, and roll the dough up from the bottom, jelly-roll style. Using a pastry brush, coat the dough with some of the remaining marinade.

6. Preheat the oven to 350°F. Wrap each dough-wrapped portion in a square of aluminum foil, and arrange on a 13-x-9-inch baking sheet. Bake for 1 hour. Then remove the foil, brush each portion with a little more marinade, and bake for about 15 additional minutes, or until the pastry is browned. Serve immediately.

Yield: 4 servings

4 chicken breasts, skinned and boned

½ white onion, cut into strips

½ green bell pepper, cut into strips

1 recipe Whole-Grain Spelt Egg Noodles (page 142), prepared up to Step 4

MARINADE

2 tablespoons canola oil

2 tablespoons plain nonfat yogurt

1 tablespoon tamari soy sauce

2 tablespoons chopped fresh tarragon, or 1 tablespoon dried tarragon

Precooking Chicken

Whenever cooked chicken is needed for a recipe—whether for a casserole dish, a skillet dish, or a salad—simply place the desired amount of chicken parts in a large pot, and cover with cold water. Bring the water to a boil over high heat. Then reduce the heat to medium, and cook uncovered for 20 to 30 minutes, depending on the size of the pieces being cooked. The chicken will be done when the juices run clear upon insertion of a sharp knife into the thickest part of the chicken. Take care to avoid overcooking the chicken, as this will make it stringy and tough, as well as reducing flavor. Remove the chicken from the liquid, and cool completely before using the meat in your recipe.

Spaghetti With Chicken, Saffron, and Ginger

Yield: 4 servings

2 tablespoons canola oil

1 clove garlic, finely minced

¼ cup finely chopped yellow onion

1 tablespoon plus 1½ teaspoons white spelt flour

1½ cups Chicken Stock (page 37)

5 ounces spelt spaghetti

2 chicken breasts, cooked and chopped

1½ cups coarsely chopped snow peas

¼ teaspoon ground ginger

¼ teaspoon herb seasoning salt

½ cup dark raisins

¼ teaspoon loosely packed saffron threads

2 heaping tablespoons plain low-fat yogurt

The nutlike taste of spelt spaghetti blends with chicken, raisins, snow peas, and a saffron-spiced ginger sauce, giving this dish an exotic Far Eastern flavor.

1. Place the oil in a 10-inch skillet over medium-high heat. Add the garlic and onions, and sauté, stirring occasionally, until the onions are golden yellow. Sprinkle the flour over the onions, and continue to cook, stirring constantly, until the flour browns. Add the chicken stock, blend well, and reduce the heat to low.

2. Break the spaghetti strands in half, and cook until al dente according to package directions. Drain the pasta well, and transfer it to a heated serving bowl. Cover and set aside.

3. Add the chicken, snow peas, ginger, and herb seasoning to the skillet mixture, and stir to mix. Continue cooking for 5 minutes to allow the flavors to blend. Add the raisins and saffron, and cook for an additional 5 minutes, stirring frequently.

4. Remove the skillet from the heat, and stir in the yogurt. Pour the mixture over the cooked spaghetti and toss lightly. Serve immediately.

Variations

• Add ¼ cup of toasted almond slivers along with the raisins and saffron.

• Create a vegetarian dish by substituting 1 cup of cooked white beans for the chicken, and 1½ cups of Veggie Stock (page 37) for the Chicken Stock.

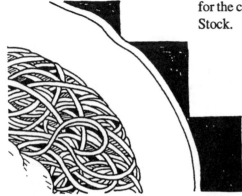

Crisp Chicken Scaloppini

The Italian word scaloppini is used to describe thin, flattened pieces of meat or poultry. In this dish, chicken scaloppini are dipped in a flavorful spelt coating and then sautéed until crisp.

1. Place the chicken pieces on a flat surface, and lightly pound with a kitchen mallet until ¼- to ½-inch thick. Sprinkle each piece with herb seasoning and pepper.

2. Place the flour in a medium-sized plastic bag and add the chicken pieces 1 at a time, shaking the bag to coat the pieces with the flour. Transfer the chicken to a plate, and set aside.

3. Lay out 2 shallow bowls. In one bowl, place the spelt flakes and the remaining coating ingredients, and stir to mix. In the other bowl, place the beaten egg.

4. One at a time, dip the chicken slices in the egg, turning the chicken several times so that both sides are well coated. Then dip the chicken in the coating mixture, again turning the pieces until they are well coated.

5. Place the oil in a 10-inch skillet over medium-high heat until hot. Reduce the heat to medium, and place the coated chicken in the skillet. Cook for 3 to 5 minutes on each side, or until well browned and tender. Transfer the sautéed slices to paper towels to drain. Serve immediately.

Serving Suggestion

• For a treat, sprinkle the cooked scallopini with freshly squeezed lemon juice, and serve with buttered and parslied spelt spaghetti.

Variations

• To make Chicken Scaloppini and Angel Hair Pasta, crush 1 large clove of garlic, and place it in 2 to 3 tablespoons of warmed olive oil. Use a wooden spoon to move the garlic around in the oil for a few minutes. Discard the garlic, and mix the olive oil with a few tablespoons of grated Parmesan cheese and 5 ounces of hot cooked spelt angel hair pasta. Top with the cooked scallopini, and serve.

• To make Crisp Tofu Scaloppini, substitute slices of firm tofu for the chicken.

Yield: 4 servings

4 slices (about 1½ pounds) boneless skinless chicken or turkey breast, each about 4 x 4-inches and about ¾-inch thick

1 tablespoon herb seasoning salt

1½ teaspoons freshly ground black pepper

¼ cup white spelt flour

1 egg, beaten (or substitute)

¼ cup canola oil

SEASONED COATING

½ cup finely ground toasted spelt flakes (page 4)

2 tablespoons finely grated low-fat Parmesan cheese

½ teaspoon herb seasoning salt

¼ teaspoon paprika

⅛ teaspoon freshly ground white pepper

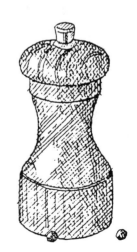

Black Bean and Burrito Bake

Yield: 4 servings

2 cups cooked or canned black beans, drained

⅓ cup sliced scallions

½ jalapeño pepper, seeded and sliced

1 clove garlic, minced

3 tablespoons fresh lime juice

1 teaspoon chili powder

1 cup Vita-Spelt Pancake/Muffin Mix (or equivalent product)

1 cup shredded cooked chicken

1 red bell pepper, cut into thin strips

½ cup shredded low-fat Monterey Jack or other low-fat cheese

¼ cup plain nonfat yogurt or nonfat sour cream (garnish)

SALSA

2 tomatoes, seeded and chopped

¼ cup finely sliced scallions

2 tablespoons seeded chopped jalapeño peppers

1 clove garlic, minced

1 tablespoon balsamic vinegar

2 teaspoons olive oil

1 tablespoon chopped fresh basil

1 tablespoon chopped fresh cilantro

1 tablespoon chopped fresh parsley

This prize-winning recipe was created by Shirley DeSantis of East Windsor, New Jersey. Shirley's recipe will be a winner with everyone who loves Mexican food.

1. To make the salsa, combine all of the salsa ingredients in a 1-quart bowl. Cover and refrigerate until needed.

2. Preheat the oven to 375°F. Lightly coat a 10-inch pie pan with nonstick cooking spray, and set aside.

3. Combine the beans, scallions, jalapeño pepper, garlic, lime juice, and chili powder in a 3-quart bowl. Using a fork, mash the ingredients together. Add the Pancake/Muffin Mix, and stir to combine.

4. Transfer the bean mixture to the prepared pie pan, spreading it evenly over the bottom and halfway up the sides. Scatter the shredded chicken and pepper strips over the bean mixture. Top with ½ cup of the salsa, and sprinkle with the cheese.

5. Bake for 30 minutes, or until the mixture is hot and bubbly. Cut into wedges and serve immediately, topping each serving with a tablespoon each of the remaining salsa and the yogurt or sour cream.

Burgundy Spaghetti

This prize-winning recipe comes from Rebecca Bien of Okemos, Michigan. Rebecca says that this delicious dish is ideal for people in a hurry, as it can be prepared when you have time and then kept in the refrigerator overnight, ready for baking the next day.

1. Place the oil in a 10-inch ovenproof skillet over medium heat. Add the turkey and onions, and sauté, stirring often, until the turkey browns. Drain off any excess fat, and add the tomato sauce, wine, mushrooms, garlic, salt, pepper, oregano, basil, rosemary, and marjoram. Reduce the heat to low, and simmer the mixture uncovered for 1 hour, stirring occasionally.

2. Cook the pasta according to package directions for 2 to 3 minutes, or just until the pasta separates. (During cooking, carefully separate the pasta with a fork as necessary.) Drain well, and transfer to a 3-quart bowl.

3. Add half the cheese to the pasta, and mix well. Add the pasta mixture to the skillet mixture, and spread it evenly in the skillet. (At this point, the mixture may be covered and refrigerated for a few hours or overnight.)

4. Preheat the oven to 325°F. Sprinkle the remaining cheese over the pasta mixture, cover, and bake for 45 minutes, or until hot and bubbly. Serve immediately.

Yield: 4 servings

3 tablespoons canola oil

1 pound ground turkey

1 medium onion, chopped

3 cans (8 ounces each) tomato sauce

1 cup Burgundy wine

½ cup sliced fresh mushrooms

2 cloves garlic, minced

½ teaspoon sea salt

¼ teaspoon freshly ground black pepper

½ teaspoon chopped fresh oregano, or ¼ teaspoon dried oregano

½ teaspoon chopped fresh basil, or ¼ teaspoon dried basil

½ teaspoon chopped fresh rosemary, or ¼ teaspoon dried rosemary

½ teaspoon chopped fresh marjoram, or ¼ teaspoon dried marjoram

8 ounces spelt angel hair pasta

2 cups shredded low-fat mozzarella cheese

SEAFOOD DISHES

Egg Noodles With Shrimp and Broccoli

Yield: 4 servings

1 pound shelled medium shrimp, deveined, rinsed, and patted dry

1 bunch broccoli (about 1½ pounds), cut into florets

¼ cup canola margarine, divided

8 ounces spelt egg noodles

2 tablespoons light olive oil

2 tablespoons finely chopped fresh parsley (garnish)

12 cherry tomatoes (garnish)

MARINADE

¼ cup light olive oil

2 cloves garlic, finely minced

¼ teaspoon herb seasoning salt

Dash freshly ground white pepper

In this dish, a garlic-and-oil marinade keeps the shrimp moist while imparting a wonderfully garlicky flavor. The marinade later becomes part of a sauce that is poured over the egg noodles at serving time.

1. Combine the marinade ingredients in a 2-quart bowl, and stir to mix. Add the shrimp, and stir to coat. Cover, and marinate in the refrigerator for 1 to 2 hours.

2. When you are ready to make the dish, place the broccoli florets in a steamer, and cook over simmering water for about 4 minutes, or just until tender. Cover, and place in a warm oven until needed.

3. Place 2 tablespoons of the margarine in a warmed 3-quart bowl, and set aside. Cook the pasta until al dente according to package directions. Drain well, transfer to the prepared bowl, and cover to keep warm. Set aside.

4. Place 2 tablespoons of olive oil and the remaining 2 tablespoons of margarine in a 10-inch skillet over medium-high heat. While the mixture is heating, drain the shrimp, reserving the marinade. Transfer the shrimp to the skillet, and sauté, tossing often, for about 2 minutes, or until the shrimp are pink.

5. Using a slotted spoon, transfer the shrimp to the bowl containing the noodles, leaving the butter and oil in the skillet. Re-cover the bowl to keep the shrimp warm.

6. Add the reserved shrimp marinade to the fat in the skillet, and cook over medium heat, stirring constantly, for about 1 minute, or until the garlic is tender but not brown. Pour the hot sauce over the noodle mixture, and toss until thoroughly blended. Add the broccoli, and mix gently.

7. To serve, mound the shrimp mixture on a large heated platter. Sprinkle the mixture with the parsley, and arrange the cherry tomatoes around the platter. Serve immediately.

Salmon–Bulgur Loaf

In this recipe, canned Alaskan salmon and spelt bulgur are combined to make a light and tasty loaf that is delicious hot or cold, for lunch or dinner.

1. Preheat the oven to 400°F. Coat a 1-pound nonstick loaf pan with nonstick cooking spray, and sprinkle lightly with 2 tablespoons of the bulgur. Set aside.

2. Place the remaining ½ cup of bulgur in a heatproof 3-quart bowl. Add the dill, and stir to mix. Pour the boiling water over the bulgur, and set aside for 5 minutes.

3. Place the egg whites in a 2-quart bowl, and beat with an electric mixer until the whites form stiff peaks. Set aside.

4. Add the salmon, scallions, lemon juice, pepper, mayonnaise, and lecithin to the bulgur, and mix well. Fold in the egg whites.

5. Pack the salmon mixture into the prepared loaf pan. Cover the pan with aluminum foil, and bake for 1 hour, or until lightly browned.

6. Run a spatula around the loaf to loosen it from the pan. Carefully invert the pan over a preheated platter, and center the loaf on the platter. Slice and serve immediately.

Serving Suggestion

• For a special treat, blanket the loaf with the Lemon Sauce variation of Basic Spelt Béchamel Sauce (page 102).

Yield: 4 servings

½ cup plus 2 tablespoons spelt bulgur, divided

2 heaping teaspoons chopped fresh dill, or 1 heaping teaspoon dried dill

½ cup boiling water

4 egg whites

1 can (14½ ounces) Alaskan salmon, drained and boned

4 scallions, white part only, finely chopped

2 tablespoons fresh lemon juice

¼ teaspoon freshly ground black pepper

¼ cup plus 2 tablespoons nonfat mayonnaise (or substitute)

1 tablespoon liquid lecithin*

*Lecithin, a by-product of soy oil refining, is available in health foods stores.

Tuna–Tomato Bread Round

Yield: 4 servings

CRUST

½ cup hot tomato juice

½ teaspoon chopped fresh basil, or
¼ teaspoon dried basil

½ teaspoon chopped fresh oregano,
or ¼ teaspoon dried oregano

¼ teaspoon garlic salt

Pinch turbinado sugar (or other
sweetener)

2¼ cups Vita-Spelt Whole Grain
Bread Mix (or equivalent
product), divided

SAUCE

1 tablespoon canola oil

1 clove garlic, finely minced

¼ cup finely chopped white onion

1 cup drained, chopped canned
Italian-style plum tomatoes

¼ cup tomato paste

1 tablespoon chopped fresh oregano,
or 1 teaspoon dried oregano

1 teaspoon chopped fresh basil, or
½ teaspoon dried basil

½ teaspoon herb seasoning salt

TOPPING

2 tablespoons canola oil

1 small onion, sliced and separated
into rings

2 tablespoons chopped green bell
pepper

1 cup chopped zucchini

10 thin slices eggplant

1 tablespoon chopped fresh basil,
or 1 teaspoon dried basil

1 tablespoon chopped fresh oregano,
or 1 teaspoon dried oregano

1 can (6 ounces) water-packed
tuna, well drained and flaked

1 teaspoon chopped fresh dill, or ½
teaspoon dried dill

2 large tomatoes, sliced

*Vita-Spelt bread mix blended with basil, oregano, and tomato juice makes
a perfect base for a savory tuna fish and vegetable topping.*

1. To make the dough, combine the tomato juice, basil, oregano,
garlic, salt, and sugar in a 1-quart bowl. Set aside.

2. Place 1¾ cups of the bread mix in a 2-quart bowl. Add the tomato
juice mixture, and thoroughly blend with a spoon to form a soft dough.
Cover the dough with a kitchen towel, and let rise in a warm place for
1 hour, or until it has doubled in size. Punch down the dough, replace
the cloth, and allow the dough to rise for an additional hour.

3. Transfer the dough to a lightly floured board. Clean the bowl, and
coat it lightly with nonstick cooking spray. Set aside.

4. Add the remaining ½ cup of bread mix to the dough, a little at a
time, kneading until the dough no longer feels sticky. Continue to knead
for about 5 additional minutes, or until the dough feels elastic.

5. Shape the dough into a round ball, and place in the oiled bowl.
Cover the dough with a clean kitchen towel, and let it rise in a warm
place for 1 to 2 hours, or until it has doubled in size.

6. While the dough is rising, make the sauce by placing the oil in a
2-quart saucepan over medium heat. Add the garlic and onion, and sauté
for 1 minute. Add the tomatoes, tomato paste, and herbs, and cook for
5 minutes. Reduce the heat to low, and cook uncovered for 15 minutes,
stirring occasionally. Remove from the heat, and set aside.

7. To make the topping, place the oil in a 10-inch skillet over medium
heat. Add the onion and green pepper, and sauté until the onions are
golden. Add the zucchini, eggplant, basil, and oregano, and continue to
cook, stirring frequently, for about 5 minutes, or until the vegetables are
soft. Remove from the heat, and set aside.

8. Preheat the oven to 375°F. Coat a 12-inch springform pan with
nonstick cooking spray, and set aside.

9. To assemble the bread round, place the dough on a lightly floured
surface, and using a floured rolling pin, roll the dough into a 12-inch
circle. Place the circle of dough in the prepared pan. Spread the sauce
evenly over the dough. Spoon the vegetable topping over the sauce.
Arrange the tuna, dill, and tomatoes over the vegetables.

10. Bake for 35 to 40 minutes, or until the bottom of the crust is crisp
and the sauce is bubbly. Unclasp the springform collar, cut the pie into
wedges, and serve immediately.

Artichoke, Squash, and Monkfish Kebabs

Although sometimes called the "poor man's lobster," monkfish is delicious in its own right. And because of its firm flesh, monkfish is a perfect kebab ingredient.

1. Place the fish chunks in a 1-quart bowl. Add the Italian dressing, tossing to coat. Cover, and place in the refrigerator for 1 hour.

2. While the fish is marinating, soak eight 9-inch bamboo skewers in cold water. Allow to soak until needed.

3. Place the dry mustard, paprika, and flour in a large plastic bag, and shake the bag to mix well. Place the squash in the bag, and shake until well coated.

4. Remove the skewers from the water, and set aside. Remove the fish from the marinade, and set aside, reserving the marinade.

5. Using 2 skewers per portion so that the ingredients will remain firmly in place during cooking, alternate 4 pieces of fish and 4 pieces of squash on each double set of skewers, placing an artichoke heart in the middle.

6. Coat the slotted insert of a broiler pan with nonstick cooking spray. Preheat the broiler, place the skewers on the coated pan, and spoon the remaining marinade over the kebabs. Place the pan 4 inches from the heat source, and broil for 6 minutes, or until evenly browned. Rotate the skewers, baste with the pan juices, and broil for an additional 6 minutes. Serve immediately.

Yield: 4 servings

1 pound monkfish fillet, cut into 16 equal chunks

¼ cup plus 2 tablespoons bottled low-calorie Italian dressing

½ teaspoon dry mustard

½ teaspoon sweet paprika

1 tablespoon white spelt flour

1 large yellow squash, cut into 16 chunks

4 canned artichoke hearts, drained

Serving Suggestions

- Place the broiled skewers on a bed of cooked spelt bulgur.
- Accompany the kebabs with any cooked spelt pasta.

Poached Yellow Perch Fillets
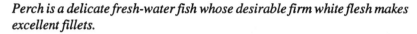

Yield: 4 servings

4 perch fillets (about 1 pound), fresh or frozen

POACHING LIQUID

4 cups water

1 leek, green part only, chopped

1 teaspoon pickling spice

$\frac{1}{2}$ teaspoon sea salt

CREAM SAUCE

2 tablespoons canola margarine

1 leek, white part only, chopped

1 tablespoon plus $1\frac{1}{2}$ teaspoons white spelt flour

$\frac{1}{4}$ teaspoon chopped fresh dill, or $\frac{1}{8}$ teaspoon dried dill

Dash freshly ground white pepper

Dash paprika

2 tablespoons nonfat sour cream

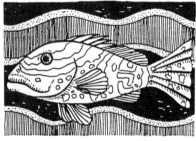

Perch is a delicate fresh-water fish whose desirable firm white flesh makes excellent fillets.

1. Place all of the poaching liquid ingredients in a 2-quart saucepan, and bring to a boil over high heat. Reduce the heat to medium-low, and simmer for 30 minutes.

2. Place the fillets in a 10-inch skillet. Using a slotted spoon, remove the leeks from the Poaching Liquid, and place over the fillets. Add 1 cup of the Poaching Liquid, cover, and simmer over medium heat for 15 minutes.

3. Scrape the leek mixture off the fish, and discard the leeks. Using a slotted spoon, remove the fillets and place them on a warm serving platter. Place in a warm oven until needed.

4. To make the sauce, pour the remaining poaching liquid through a fine sieve. Discard the solids, and reserve the remaining stock. Set aside.

5. Place the margarine in a 2-quart saucepan, and melt over medium-high heat. Add the leek, and sauté, stirring constantly, until the leek is lightly browned.

6. Add the flour to the leek mixture, and stir until the mixture is slightly brown. Add 1 cup of the reserved poaching liquid and the dill, pepper, and paprika. Continue to cook and stir until the mixture is well blended.

7. Remove the pan from the heat, and stir in the sour cream. Spoon the sauce over the fish fillets, and serve immediately.

Serving Suggestions

• Serve with cooked spelt pasta or kernels.

• Serve with Fresh Green Bean Bulgur Salad (page 59).

• Flake the cooked fillets, and place them in Basic Spelt Crêpes (page 148). Top with the Anchovy Sauce or Herb Sauce variations of Basic Spelt Béchamel Sauce (page 102).

VEGETARIAN DISHES

Buckwheat Pasta With Eggs and Peppers

With significant amounts of vitamins and minerals, buckwheat pasta is a boon to the health-conscious cook. When this pasta also contains spelt, the nutritional value—and the satisfying flavor—of the dish is all the greater.

1. Cook the pasta until al dente according to package directions. Drain well, transfer to a large bowl, and set aside.

2. Place 1 tablespoon of the margarine in a 10-inch nonstick ovenproof skillet, and melt over medium heat. Add the peppers, onion, tarragon, herb seasoning, and pepper, and sauté, stirring often, for 6 to 8 minutes, or until the onions are golden brown and the peppers are soft. Transfer the mixture to a dish, and set aside.

3. Wipe the skillet clean with a paper towel, and add the remaining tablespoon of margarine and the garlic. Place over medium heat, and, using the back of a wooden spoon, move the garlic around in the margarine as it melts. Remove and discard the garlic.

4. Place the cooked pasta in the skillet, and turn off the heat. Using the back of the wooden spoon, make 4 separate wells in the spaghetti, and break an egg into each well. Top the eggs with the cheese, and spoon the cooked peppers and onions around the eggs. Arrange the olives over the top of the dish.

5. Preheat the oven to 350°F. Place the bouillon cube and water in a 1-quart bowl, and stir to dissolve. Pour the liquid around the inside edge of the skillet, cover the skillet with aluminum foil, and bake for about 12 minutes, or until the egg whites are firm and the yolks are still soft. Serve immediately.

Serving Suggestion

• For an impressive brunch, serve this savory dish with a selection of spelt muffins.

Yield: 4 servings

4 ounces spelt buckwheat spaghetti

2 tablespoons canola margarine, divided

½ small red bell pepper, cut into thin strips

½ small green bell pepper, cut into thin strips

½ small yellow bell pepper, cut into thin strips

1 small white onion, chopped

1 tablespoon chopped fresh tarragon, or 1 teaspoon dried tarragon

Pinch herb seasoning salt

Pinch freshly ground black pepper

1 small clove garlic, crushed

4 eggs

¼ cup grated low-fat Parmesan cheese

6 pitted black olives, sliced

1 vegetable bouillon cube

½ cup hot water

Macaroni and Cheese With Feta

Yield: 4 servings

½ cup low-fat milk (or substitute)

1 package (7¼ ounces) Vita-Spelt Macaroni and Cheese (or equivalent product)

3 tablespoons chopped fresh dill, or 1½ teaspoons dried dill, divided

1 cup crumbled feta cheese

2 tablespoons diced green bell pepper

¼ teaspoon paprika

Pinch freshly ground white pepper

4 egg whites

4 tomatoes, thinly sliced

This dish is first made wholesome and easy-to-prepare with Vita-Spelt Macaroni and Cheese, and then made special with a "stuffing" of seasoned feta cheese.

1. Preheat the oven to 375°F. Coat a deep 3-quart casserole dish with nonstick cooking spray. Pour the milk into the dish, and set aside.

2. Prepare the macaroni mix according to package directions, and when blending the supplied cheese-milk mixture with the cooked macaroni, add 1½ teaspoons of the dill. Transfer the mixture to a 3-quart bowl, and set aside.

3. Combine the feta cheese, the remaining 1½ teaspoons of dill, and the green pepper, paprika, and pepper in a 1-quart bowl. Set aside.

4. Place the egg whites in a 2-quart bowl, and beat with an electric mixer until the whites form stiff peaks. Fold the egg whites into the macaroni mixture. Transfer half of this mixture to the prepared dish, placing it over the milk. Top with the feta cheese mixture, and finish with the remaining marcaroni mixture. Arrange the tomato slices over the top.

5. Bake for 35 to 40 minutes, or until the mixture bubbles and the tomatoes are soft. Serve immediately.

Making Savory Garni

Savory garni—a blend of flavorful fresh herbs and oil—is a wonderful addition to salad dressings, stuffings, and many other dishes, including the Savory Spelt Kernel Roast presented in this chapter (page 130). Once made and stored in an airtight container, this delightful seasoning aid will keep fresh in your refrigerator for up to three weeks.

Savory Garni

12 fresh sage leaves, finely chopped

2–3 sprigs fresh thyme, finely chopped

6 stalks fresh parsley, finely chopped

¼ cup plus 2 tablespoons finely chopped fresh chives

½ cup canola oil

1. Combine the sage, thyme, parsley, and chives in a small bowl, and mix thoroughly. Top with the oil, and mix well.

2. Transfer the mixture to a screw-top jar or other airtight container, and store in the refrigerator for up to 3 weeks.

Baked Pasta Olé

This prize-winning Mexican-style dish, created by Gail Dean of St. Augustine, Florida, deserves an "olé" not only for its taste, but also for its colorful appearance.

1. Preheat the oven to 350°F. Coat a 2-quart casserole dish with nonstick cooking spray, and set aside.

2. Cook the pasta until al dente according to package directions. Drain, rinse, and drain again. Transfer to a 3-quart bowl.

3. Add the sour cream, jalapeño peppers, garlic, parsley, scallions, cumin, cilantro, salt, and pepper to the pasta, and toss to mix well. Transfer the mixture to the prepared baking dish, and sprinkle with the cheese.

4. Bake uncovered for 30 minutes, or until hot and bubbly. Arrange the garnishes attractively over the top, and serve immediately.

Yield: 4 servings

5 ounces spelt elbow pasta

1 cup low-fat sour cream

2 teaspoons minced jalapeño peppers

2 teaspoons minced garlic

2 tablespoons chopped fresh parsley

1 cup sliced scallions

½ teaspoon cumin

1 teaspoon chopped fresh cilantro

¼ teaspoon sea salt

½ teaspoon freshly ground black pepper

1 cup grated low-fat Monterey Jack or Cheddar cheese

1 cup diced fresh tomatoes (garnish)

1 ripe avocado, peeled, pitted, and cut into 8 wedges (garnish)

Several sprigs fresh cilantro or parsley (garnish)

Whole or sliced black olives (garnish)

Spinach-Spelt Balls

Yield: 4 servings

¾ cup spelt kernels

1 bay leaf

1 tablespoon herb seasoning salt

1 tablespoon canola oil

1 clove garlic, chopped

1 small red onion, chopped

1 cup chopped fresh spinach, packed (about 12 large leaves)

1 slice stale spelt bread

1 egg, beaten (or substitute)

½ cup finely ground toasted spelt flakes (page 4)

2 tablespoons chopped fresh oregano, or 1 tablespoon dried oregano

1 tablespoon chopped fresh basil, or 1 teaspoon dried basil

¼ cup tomato paste

¼ teaspoon freshly ground white pepper

2 tablespoons canola oil

Spinach-Spelt Balls make a splendid vegetarian substitute for conventional meatballs.

1. Place the spelt kernels in a sieve, and rinse under cool running water. Transfer the kernels to a 2-quart bowl, and add water to cover. Cover the bowl, and allow to soak overnight at room temperature.

2. Drain the water from the kernels, and transfer the kernels to a 2-quart saucepan. Cover with fresh water, add the bay leaf and herb seasoning, and bring to a boil over medium-high heat.

3. Reduce the heat to low, cover, and simmer for about 1 hour, or until the kernels are tender, stirring several times and adding more water if necessary. Remove the pan from the heat, drain off the water, and allow the kernels to cool completely.

4. Place the oil in a 2-quart saucepan over medium heat. Add the garlic and onions, and sauté for 2 to 3 minutes, or until the onions are soft. Add the spinach, and cook for another minute or 2, or just until the spinach wilts.

5. Place the cooled spelt kernels and the spinach mixture in a food processor, and, using a fine cutting circle, process on "grind." Place the bread in the processor, and process to force all of the kernels through the grinder. Transfer the mixture to a 2-quart bowl, and add the egg, spelt flakes, oregano, basil, tomato paste, and pepper. Mix thoroughly.

6. Using wet hands, form the mixture into 12 equal-sized balls. Place the oil in a 10-inch skillet, and cook the balls over medium heat, turning frequently, for about 5 minutes, or until all sides are browned. Serve immediately.

Serving Suggestion

• Arrange the balls over spelt spaghetti, and top with Make-Ahead Tomato Sauce (page 105) and a sprinkling of grated Parmesan cheese.

Pinto Pie

This prize-winning recipe was created by Cindy Thoreson of Austin, Texas. Cindy says: "As a vegetarian and being allergic to wheat, I developed a version of my mother's tamale pie that everyone can enjoy."

1. To make the filling, place the oil in a 10-inch skillet over medium heat. Add the onion, potato, green pepper, and garlic, and sauté until the vegetables are lightly browned. Stir in the beans, corn, olives, and tomato sauce, adding salt and pepper to taste. Reduce the heat to low, and allow the mixture to simmer uncovered for about 30 minutes, or until the potatoes are tender, stirring occasionally.

2. While the filling is simmering, make the biscuit mixture by combining all of the biscuit ingredients in a 3-quart bowl. Turn the mixture onto a floured board, and knead for 3 minutes, or just until a dough forms.

3. Using a lightly floured rolling pin, roll the dough until it forms a ½-inch-thick sheet. Use a biscuit cutter to cut the dough into 6 to 8 biscuits.

4. Preheat the oven to 400°F. Pour the bean mixture into an ungreased 13-x-8-inch baking pan, and arrange the biscuits on top of the mixture. Bake for 12 minutes, or until the biscuits are browned. Serve immediately.

Yield: 6 servings

FILLING

2 tablespoons canola oil

1 onion, cut into ¼-inch squares

1 medium potato, peeled and cut into ¼-inch cubes

1 green bell pepper, cut into ¼-inch squares

1 clove garlic, minced

1 can (1 pound) pinto beans, drained

1 can (10 ounces) whole kernel corn, drained

¼ cup sliced black olives

2 cups tomato sauce

Pinch sea salt

Pinch freshly ground black pepper

BISCUIT TOPPING

1¼ cups white or whole-grain spelt flour

¾ cup cornmeal

1 tablespoon nonaluminum baking powder

½ teaspoon sea salt

¼ cup canola oil

¾ cup low-fat milk (or substitute)

Egg Noodles Indonesian

Yield: 4 servings

8 ounces spelt egg noodles

2 cups broccoli florets, cut into bite-sized pieces

6 scallions, finely chopped

1 red bell pepper, quartered and cut into ⅛-inch slivers

PEANUT SAUCE

¼ cup plus 2 tablespoons smooth peanut butter

2 tablespoons hot water

2 tablespoons peanut oil

¼ cup soy sauce

2 tablespoons apple cider vinegar

2 cloves garlic, minced

2 teaspoons grated fresh ginger

⅛ teaspoon cayenne pepper

This prize-winning recipe, which comes to us from Leisla Sansom of Alexandria, Virginia, is ideal for people in a hurry. Fifteen minutes is all you'll need to get this tasty dish onto the table.

1. To make the peanut sauce, combine the peanut butter and water in a 1-quart bowl, stirring until the ingredients are thoroughly blended. Add the oil, soy sauce, and vinegar, mixing thoroughly. Stir in the garlic, ginger, and cayenne pepper, and set aside.

2. Cook the egg noodles until al dente according to package directions. Drain well, and transfer to a serving dish. Place in a warm oven.

3. Place the broccoli in a steamer, and cook over simmering water for 4 to 6 minutes, or just until tender.

4. Add the broccoli, peanut sauce, scallions, and red pepper to the noodles, and toss to mix. Serve immediately.

Spanish Pasta Roll

This prize-winning recipe was created by Desiree Witkowski of Buellton, California. Desiree says that this versatile dish is not only delicious, but also a great way to use up leftovers.

1. Preheat the oven to 375°F. Coat a 16-x-14-inch cookie sheet with nonstick cooking spray, and set aside.

2. To make the filling, combine all of the filling ingredients in a 3-quart bowl. Set aside.

3. To make the dough, place the flour in a 2-quart bowl. Make a well in the flour, and pour in the melted margarine, beaten eggs, and salt. Use a spoon to lightly mix just until a dough forms.

4. Shape the dough into a ball, and transfer to a floured board. Using a floured rolling pin, roll the dough out into a 14-x-14-inch square. Spread the filling evenly over the dough to within $1\frac{1}{2}$ inches of each edge, and roll the dough up jelly-roll style. Moisten your fingers, and seal the edges of the roll by pinching them together.

5. Place the roll on the prepared cookie sheet, and bake for about 25 minutes, or until the dough is browned. Serve immediately, accompanying the roll with salsa, if desired.

Yield: 4 servings

PASTA

$1\frac{1}{4}$ cups whole-grain or white spelt flour

2 tablespoons melted canola margarine

2 eggs, beaten (or substitute)

Dash sea salt

FILLING

2 cups low-fat ricotta cheese

$\frac{3}{4}$ cup fresh, canned, or frozen whole kernel corn

$\frac{3}{4}$ cup chopped tomatoes

$\frac{1}{4}$ cup chopped scallions

1 can (4 ounces) green chilies, drained and chopped

$\frac{1}{4}$ cup chopped fresh cilantro

$\frac{1}{2}$ teaspoon chopped fresh oregano, or $\frac{1}{4}$ teaspoon dried oregano

$\frac{1}{4}$ teaspoon garlic powder

$\frac{1}{4}$ teaspoon sea salt

$\frac{1}{8}$–$\frac{1}{4}$ teaspoon crushed red pepper

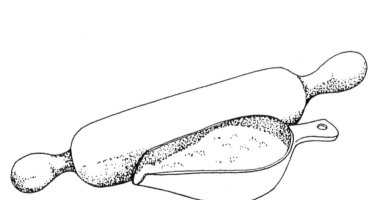

Savory Spelt Kernel Roast

Yield: 4 servings

2 egg whites

2 cups cooked spelt kernels (page 3)

1 cup crumbled firm tofu

1 slice stale spelt bread

3 tablespoons canola oil

2 tablespoons minced red onion

1 tablespoon prepared Savory Garni (page 124)

1 teaspoon herb seasoning salt

¼ teaspoon freshly ground white pepper

1 teaspoon tamari soy sauce

1 cup cooked kidney beans

2 carrots, cut into thin strips

This vegetarian roast is both tasty and nutritious. The herbs in the Savory Garni add zest to the ground kernel mixture, giving the roast a unique flavor.

1. Place the egg whites in a 2-quart bowl, and beat with an electric mixer until the whites form stiff peaks. Set aside.

2. Place the spelt kernels and tofu in a food processor, and, using a fine cutting circle, process on "grind." Place the bread in the processor, and process to force all the kernels through the grinder.

3. Transfer the ground mixture to a 2-quart bowl. Add the oil, onion, Savory Garni, herb seasoning, pepper, and tamari sauce, and mix thoroughly. Fold in the beaten egg whites.

4. Preheat the oven to 425°F. Fill a 16-x-11-inch baking pan with 1 inch of water, and set aside. Coat a 1-quart oval casserole dish with nonstick cooking spray, and sprinkle the inside with finely ground bread crumbs.

5. Spread a third of the kernel mixture over the bottom of the prepared dish. Arrange the kidney beans over the mixture, and use a spoon to push the beans into the mixture. Spread another third of the kernel mixture over the beans, and arrange the carrot strips over the mixture, again pushing the vegetables into the mixture. Spread the remaining kernel mixture over the carrots, and, using wet hands, push the edges of the mixture down to seal the layers together.

6. Cover the dish with aluminum foil, and place it in the water-filled pan. Bake for 1 hour and 15 minutes, or until the roast is evenly browned. Serve immediately.

Serving Suggestions

• For a complete dinner, serve the roast with cooked potatoes and steamed in-season vegetables.

• For a fast lunch, heat a small amount of canola oil in a skillet, and sauté slices of leftover roast along with any vegetables you have on hand.

Tofu⁄Spelt Roast

This roast combines whole-grain spelt flour with nutritious tofu, flavorful sunflower seeds, fresh green peppers, and fragrant rosemary, for a delicious protein-packed dish that your family is sure to love.

1. Place the sunflower seeds in a blender, and process on high speed for 1 minute, or until finely ground. Set aside.

2. Place the bouillon cube and hot water in a small bowl, and stir to dissolve. Allow to cool to room temperature. Stir in the tamari, and set aside.

3. Place the flour in a 2-quart bowl. Add the bouillon mixture, and mix until the ingredients form a stiff mixture. Form this flour base into a ball, and thoroughly knead it in the bowl for about 5 minutes, or until pliable.

4. Add enough cool water to the bowl to cover the flour base. Cover, and refrigerate overnight.

5. The next day, drain the water from the flour base, reserving the water, which will later be added to the roast and used to make the basting sauce. Rinse the starch from the base by holding the bowl under running water as you squeeze the base gently, continuing for about 1 minute, or until the water in the bowl is almost clear.

6. Place the flour base in a food processor, and, using a fine cutting circle, process on "grind." Place the bread in the processor, and process to force all of the base through the grinder. Transfer the ground base to a 3-quart bowl, and set aside.

7. Preheat the oven to 375°F. Lightly coat a 2-quart casserole dish with nonstick cooking spray, and set aside.

8. To make the basting sauce, place the sauce ingredients in a 2-cup bowl, and mix thoroughly. Set aside.

9. Place 1 cup of the reserved flour base water in a 1-quart saucepan, and bring to a boil over high heat. Add 1 bay leaf and the rosemary, and reduce the heat to low. Simmer uncovered for 5 minutes. Remove and discard the bay leaf, and allow the mixture to cool to room temperature.

10. Add the tofu, green pepper, and sunflower seeds to the ground flour base, and mix well. Pour in the cooled bay leaf mixture and the lecithin, and blend thoroughly.

11. Place the dough on an unfloured board, and shape it into a loaf. Transfer the loaf to the prepared dish, and pour half of the basting sauce over the mixture. Add 1 bay leaf.

Yield: 4 servings

2 cups lightly salted hulled sunflower seeds

1 vegetable bouillon cube

3⁄4 cup hot water

1 teaspoon tamari soy sauce

2 cups whole-grain spelt flour

1 slice stale spelt bread

2 bay leaves, divided

1 tablespoon chopped fresh rosemary, or 1 teaspoon dried rosemary

1 1⁄2 cups mashed firm tofu

1 medium green bell pepper, finely chopped

1⁄4 cup liquid lecithin*

BASTING SAUCE

1⁄2 cup reserved flour base stock

1⁄4 cup canola oil

1 tablespoon tamari soy sauce

*Lecithin, a by-product of soy oil refining, is available in health foods stores.

12. Cover the dish with aluminum foil, and bake for 2 hours and 30 minutes, or until evenly browned, basting frequently with the remainder of the basting sauce. Serve immediately.

Variations

• To make Tofu-Spelt Cutlets, shape the roast mixture into 4-x-3-inch squares ½-inch thick, place on a greased pan, and bake in a 375°F for about 35 minutes, or until the cutlets are crisp and brown.

• To make Tofu-Spelt Balls, shape the roast mixture into 1½-inch balls, and drop into a pot of simmering stock. Simmer for 40 minutes, remove with a slotted spoon, and serve with vegetables or over spelt pasta.

Spinach Fettuccine With Cauliflower

Yield: 4 servings

2 cups cauliflower florets

1 teaspoon canola oil

1 clove garlic, split

⅛ teaspoon crushed red pepper

2 cups cooked Spinach Noodles (page 143)

2 tablespoons chopped fresh parsley

¼ cup grated Romano cheese

Colorful and delicious, this dish is a wonderful showcase for homemade whole-grain spelt noodles.

1. Place the cauliflower in a steamer, and cook over simmering water for about 4 minutes, or until nearly tender. Set aside.

2. Place the oil in a 10-inch nonstick skillet over medium heat. Add the garlic, and sauté just until the garlic is lightly browned. Remove and discard the garlic.

3. Add the cauliflower and red pepper to the skillet, and sauté for 2 to 3 minutes, or just until the cauliflower is tender. Add the pasta, and toss gently to mix.

4. Transfer the pasta mixture to individual plates. Top each serving with parsley and Romano, and serve immediately.

Variation

• Make Egg Noodles With Cauliflower by replacing the homemade pasta with cooked store-bought spelt egg noodles. While the green color will be lost, the dish will still be delicious.

Zucchini and Tomato Pizza

Although most of us think of the pizza as an Italian creation, some sources suggest that the pizza originated in ancient Egypt, where a flat bread was heaped with whatever foods were available. Wherever the pizza started, it is clear that this versatile food is now a favorite throughout the United States. And when made with whole-grain spelt flour, as this one is, pizza is as healthful as it is delicious.

1. To make the crust, place the yeast, sugar, and water in a 2-cup bowl, and stir until the yeast and sugar are dissolved.

2. Combine the 1½ cups of flour with the sea salt in a 2-quart bowl. Slowly stir in the yeast mixture, mixing thoroughly with a wooden spoon until the ingredients form a soft dough.

3. Transfer the dough to a well-floured board, and knead in as much of the remaining ⅓ cup of flour as necessary to prevent the dough from sticking to the board. Continue kneading for about 5 minutes, or until the dough becomes smooth and elastic.

4. Coat a 3-quart bowl with nonstick cooking spray. Shape the dough into a round ball, and place in the oiled bowl. Cover the bowl with a clean kitchen towel, and let it rise at room temperature for 1½ to 2 hours, or until it has doubled in size.

5. While the dough is rising, make the sauce by placing the oil in a 2-quart saucepan over medium heat. Add the garlic and onion, and sauté for about 1 minute. Add the tomatoes, tomato paste, oregano, basil, and herb seasoning, and cook for an additional 5 minutes. Reduce the heat to low, and cook uncovered for 15 minutes, stirring occasionally. Remove the pan from the heat, and set aside.

6. Preheat the oven to 450°F. Spread about 1 tablespoon of olive oil over the bottom and sides of a 10-inch springform pan. Sprinkle the pan lightly with bread crumbs or cornmeal, and set aside.

7. Transfer the dough to a lightly floured board, and, using a lightly floured rolling pin, roll the dough into a 12-inch circle. Transfer the circle to the prepared pan.

8. Spread the sauce evenly over the dough, and top with the zucchini and tomatoes. Bake on the middle rack for 20 minutes. Sprinkle the cheese over the pizza, lower the heat to 400°F, and bake for an additional 12 minutes, or until the bottom of the crust is crisp. Unclasp the springform collar, cut the pie into wedges, and serve immediately.

Yield: One 10-inch pie

CRUST

1 package (2¼ ounces) dry active yeast

¼ teaspoon turbinado sugar (or other sweetener)

¾ cup very warm water (105°F to 115°F)

1½ cups whole-grain spelt flour

1 teaspoon sea salt

⅓ cup whole-grain spelt flour

SAUCE

1 tablespoon canola oil

1 clove garlic, finely minced

¼ cup finely chopped white onion

1 cup drained and chopped canned Italian-style plum tomatoes

¼ cup tomato paste

1 tablespoon chopped fresh oregano, or 1 teaspoon dried oregano

1 teaspoon chopped fresh basil, or ½ teaspoon dried basil

½ teaspoon herb seasoning salt

TOPPING

1 small zucchini, thinly sliced

2 large tomatoes, thinly sliced

1 cup finely chopped Tilsiter cheese

Bean and Vegetable Lasagna

Yield: 6 servings

9 spelt lasagna noodles

3 cups Make-Ahead Tomato
Sauce (page 105)

1 can (14½ ounces) Italian-style
stewed tomatoes, drained

8 ounces shredded low-fat
mozzarella cheese

TOFU FILLING

8 ounces firm tofu, cut into 8
equal slices

½ teaspoon paprika

¼ teaspoon freshly ground white
pepper

2 tablespoons tamari soy sauce

1 small zucchini, coarsely grated

1 clove garlic, minced

½ teaspoon herb seasoning salt

2 tablespoons canola oil

½ cup grated low-fat Parmesan
cheese

BEAN FILLING

1½ cups canned white lima
beans, drained and mashed

¼ cup chopped green bell pepper

½ teaspoon herb seasoning salt

1 tablespoon chopped fresh basil,
or 1 teaspoon dried basil

1 tablespoon chopped fresh
oregano, or 1 teaspoon dried
oregano

This delicious spelt-noodle lasagna has a tomato sauce base and two fillings: an Italian-style white lima bean filling, and a tofu, cheese, and zucchini filling.

1. Place the tofu slices in a shallow dish. Sprinkle with the paprika, pepper, and tamari sauce, turning the slices so that they become evenly coated. Cover, and allow to marinate in the refrigerator overnight.

2. The next day, cook the lasagna noodles until al dente according to package directions. Drain, rinse, and drain again. Set aside.

3. To make the bean filling, combine all of the bean filling ingredients in a 2-quart bowl. Set aside.

4. To make the tofu filling, crumble the marinated tofu slices into a 2-quart bowl. Add the remaining tofu filling ingredients, and mix well. Set aside.

5. Preheat the oven to 400°F. To assemble the lasagna, spread 1 cup of the tomato sauce over the bottom of an 11-x-8-inch baking dish. Arrange 3 of the cooked noodles over the sauce. Arrange the bean filling over the noodles, spreading the filling into an even layer. Follow this with the stewed tomatoes, another 3 noodles, and another cup of sauce. Arrange the tofu filling over the sauce, and top with the remaining 3 noodles and the remaining cup of sauce. Sprinkle with the mozzarella cheese.

6. Cover the dish with aluminum foil, and bake for 45 minutes. Remove the foil, increase the heat to 425°F, and bake for an additional 15 minutes, or until the sauce is bubbly and the cheese has melted. Let the lasagna sit at room temperature for 10 minutes before cutting into squares and serving.

Serving Suggestion

• To balance the lasagna's richness and bring out its flavors, accompany the dish with a tossed green salad and garlic bread.

Pasta and Carrots in Cumin Yogurt Sauce

A pungent seed, cumin is widely used in Middle Eastern dishes. In this recipe, cumin is blended with carrot juice and yogurt, giving the dish an exotic flavor and an alluring aroma.

1. Cook the pasta until al dente according to package directions. Drain well, rinse, and drain again. Set aside.

2. Place the margarine in a 10-inch skillet, and melt over medium heat. Add the carrot strips, and sauté, stirring frequently, for 3 to 5 minutes, or until the carrots are barely tender.

3. Sprinkle the cumin over the carrots. Add the tamari sauce, and mix thoroughly.

4. Move the carrots to one side of the skillet, and add the spaghetti. Sauté the spaghetti for a few minutes, stirring frequently.

5. Add the carrot juice to the skillet mixture, and reduce the heat to low. Cook for about 3 minutes, or just until the juice is warm.

6. Remove the skillet from the heat, and add the yogurt and parsley. Combine all of the ingredients in the skillet by stirring gently. Check the seasoning, adding more cumin if necessary, and serve immediately.

Variation

• For a heartier dish, just before adding the carrot juice, add 1 cup of diced cooked chicken and $\frac{1}{2}$ cup of cooked green peas.

Yield: 4 servings

5 ounces spelt spaghetti

1 tablespoon canola margarine

2 large carrots, peeled and cut into julienne strips

$\frac{1}{4}$ teaspoon cumin

$\frac{1}{2}$ teaspoon tamari soy sauce

$\frac{1}{4}$ cup carrot juice

$\frac{1}{4}$ cup plus 2 tablespoons plain nonfat yogurt

2 tablespoons chopped fresh parsley

VEGAN DISHES

Pumpkin Primavera Pasta

Yield: 4 servings

1 cup bite-sized broccoli florets

4 asparagus spears, cut into 1-inch pieces

8 ounces silken tofu

1 cup packed cooked or canned pumpkin

1 teaspoon sea salt

2 tablespoons frozen apple juice concentrate

2 tablespoons tahini

1 tablespoon chopped fresh basil, or 1 teaspoon dried basil

1 tablespoon fresh lemon juice

2 tablespoons water

8 ounces spelt rotini pasta

2 to 3 tablespoons canola oil

2 cloves garlic, minced

1 onion, chopped

6 large fresh mushrooms, sliced

1 small zucchini, cut into julienne strips

1 small red pepper, diced

Lauren Kruss of Colts Neck, New Jersey, created this prize-winning dish, which is unbelievably rich and creamy despite the fact that it contains absolutely no dairy products.

1. Place the broccoli and asparagus in a steamer, and cook over simmering water for about 3 minutes, or just until tender. Set aside to cool.

2. Place the tofu, pumpkin, salt, apple juice concentrate, tahini, basil, lemon juice, and water in a blender, and process on "purée" for 2 minutes, or until smooth. Allow the mixture to remain in the blender until needed.

3. Cook the pasta until al dente according to package directions. Drain well, transfer to a bowl, and place in a warm oven until needed.

4. Place the oil in a wok or a 10-inch skillet over medium-high heat. Add the garlic, onion, mushrooms, and zucchni, and stir-fry for 2 minutes. Add the broccoli and asparagus, and stir-fry just until the vegetables are heated through.

5. Pour the tofu mixture over the vegetables. Add the red pepper, stir, and heat to boiling, stirring frequently.

6. Transfer the primavera mixture to a warmed bowl. Add the pasta, and gently fold it into the mixture. Serve immediately.

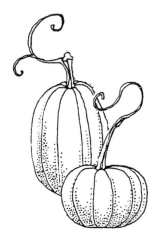

Chinese Strudel

This prize-winning recipe was created by Margaret Wittenberg of Buda, Texas. Margaret says that this easy-to-make dish provides a tempting taste of the Orient.

1. To make the filling, place the canola oil in a wok or a 10-inch skillet over medium-high heat. Add the garlic, ginger, sesame seeds, and onion, and stir-fry for 1 minute.

2. Add the celery and cabbage to the skillet mixture, and stir-fry for 1 minute.

3. Add the mushrooms and carrots to the skillet mixture. Sprinkle the mixture with the soy sauce, extracts, pepper, and sesame oil, and stir-fry for 1 minute.

4. Add the bean sprouts to the skillet mixture, cover the wok or skillet, and steam for 2 minutes at medium-low heat. Transfer the contents of the wok or skillet to a colander, and set aside to drain for 20 minutes. (If desired, you may collect the drained juices in a bowl and use them as vegetable stock in other recipes. Also note that the drained mixture may be prepared in advance and stored in the refrigerator for up to 3 days before completing the recipe.)

5. To make the strudel dough, combine the flour and salt in a 2-quart bowl. Slowly add the canola oil, stirring with a fork until the mixture becomes crumbly. Still stirring, slowly add the water until a dough forms. Shape the dough into a smooth, damp ball, and allow it to sit in the bowl for 5 minutes.

6. Preheat the oven to 350°F. Coat a 16-x-14-inch cookie sheet with nonstick cooking spray, and set aside.

7. Transfer the dough to a floured surface. Using a lightly floured rolling pin, roll the dough into a ¼-inch-thick 18-x-8-inch rectangle. Arrange the drained filling along the length of the dough in a sausage shape, extending the filling to within 1 inch of each end. Fold the long sides of the rectangle over the filling until the sides meet, and pinch the edges together. Close the ends by pinching the edges together.

8. Carefully transfer the strudel to the prepared cookie sheet, placing the roll seam side down. Using a sharp knife, make slits along the top, spacing them every 1½ inches. This will prevent cracking by allowing the steam to escape during baking.

9. Bake for about 40 minutes, or until golden brown. Allow to cool at room temperature for 5 minutes before slicing and serving.

Yield: 12 servings

FILLING

2 teaspoons canola oil

3 cloves garlic, minced

1 teaspoon grated fresh ginger

1 tablespoon sesame seeds

1 small onion, chopped

1 cup diced celery

1½ cups shredded cabbage

1 cup finely sliced fresh mushrooms

1½ cups grated carrots

2 tablespoons soy sauce

¼ teaspoon orange extract

½ teaspoon lemon extract

Dash freshly ground black pepper

2 teaspoons sesame oil

3 cups fresh mung bean sprouts

STRUDEL DOUGH

3 cups white or whole-grain spelt flour

¼ teaspoon sea salt

⅓ cup plus 1 tablespoon canola oil

¼ cup water

Soy~Curry Casserole

Yield: 6 servings

⅓ cup white or whole-grain spelt flour

½ teaspoon sea salt

1 teaspoon curry powder

8 ounces spelt elbow pasta

12 ounces soy Cheddar cheese, grated

1 package (10 ounces) frozen chopped broccoli, thawed and drained

1 cup chopped almonds

½ cup chopped onion

1 cup sliced carrots

3 cups soymilk

This prize-winning recipe comes to us from Cathy Teal of Midland, Michigan. Cathy says that this casserole is perfect as either a main dish or a side dish.

1. Combine the flour, salt, and curry powder in a 2-quart bowl. Set aside.

2. Cook the pasta according to package directions, but for 2 minutes *less* than specified on the package. Drain well, and set aside.

3. Preheat the oven to 375°F. In a 3-quart casserole dish, arrange all of the pasta over the bottom of the dish. Then add layers of each of the following: ⅔ of the cheese, all of the broccoli, ⅔ of the almonds, all of the flour mixture, all of the onion, and all of the carrots. Mix the remaining cheese and almonds together in a small bowl, and sprinkle over the carrots.

4. Place the soymilk in a 2-quart saucepan, and heat over medium-low heat until the milk is very warm, but not too hot to touch with your finger. Pour the soymilk over the top of the casserole.

5. Cover the dish loosely with aluminum foil, and bake for 1 hour. Remove the foil, and bake for an additional 10 to 15 minutes, or just until the mixture is bubbly. Serve immediately.

Spaghetti With Spicy Peanut Sauce

Yield: 8 servings

1 package (10 ounces) frozen butternut squash

8 ounces spelt spaghetti

½ cup smooth peanut butter

3 tablespoons hoisin sauce

1 tablespoon honey

2–3 drops hot pepper oil

¼ cup fresh lemon juice

3 tablespoons sesame or peanut oil

2 to 3 teaspoons grated fresh ginger

Scallion and radish slices (garnish)

This prize-winning recipe was created by Anne Frederick of New Hartford, New York. Quick and easy to make, the spicy peanut sauce gets its uniquely Oriental flavor from hoisin sauce—a blend of fermented soybeans and spices.

1. Prepare the squash according to package directions. Set aside.

2. Cook the pasta until al dente according to package directions. Drain well, transfer to a heated serving platter, and place in a warm oven until needed.

3. Place the peanut butter, hoisin sauce, honey, hot pepper oil, lemon juice, sesame or peanut oil, ginger, and squash in a blender, and process at medium speed for 2 minutes, or until the mixture is smooth.

4. Pour the peanut sauce over the pasta, and toss to mix. Garnish with the scallion and radish slices, and serve immediately.

9

Pasta, Dumplings, and Crêpes

When planning menus, whether for weekday family dinners or for festive weekend gatherings, perhaps the greatest challenge facing any cook is the need to keep meals interesting, either by modifying old standbys or by creating entirely new dishes. If this is a dilemma that you face, this chapter offers three delicious solutions: pasta, dumplings, and crêpes.

During the last two decades, many of us have learned how pasta, in all its varied shapes and with all its many toppings, can add exciting new textures and tastes to our diet. Similarly, dumplings and crêpes can bring welcome relief from the usual entrées and side dishes, and can put a new spin on old favorites, as well. Of course, when these dishes are made with spelt flour and other spelt products, you will enjoy more than just a change of pace. Spelt pasta, dumplings, and crêpes all have the delicate nutty taste and high nutritional value that you have come to expect from spelt foods.

MAKING PASTA

Americans have long had a love affair with pasta. For many years, macaroni, noodles, and spaghetti were the only types of pasta with which most of us were familiar. During the 1970s, though, pasta emerged in a dazzling variety of shapes and flavors, and topped with a wide array of sauces. Now we know that pasta is not only delicious, but also a low-fat source of healthful complex carbohydrates, vitamins, and minerals. Just as important, pasta is a versatile food that can be served as either an entrée or a side dish, and can be easily adapted for different appetites and occasions.

Of course, ready-made pasta—including a variety of whole-grain spelt pastas—is now widely available. But for the freshest, most nutritious dishes possible, nothing can compare with homemade pasta. True, the pasta-making process will require about two hours of your time. But the result will be well worth the effort, especially when the pasta is made with spelt flour.

This chapter presents recipes for three types of pasta. Whole-Grain Spelt Egg Noodles is a versatile recipe that includes a number of variations, including Spinach Noodles, Lemon Noodles, Curry Noodles, and even Cocoa Noodles. Potato Spelt Noodles combine potatoes, spelt flour, and ground spelt bulgur for a heartier pasta. Spelt Drop Noodles are a healthy version of an old German favorite. Each of these recipes may be served with a variety of sauces and toppings, some of which are mentioned in the recipes. (For more ideas, turn to Chapter 7, "Sauces, Stuffings, and Dressings.")

Because most people don't own pasta machines, the recipes in this chapter give directions for hand-cutting pasta. This process, of course, does contribute to preparation time. But, as with most things, practice makes perfect, and if you make pasta frequently, the task will become quicker and easier. Of course, if you do have a pasta machine, you can use it to speed the preparation of your spelt pasta.

When cooking homemade pasta, use a pot large enough to hold an amount of water three times the volume of the pasta. If desired, add a teaspoon or so of vegetable oil to prevent the pasta from sticking together during cooking. To prevent the pasta from overcooking, check it for doneness a few minutes before the end of the suggested cooking time. The finished product should be *al dente*—tender, but still firm to the tooth. Drain the pasta well before serving.

Although, ideally, you will want to cook your fresh pasta as soon as possible, once your pasta has been dried, you may place it in an airtight container and refrigerate it for five days, or store it in the freezer for thirty days. Any leftover cooked pasta may be stored in the refrigerator in an airtight container for up to three days. For best results, moisten the pasta with a little vegetable oil, vegetable stock, or milk before placing it in the refrigerator. Then reheat the pasta in a steamer basket or a microwave oven.

MAKING DUMPLINGS

Although popular in many countries, dumplings are rarely found on the American dinner table. This is a shame, as the dumpling is a satisfying and highly versatile food. Depending on your choice of ingredients and on the other dishes in your menu, the dumpling can be part of the entrée itself; can be used as a side dish in place of potatoes, pasta, or rice; or can be a hearty addition to an otherwise unsubstantial soup. Dumplings can even make a deliciously different dessert!

This chapter contains two dumpling recipes. Parslied Spelt Dumplings make an ideal accompaniment to any main dish. Highly adaptable, this recipe can be easily varied by replacing the parsley with dill, rosemary, chives, or other herbs. Sugarplum Dumplings—sweet dumplings filled with fresh sugarcoated plums—can be used to accompany a main dish such as baked chicken, or can be served as a luscious dessert.

If you will be making dumplings for the first time, keep in mind that dumpling dough should be of a firm consistency. If your dough seems too soft, it may be thickened with spelt flour or fine spelt bread crumbs. Once the dough seems right, form and cook a test dumpling to determine if it is, in fact, of the proper consistency. If not, adjust the dough accordingly.

Always use ample liquid when cooking dumplings, and always use a wide-topped pot. When you place your dumplings in the cooking liquid, they will lie on the bottom of the pot for one or two minutes before rising slightly and turning. Sufficient water and space will allow the dumplings to move and expand as they cook. If your dumplings don't rise and turn as expected, help them by moving them with a wooden spoon.

After another minute or two, your dumplings will rise fully to the surface. Be sure to turn down the heat the moment your dumplings reach the top. Most dumplings are bound together by egg, which can toughen at high temperatures. By cooking them in a simmering—but not boiling—liquid, you will ensure that your dumplings cook up light and tender. After reducing the heat, cover the pot, and allow the dumplings to cook for the required time.

When your dumplings look fluffy, test one for doneness with a toothpick. When the dumplings are done, the toothpick will come out clean. If desired, remove one dumpling and cut it in half for inspection. An underdone flour-based dumpling will be doughy in the center, while an underdone potato-based dumpling will have a soggy center. Fully cooked dumplings are even in consistency. If your dumplings have been cooked in water or stock, rather than a soup or stew, remove them from the liquid with a slotted spoon, and serve them immediately.

MAKING CRÊPES

Elegant restaurants have long had a monopoly on crêpes. Now, using spelt flour, it's your turn to discover just how easy it is to make these light, thin pancakes—pancakes that can be served at virtually any meal of the day.

This chapter features three crêpe recipes. Basic Spelt Crêpes can be filled with a variety of mixtures, from vegetables to seafood to chicken. As suggested in the recipe, the pancake itself may also be varied through the addition of new ingredients, giving you endless possibilities. The second recipe, Fresh Corn and Spelt Crêpes, produces heartier pancake-type crêpes that may be used unfilled to accompany virtually any entrée. Finally, to round off your next dinner party, try Lemon Dessert Crêpes. Whether stuffed with a filling of fresh fruit or left unfilled and sprinkled with sugar and lemon juice, these elegant crêpes are the perfect finale to an elegant meal.

Even if you are a novice crêpe maker, you will enjoy success if you pay attention to three important factors: the mixing of the batter, the temperature of the pan, and the style of the pan. When making the batter, quickly mix the liquid ingredients into the dry ingredients. Then beat with a wire whisk only until the ingredients are moistened and all of the lumps have disappeared. Add the batter to the pan when the oil has been heated to the point where a few drops of water dropped onto the pan bounce and sputter, rather than being absorbed. Finally, always use a genuine crêpe pan—a pan with rounded sides. This will allow you to cook and remove the crêpe without breaking it.

Contrary to what you may think, crêpes need not be mixed and cooked at the last minute. Both crêpe batters and finished crêpes can be prepared ahead of time, covered, and stored in the refrigerator for up to forty-eight hours. After removing batter from the refrigerator, simply stir the batter and continue with your recipe. When storing crêpes, prevent sticking by separating the individual crêpes with waxed paper. To reheat, simply place them in a 350°F oven for a few minutes, or heat them in a microwave oven. Then delight family and friends with a treat that's as easy to make as it is healthy and delicious!

PASTA

Whole-Grain Spelt Egg Noodles

Yield: 4 servings

1½ cups whole-grain spelt flour

2 eggs (or substitute)

¼ teaspoon sea salt

1 tablespoon canola oil

3–5 tablespoons cold water

Once mastered, this is a pasta you will want to make often. For a lighter pasta, replace half of the whole-grain spelt flour with white spelt flour. Experiment as you become more proficient, and try making this pasta in different shapes and with different flavorings.

1. Heap the flour onto a large wooden board. Make a medium-sized well in the middle of the flour mound, and set aside.

2. Break the eggs into a 2-cup bowl or measuring cup. Add the salt and oil, and mix well. Pour the egg mixture, a little at a time, into the well in the flour, gradually drawing flour from the inner edge of the well into the center. Mix first with a fork and then with your fingertips until all of the egg mixture has been added.

3. Using both hands, knead the flour and egg mixture for about 3 minutes, adding just enough of the water to make a pliable dough that does not adhere to your hands or the board. Roll the dough into a ball, and either wrap it in plastic wrap or lay it on a plate and cover it with an inverted bowl. Set aside for 1 hour.

4. Cut the dough into 4 equal pieces. Working with 1 piece at a time, place the dough on a floured board and use a floured rolling pin to roll the dough into a 12-x-8-inch rectangle. The dough should be paper thin and translucent.

5. Drape the dough over racks—or over the backs of plastic- or kitchen towel-covered chairs—and allow it to dry for about 10 minutes. You will know that the dough is ready to be cut when its surface is dry, but it is still pliable.

6. Using your hands, roll each sheet into a scroll. Place the scrolls on a board, and use a sharp knife to cut the scrolls into strips, slicing the scrolls on the bias (diagonally). Cut the pasta about ⅛ inch wide for most uses, or about ¼ inch wide for fettuccini.

7. Arrange the cut noodles, still in coils, on large baking sheets, and allow them to dry for at least another 20 minutes, turning occasionally to prevent sticking. At this point, the noodles may be placed in an airtight container and stored in the refrigerator for up to 5 days, or in the freezer for up to 30 days.

8. Place 3½ quarts of water and, if desired, a dash of salt in a 5-quart kettle, and bring to a boil over high heat. Add the noodles and cook at a boil, stirring frequently to prevent sticking. Cook for about 12 minutes for narrow noodles, and a few minutes longer for fettuccini. Drain the noodles well. If using the noodles immediately, toss with your favorite sauce and serve. If storing for later use, toss with a small amount of vegetable stock or other liquid, and refrigerate in an airtight container for up to 3 days.

Serving Suggestions

• Toss the cooked pasta with 2 tablespoons of melted margarine mixed with 1 tablespoon of Savory Garni (page 124), or top with Pesto Sauce (page 103), Zucchini-Cilantro Sauce (page 101), or Make-Ahead Tomato Sauce (page 105).

Variations

• To make Spinach Noodles, prepare the mound of flour as explained in the basic recipe. Remove the stems of 8 ounces of fresh spinach, and rinse well. Place the spinach in a 1-quart pot of boiling water, and cook over high heat for about 2 minutes, or just until wilted. Drain, rinse until cool, and squeeze dry. Place the spinach in a food processor, and process on "purée" until the spinach is finely puréed. Add only 1 egg to the spinach, and process until well-blended. Add the salt and oil, and mix well. Then continue with the basic recipe instructions, substituting the spinach-egg mixture for the original egg mixture. Toss the cooked Spinach Noodles with 2 tablespoons of melted margarine mixed with 1 tablespoon of Savory Garni (page 124), or top with Sweet Paprika Walnut Sauce (page 103) or Pesto Sauce (page 103).

• To make Lemon Noodles, replace the whole-grain spelt flour with white spelt flour. Also, replace the 2 whole eggs with 1 whole egg and 1 egg yolk; replace the water with lemon juice; and add 2 tablespoons of finely grated lemon peel to the dry ingredients. Toss the cooked Lemon Noodles with 2 tablespoons of melted margarine mixed with 1 tablespoon of Savory Garni (page 124), or top with Sweet Paprika Walnut Sauce (page 103), Pesto Sauce (page 103), or Zucchini-Cilantro Sauce (page 101).

• To make Curry Noodles, add 1 tablespoon of prepared curry powder to the egg mixture. Toss the cooked Curry Noodles with 2 tablespoons of melted margarine mixed with 1 tablespoon of Savory Garni (page 124), or top with Basic Spelt Béchamel Sauce (page 102).

• To make Cocoa Noodles, replace the whole-grain spelt flour with $1\frac{1}{3}$ cups of white spelt flour, and sift with $\frac{1}{4}$ cup of cocoa or carob powder. Serve with a dessert sauce.

Potato Spelt Noodles

Yield: 4 servings

4 medium potatoes

$\frac{1}{4}$ cup finely ground spelt bulgur (page 4)

1 cup whole-grain spelt flour

1 egg (or substitute)

$\frac{1}{2}$ teaspoon sea salt

Pinch ground nutmeg

1 teaspoon herb seasoning salt

A combination of riced potatoes, finely ground spelt bulgur, and spelt flour gives these finger-like noodles a hearty taste.

1. Place 2 quarts of water and the potatoes in a 3-quart saucepan, and bring to a boil over high heat. Reduce the heat to medium-low, cover, and simmer for about 20 minutes, or until tender. Drain well, cool until comfortable to handle, and peel. Cover, and refrigerate overnight.

2. Force the cold potatoes through a potato ricer or a fine sieve, and transfer to a 3-quart bowl. Add the bulgur, flour, egg, salt, and nutmeg, and stir together. Using well-floured hands, knead the dough until it is no longer crumbly, adding flour as necessary to prevent the dough from sticking to your hands.

3. Turn the dough onto a floured board, and shape it into a 2-inch-thick log. Using a sharp knife, cut the log into $\frac{1}{4}$-inch slices.

4. Using floured hands, roll each piece of dough between your fingers, leaving the middle thick, and tapering the ends.

5. Place 2 quarts of water and the herb seasoning salt in a 3-quart kettle, and bring to a boil over high heat. Add the noodles, and simmer for about 7 minutes, or until the noodles rise to the surface. Remove the noodles with a slotted spoon. If using the noodles immediately, toss with your favorite sauce and serve. If storing for later use, cool to room temperature and refrigerate in an airtight container for up to 3 days.

Variations

• To make Sautéed Spelt Noodles, place a small amount of canola oil in a skillet, and sauté the cooked noodles over medium heat until brown and crisp. Sprinkle with chopped fresh parsley or chives, and serve.

• To make Glazed Spelt Dessert Noodles, drizzle $\frac{1}{2}$ cup of honey over the cooked noodles, and sprinkle with poppy seeds. Place the mixture in a well-greased 3-quart casserole dish, and bake at 400°F for 25 minutes. Serve with stewed fruit, marmalade, or rose hip jam.

Spelt Drop Noodles

When nineteenth-century German immigrants arrived in this country, they brought with them many cooking implements, one being a noodle-mill. In those days, it was the custom to present a bride with such a mill as a wedding gift. It was believed that the number of the first few noodles to drop through the mill into the boiling water indicated the size of her future family. Now that these mills are found only in museums, making drop noodles is a little more challenging, but this dish is well worth the effort.

1. Place the eggs and stock in a 2-cup measuring cup, and mix. Set aside.

2. Combine the flour, salt, and baking powder in a 2-quart bowl. Slowly poor the egg mixture into the flour mixture, stirring continuously for about 2 minutes, or until the dough bubbles.

3. In a 3-quart saucepan, bring 2 quarts of water to a boil. Spoon enough of the dough onto a wet hand-held wooden board to make a circle about 6 inches in diameter. Tilt the board slightly over the pan of boiling water. As the dough runs towards the end of the board, use a sharp knife to quickly cut into the boiling water small (about 2½-x-¼-inch) pieces of dough. Continue as quickly as possible until all the dough has been used. Alternatively, use a sliding noodle cutter, or a colander with ¼-inch holes. Reduce the heat to medium-low, and simmer for 10 minutes, or until the noodles are no longer doughy inside when cut.

4. Drain the noodles well. If using the noodles immediately, toss with your favorite sauce and serve. If storing for later use, toss them with a small amount of vegetable stock or other liquid, and refrigerate in an airtight container for up to 3 days.

Yield: 4 servings

2 eggs, beaten (or substitute)

½ cup Veggie Stock (page 37) or water

1½ cups whole-grain spelt flour

Dash sea salt

Dash nonaluminum baking powder

Variations

• Rinse the cooked noodles with cold water, and drain well. Mix with 1 cup of grated Swiss Emmenthaler cheese, and serve.

• Make a bed of sauerkraut at the bottom of a 3-quart dish, and arrange the drained noodles over the sauerkraut. Top with well-browned onions, and sprinkle with a little brown sugar. Bake in a 400°F oven for 30 minutes, top with a tablespoon of nonfat sour cream, and serve.

DUMPLINGS

Sugarplum Dumplings

Yield: 6 dumplings

6 medium potatoes

1¼ cups white spelt flour

1 egg plus 1 egg yolk, beaten (or substitute)

Dash sea salt

3 plums, halved and pitted

1 tablespoon turbinado sugar

These luscious dumplings are filled with sugar-coated fresh plums. In the winter, when plums are not available, try using prunes soaked overnight in apple juice and sugar.

1. Place 2 quarts of water and the potatoes in a 3-quart saucepan, and bring to a boil over high heat. Reduce the heat to medium, cover, and simmer for about 20 minutes, or until tender. Drain well, cool until comfortable to handle, and peel. Cover, and refrigerate overnight.

2. Force the cold potatoes through a potato ricer or a fine sieve, and transfer the riced potatoes to a well-floured board. Add the flour, eggs, and salt to the potatoes, and knead the mixture together, adding more flour, if necessary, to prevent the dough from sticking to your hands.

3. Using your hands, shape the dough into a 4-inch-thick log. Cover with a clean kitchen towel, and set aside for 20 minutes.

4. Place the plum halves on a flat surface, and generously sprinkle them with the sugar, coating all sides. Using a sharp knife, cut the log of dough into 6 equal-sized pieces. Flour your hands well, and place 1 piece of dough in the palm of 1 hand. Push a plum half into the middle of the dough, and close your hand around it so that the dough encloses the plum. Finally, shape the dough into a round ball by rolling it between both your hands. Repeat with the remaining dough until you have 6 dumplings.

5. Place 2 quarts of water and a dash of salt in a 3-quart kettle, and bring to a boil over high heat. Drop the dumplings into the boiling water. After they have turned and risen to the top, reduce the heat to low, and simmer covered for 20 minutes. When the dumplings test done—when a toothpick inserted in the center comes out clean—remove them from the water, and transfer to a serving bowl. Serve immediately.

Serving Suggestions

• For a side dish to accompany a poultry entrée, place 2 tablespoons of canola margarine in a small skillet, and melt over medium heat. Add ¼ cup of spelt bread crumbs, a sprinkling of nutmeg and turbinado sugar, and cook, stirring constantly, until the bread crumbs are lightly browned. Top each dumpling with a tablespoon of the crumb mixture, and serve.

- For a simple but memorable dessert, sprinkle the cooked dumplings with cinnamon and turbinado sugar, and serve.

- To make a baked pudding, slice leftover dumplings, and place half of the slices in a well-greased 3-quart casserole dish. Top with 3 sliced plums or prunes, $\frac{1}{2}$ cup of dark raisins, and $\frac{1}{4}$ cup of maple syrup. Add the remaining dumpling slices, and sprinkle them with cinnamon and $\frac{1}{2}$ cup of low-fat milk. Top with spelt bread crumbs, and bake at 400°F for 35 minutes, or until lightly browned on top. Serve immediately.

Parslied Spelt Dumplings

The vegetable milk used in this recipe gives the dumplings a creamy country taste. However, they will also be delicious if made with another milk substitute or with low-fat or nonfat milk.

1. Sift the flour into a 3-quart bowl. Add the potato starch, baking powder, and salt, and mix well. Set aside.

2. In a 2-quart bowl, cream together the margarine, egg, and milk substitute. Slowly add the egg mixture to the flour mixture, beating the mixture with a fork until the batter begins to bubble. Stir in the parsley.

3. Place 2 quarts of water and the herb seasoning in a 3-quart kettle, and bring to a boil over high heat. Using a wet tablespoon, cut rounded spoonsfuls of dough from the bowl, and drop the dough into the boiling water. After the dumplings have turned and risen to the top, reduce the heat to low, and simmer covered for 12 minutes. When the dumplings test done—when a toothpick inserted in the center comes out clean—remove them from the water with a slotted spoon, and transfer to a serving bowl. Serve immediately.

Variations

- To make Cheese Dumplings, blend 2 tablespoons of finely grated cheese into the mixed batter.

- To make Spinach Dumplings, substitute chopped fresh spinach for the parsley.

Yield: 12 dumplings

1 $\frac{1}{4}$ cups sifted white spelt flour

$\frac{1}{4}$ cup potato starch

$\frac{1}{2}$ teaspoon nonaluminum baking powder

$\frac{1}{4}$ teaspoon sea salt

$\frac{1}{4}$ cup softened canola margarine

1 egg (or substitute)

$\frac{1}{3}$ cup vegetable milk* or low-fat milk

2 tablespoons finely chopped fresh parsley

1 teaspoon herb seasoning salt

*Made from dehydrated vegetables, vegetable milk powder is available from health foods stores under the name Vegelicious. To prepare the milk, you mix the white powder with water.

CRÊPES

Basic Spelt Crêpes

Yield: 8 crêpes

½ cup whole-grain spelt flour

¾ cup low-fat milk (or substitute)

1 egg, beaten (or substitute)

Dash sea salt

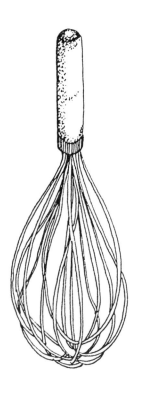

These basic crêpes can be filled with almost any mixture, sweet or savory, making this dish not only versatile, but also a great way of using up leftover vegetables, cheese, poultry, and fish.

1. Place the flour in a deep 1-quart bowl. (A deep bowl makes it easier to spoon out the batter.)

2. Combine the milk, egg, and salt in a 2-cup measuring cup, and quickly add the mixture to the flour, beating with a wire whisk just until no lumps remain.

3. Place 1 teaspoon of canola oil in a 6-inch crêpe pan over medium heat, and tilt the pan so that the oil coats its entire surface. When the oil is hot but not smoking, tilt the pan slightly to one side, and place 2 to 3 tablespoons of batter in the pan. Quickly rotate the pan so that the batter covers the bottom in a thin, even layer. Cook the crêpe for about 1 minute, or until the bottom is lightly browned. Carefully turn the crêpe over, and cook for an additional 45 seconds.

4. Invert the pan over paper towels, and let the crêpe drop out, using a spatula if necessary to loosen it from the pan. After a few moments, use a spatula to carefully transfer the crêpe to a plate, and place in a warm oven. Repeat the crêpe-making process until all of the batter has been used, adding more oil to the pan as necessary.

5. Fill or top the crêpes as desired (see the inset on page 149), and serve immediately.

Variation

• To make Parmesan Crêpes, substitute white spelt flour for the whole-grain flour, and add 2 tablespoons of finely grated Parmesan cheese to the liquid mixture.

Fresh Corn and Spelt Crêpes

Fresh sweet corn is an essential ingredient in these 6-inch pancake-type crêpes.

1. To blanch the corn, place 2 quarts of water in a 3-quart pot, and bring to a boil over high heat. Add the corn to the pot, and boil for 5 minutes. Drain well, and cool quickly by rinsing under cool running water.

2. Hold an ear of corn upright over a board, and, using a sharp knife, slice the kernels off the cob. Repeat with the remaining corn until you have 1 cup of kernels.

3. Place the corn kernels in a blender, and process at medium speed until the kernels are finely chopped. Set aside.

Yield: 16 crêpes

2–3 ears fresh sweet corn

3 tablespoons cornstarch

¾ cup nonfat milk (or substitute)

2 eggs, beaten (or substitute)

⅓ cup whole-grain spelt flour

2 tablespoons canola oil

¼ teaspoon sea salt

Pinch ground nutmeg

Crêpe Fillings and Toppings

A wonderfully versatile food, crêpes can be served for breakfast, lunch, or dinner. When using crêpes, experiment with different ways of folding them. For instance, after spreading one side of a crêpe with the filling of your choice, you can either roll it up jelly-roll style, or fold it in half, and then fold again to make a triangular shape. You can also arrange the filling in a line near one edge, and then roll up the crêpe to enclose the filling. Or you can spread each crêpe with your filling, stack the crêpes, and cut them into wedges like a cake.

Also feel free to experiment with crêpe fillings and toppings. Almost any ingredient—from cooked fruit, to steamed vegetables, to leftover poultry or seafood—can be used to fill your crêpes. While the following suggestions should get you started, the possibilities are limitless.

• For a light breakfast, arrange a line of sliced fresh fruit on Basic Spelt Crêpes, and roll up. Top the crêpes with nonfat yogurt, and serve.

• For brunch, spread softened low-fat cream cheese over Basic Spelt Crêpes, and roll up. Top the crêpes with your choice of preserves, and serve.

• For a quick entrée, arrange a line of cooked shrimp and steamed broccoli on Basic Spelt Crêpes, and roll up. Place the crêpes in a casserole dish coated with nonstick cooking spray, and generously brush them with Pesto Sauce (page 103). Bake in a 350°F oven for 20 minutes, or until lightly browned, and serve.

• For a flavorful main dish, arrange strips of leftover Tofu-Spelt Roast (page 131) in a line on Basic Spelt Crêpes, and sprinkle with low-fat Cheddar cheese. Roll up the crêpes, and place them in a casserole dish coated with nonstick cooking spray. Top with Zucchini-Cilantro Sauce (page 101), and bake at 350°F for 20 minutes, or until the sauce is hot and bubbly.

• For a no-fuss dessert, spread the preserves of your choice over Lemon Dessert Crêpes. Fold the crêpes in half, and then in half again, forming a triangle. Top with whipped cream or nondairy whipped topping, and serve.

• For a more impressive dessert, arrange fresh or stewed fruits in a line on Lemon Dessert Crêpes. Roll up the crêpes, and place them in a casserole dish coated with nonstick cooking spray. Whip egg whites until they form stiff peaks, and pipe the whites around the edge of the dish. Bake at 325°F for 20 minutes, or until the piping is slightly brown, and serve.

4. Place the cornstarch in a deep 2-quart bowl. (A deep bowl makes it easier to spoon out the batter.) Gradually stir in the milk, beating with a wire whisk just until the mixture is smooth. Add the remaining ingredients, including the corn mixture, and whisk just until no lumps remain.

5. Place 1 teaspoon of canola oil in a 6-inch crêpe pan over medium heat, and tilt the pan so that the oil coats its entire surface. When the oil is hot but not smoking, tilt the pan slightly to one side, and place 2 to 3 tablespoons of batter in the pan. Quickly rotate the pan so that the batter covers the bottom in a thin, even layer. Cook the crêpe for about 1 minute, or until the bottom is lightly browned. Carefully turn the crêpe over, and cook for an additional 45 seconds.

6. Invert the pan over paper towels, and let the crêpe drop out, using a spatula if necessary to loosen it from the pan. After a few moments, use a spatula to carefully transfer the crêpe to a plate, and place in a warm oven. Repeat the crêpe-making process until all of the batter has been used, adding more oil to the pan as necessary.

7. Arrange the crêpes in stacks, and serve either plain or spread with the filling of your choice.

Lemon Dessert Crêpes

Even when topped with just a light sprinkling of sugar and lemon juice, these crêpes make an elegant dessert.

Yield: 16 crêpes

1. Place the flour in a deep 1-quart bowl. (A deep bowl makes it easier to spoon out the batter.)

2. Combine the milk, eggs, honey, vanilla, oil, and lemon peel in a 2-cup measuring cup, and quickly add the mixture to the flour, beating with a wire whisk just until no lumps remain.

3. Place 1 teaspoon of canola oil in a 6-inch crêpe pan over medium heat, and tilt the pan so that the oil coats its entire surface. When the oil is hot but not smoking, tilt the pan slightly to one side, and place 2 to 3 tablespoons of batter in the pan. Quickly rotate the pan so that the batter covers the bottom in a thin, even layer. Cook the crêpe for about 1 minute, or until the bottom is lightly browned. Carefully turn the crêpe over, and cook for an additional 45 seconds.

4. Invert the pan over paper towels, and let the crêpe drop out, using a spatula if necessary to loosen it from the pan. After a few moments, use a spatula to carefully transfer the crêpe to a plate, and place in a warm oven. Repeat the crêpe-making process until all of the batter has been used, adding more oil to the pan as necessary.

5. Fill or top the crêpes as desired (see the inset on page 149), and serve immediately.

1 cup white spelt flour

1½ cups low-fat milk (or substitute)

2 eggs (or substitute)

1 tablespoon honey

Several drops vanilla extract

1 teaspoon canola oil

1 tablespoon finely grated fresh
   lemon peel

Variation

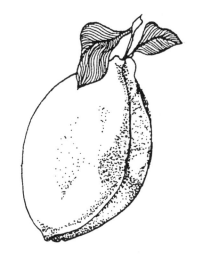

• To make Coffee Dessert Crêpes, substitute rum extract for the vanilla, and instant coffee powder for the lemon peel.

10

Side Dishes

Not too long ago, a side dish was often nothing more than an uninspired bowl of vegetables—overcooked vegetables, at that. The really important dish, it was thought, was the entrée, and any accompanying fare was given short shrift.

Fortunately, times have changed. Our new understanding of what constitutes a complete meal, our movement away from processed foods, and our higher regard for vegetables and other wholesome ingredients have breathed life into the side dish. And, of course, now that a wide variety of spelt products is so readily available, it is easier than ever to create dishes that are varied, tempting, and packed with nutrients.

Just how can spelt expand and improve your repertoire of side dishes? Spelt pasta is, of course, a wonderful side dish in itself, and becomes even more delicious and healthful when combined with vegetables, as in Rotini With Sweet Onion Jam, or when blanketed with cheese, as in Macaroni-and-Cheese Puff. Often, yesterday's main-dish pasta can easily be turned into today's side dish with the addition of some vegetables, an oil-and-vinegar dressing, or a few pinches of fresh herbs. Similarly, by quickly cooking up some pasta, you can turn any number of leftovers into an "instant" side dish.

Spelt kernels, too, are a boon to menu planners, and may be cooked and served plain; baked in a piquant casserole, such as Baked Spelt Kernels and Paprika Peas; or used in a spirited skillet dish, such as Sauerkraut-Spelt Kernel Skillet. In fact, the versatile spelt kernel can be used in any recipe that calls for rice, and so can add a new dimension to many old standbys.

Spelt bulgur, like spelt kernels and pasta, is delicious on its own, or may be combined with other ingredients. Scalloped Spinach and Bulgur Casserole, for instance, blends this golden grain product with fresh spinach, eggs, onion, and seasoning, creating a side dish that will complement almost any entrée.

Toasted spelt flakes are yet another invaluable asset when preparing side dishes. In Spelt-Crusted Oven Fries, these high-nutrient flakes are mixed with other coating ingredients to make crisp oven-baked French fries. In Leek and Potatoes au Gratin, the flakes are used to make a tempting casserole topping. And in Cranberry-Spelt Onion Skins, the flakes add their special flavor to a fruit-filled stuffing.

Of course, while spelt products figure prominently in all of the recipes in this chapter, it is important to pay equal attention to another ingredient—the vegetable. As already mentioned, for many years, vegetables were simply not given the respect they deserved. Too often, side-dish vegetables came out of a can, tasteless and mushy. Even when fresh produce was used, overcooking often robbed it of its unique flavors, its bright colors, and its nutrients. Now, most of us know the importance of buying fresh produce and preparing it in a way that preserves its flavor, color, and goodness. The following guidelines will assist you in choosing, storing, and preparing vegetables for maximum taste and nutrition.

• Try to use vegetables at the peak of ripeness. Vegetables that are immature or overgrown not only have less eye appeal, but also contain less nutrients and have a less pleasing flavor.

• Whenever possible, choose organic vegetables— vegetables grown without pesticides. When organic produce is not available, be sure to peel vegetables or to wash them thoroughly.

• Choose unwaxed apples, cucumbers, peppers, and other produce. When unwaxed produce is not available, consider peeling it, as waxes cannot be washed away.

• Be aware that some fruits and vegetables should not be stored together. For instance, apples give off a gas that makes carrots taste bitter, and onions cause potatoes to decay more rapidly. Test other combinations for compatibility.

• Place most vegetables in the refrigerator as soon as you get them home. Place potatoes and onions in a cool dry place, such as a cellar.

• For maximum freshness and nutritional value, wash and cut vegetables just before cooking.

While it is important to use only the freshest, most wholesome ingredients when creating your side dishes, it is also important to keep your entrée in mind when choosing the foods that will accompany it. A side dish should complement a main dish—not overwhelm it or fight with it. In some cases, you may want your dish to supplement an entrée that is not nutritionally complete. In other cases, you may want to add a splash of color to a monochromatic meal, or to introduce a fresh, light taste to a meal that is somewhat heavy. Whatever your need may be, spelt will help you fill it deliciously!

Angel Hair
With Almond/Raisin Topping

In this dish, angel hair—the most delicate form of pasta—is combined with zucchini and topped with almonds and raisins for a sweet and savory side dish.

1. Place the raisins in a 1-quart bowl. Pour the apple juice over the raisins, and set aside to soak at room temperature for at least 3 hours, or overnight in the refrigerator.

2. The next day, cut the zucchini into 3 equal sections. Cut each section lengthwise into strips ¼ inch wide and ¼ inch thick. Place the zucchini strips in a small bowl, and sprinkle with the lemon juice, herb seasoning, and pepper. Set aside.

3. Place 1 tablespoon of the margarine in a 10-inch skillet, and melt over medium heat. Add the almonds, and sauté, stirring constantly, for about 3 minutes, or until the nuts are golden brown. Transfer the almonds to a small dish, and set aside.

4. Wipe the skillet clean with a paper towel. Add the oil to the skillet, and place over medium heat. When the oil is hot, add the zucchini, and sauté for about 2 minutes, or until the strips are barely tender. Transfer the zucchini to a warmed plate, and place in a warm oven until needed.

5. Wipe the skillet clean with a paper towel. Place the remaining 3 tablespoons of margarine in the skillet, and melt over medium heat. Add the uncooked pasta, and sauté, stirring constantly, for about 5 minutes, or until the pasta is golden brown.

6. Add half of the chicken stock to the pasta, and continue to cook the pasta uncovered for 5 minutes, stirring often. Add a small amount of the remaining stock, and continue to cook and stir until the stock is absorbed. Continue to add the stock in small amounts, stirring often, until the pasta is tender.

7. Stir the zucchini mixture and the parsley into the pasta. Top with the raisin-apple juice mixture and the almonds, and serve immediately.

Yield: 6 servings

¼ cup dark raisins

1 cup apple juice

1 medium zucchini

2 tablespoons fresh lemon juice

Dash herb seasoning salt

Dash freshly ground white pepper

4 tablespoons canola margarine, divided

½ cup slivered almonds

1 tablespoon canola oil

8 ounces spelt angel hair pasta

2 cups Chicken Stock (page 37)

2 tablespoons chopped fresh parsley

Variations

• To make Angel Hair With Smoked Turkey, omit the raisins, apple juice, and almonds, and add 12 ounces of smoked turkey strips to the chicken stock when cooking the pasta. Top with crumbled feta cheese, and serve.

• Substitute carrots for the zucchini, cutting them as you would cut the zucchini, and lightly steaming them prior to adding them to the pasta. When sautéing the almonds, toss in $\frac{1}{4}$ cup of coconut flakes for a sweeter topping.

Rotini With Sweet Onion Jam

Yield: 4 servings

8 ounces spelt rotini pasta

2 large yellow onions, peeled

1 tablespoon canola oil

4 tablespoons canola margarine, divided

1 teaspoon herb seasoning salt

$\frac{1}{8}$ teaspoon freshly ground white pepper

2 tablespoons turbinado sugar (or other sweetener)

1 bay leaf

2 tablespoons grated low-fat Parmesan cheese (garnish)

2 tablespoons chopped fresh parsley (garnish)

This simple but tasty side dish complements almost any entrée. The tender onions add just the right degree of sweetness.

1. Cook the pasta until al dente according to package directions. Drain well, and set aside.

2. Cut each onion in half lengthwise. Finely slice the onion and separate it into half rings. Set aside.

3. Place the oil and 3 tablespoons of the margarine in a 10-inch skillet, and melt over over medium-low heat. Add the onions, herb seasoning, pepper, sugar, and bay leaf, and sauté, stirring often, for about 20 minutes, or until the onions are soft. Increase the heat to medium-high, and cook, stirring constantly, for about 5 minutes, or until the onions are light brown. Discard the bay leaf, and reduce the heat to low.

4. Add the cooked rotini and the remaining tablespoon of margarine to the onion mixture, and toss gently until the margarine has melted and the ingredients are well mixed and heated through. Serve immediately, garnishing each portion with Parmesan cheese and parsley.

Variation

• To make Rotini With Sweet Onions and Cabbage, add a cup of finely chopped white cabbage to the skillet along with the onions, and increase the oil by 1 to 2 tablespoons.

Baked Spelt Kernels and Paprika Peas

A smooth paprika sauce and peas cooked in honey-water give this casserole side dish a delightfully different flavor.

1. Place the peas in a 3-quart saucepan, and cover with water. Add the honey, cover, and cook over medium heat for 15 minutes, checking the water level periodically, and adding more water if necessary. Add the cooked kernels, and cook for an additional 5 minutes, or until the peas are tender. Drain and reserve the cooking liquid for use in making the sauce, and cover the pan to keep the contents warm.

2. To make the sauce, place the margarine in a 10-inch skillet, and melt over medium heat. Add the onion, and sauté for 8 to 10 minutes, or until the onion is golden brown.

3. Slowly stir the flour into the onion mixture. Reduce the heat to low, and, stirring constantly, allow the flour to brown slightly. Still stirring, add the salt, pepper, paprika, reserved cooking liquid, and milk, and cook until the mixture is smooth.

4. Preheat the broiler. Place the pea mixture in a 12-x-8-inch casserole dish, and pour the sauce over the mixture. Sprinkle the cheese over the sauce, and place the dish under the broiler for about 5 minutes, or just until the cheese bubbles. Serve immediately.

Yield: 6 servings

5 cups shelled fresh green peas

1 teaspoon honey

1 cup Simmered Spelt Kernels (below)

$\frac{1}{2}$ cup grated low-fat Cheddar cheese

SAUCE

$\frac{1}{4}$ cup canola margarine

1 small white onion, minced

$\frac{1}{4}$ cup whole-grain spelt flour

1 teaspoon sea salt

$\frac{1}{4}$ teaspoon freshly ground white pepper

1 teaspoon paprika

$\frac{3}{4}$ cup low-fat milk (or substitute)

Simmered Spelt Kernels

Simmered Spelt Kernels is a delicious side dish that can be seasoned to accompany many different entrées. In addition, the $4\frac{1}{2}$ cups of cooked kernels yielded by the recipe may be dried, stored in the refrigerator, and used whole or ground in a variety of recipes.

1. Place the spelt kernels in a large sieve—not a colander, which might let some kernels fall through. Rinse the kernels by holding them under cool running water. Transfer the kernels to a 1-quart bowl, and cover them with 2 cups of water. Allow the kernels to soak for 8 hours or overnight.

2. After soaking, discard any remaining water, and again rinse the kernels in a sieve. Transfer the kernels to a 2-quart saucepan, add the herbs, and add water until the kernels are covered by 2 inches of liquid. Place over high heat, and bring to a boil.

Yield: 4 servings

1$\frac{1}{2}$ cup spelt kernels

Dried or fresh herbs to taste

3. Reduce the heat to medium-low, cover, and simmer for 20 minutes. Remove the pan from the heat, and allow the kernels to soak uncovered for an additional 30 minutes. Drain off any remaining water, and serve immediately.

Variation

• To dry the kernels for storage, spread the cooked, drained kernels on a 17-x-11-inch baking sheet, and air-dry them at room temperature for at least 2 hours. Transfer the dried kernels to an airtight container, and store in the refrigerator for up to 5 days.

Sauerkraut⁄Spelt Kernel Skillet

Yield: 4 servings

3 large tomatoes

2 tablespoons canola oil

2 yellow onions, chopped

1 pound sauerkraut, drained

1½ cups Simmered Spelt Kernels (page 157)

¼ teaspoon sea salt, or to taste

⅛ teaspoon lemon pepper, or to taste

1 tablespoon caraway seeds, or to taste

1 cup Chicken Stock (page 37) or Veggie Stock (page 37)

½ cup grated low-fat Gouda or Swiss cheese

First introduced to the United States by German and Russian immigrants, sauerkraut is a healthful food that aids in digestion. When making this dish, keep in mind that sauerkrauts differ in their degree of sourness. If your sauerkraut is too sour for your taste, try rinsing it in a colander prior to cooking.

1. Fill a 3-quart pot with water, and bring to a boil over high heat. Place the tomatoes in the water, and cook at a boil for 1 minute. Using a slotted spoon, remove the tomatoes from the pot and place in a bowl of cold water. When cool enough to handle, remove the skins from the tomatoes, and chop the remaining flesh into 1-inch pieces.

2. Place the oil in a 10-inch skillet over medium heat. Add the onions, tomatoes, sauerkraut, and kernels, and cook, stirring frequently, for about 7 minutes, or until the onions are lightly browned. Reduce the heat to low, and stir in the salt, lemon pepper, caraway seeds, and stock, adding only a small amount of seasoning at first, and making adjustments according to taste. Cover and cook for 20 minutes.

3. Add the cheese to the sauerkraut mixture, stir to blend, and continue cooking until the cheese has melted. Serve immediately.

Spelt-Crusted Oven Fries

These spelt-crusted potatoes are far healthier than the usual fries. Serve them to the potato lovers in your house.

1. Preheat the oven to 400°F. Coat a 13-x-9-inch baking sheet with nonstick cooking spray, and set aside.

2. To make the coating, place all of the coating ingredients in a 1-quart bowl, and mix thoroughly with a fork. Set aside.

3. Cut each potato lengthwise into 4 equal-sized wedges. Using your fingers, pack the coating mixture around the potato pieces, pressing firmly. Place the pieces cut side down on the prepared baking sheet, and bake for 45 minutes, or until the potatoes are soft inside and the coating is crisp. Serve immediately.

Variation

• Substitute sliced zucchini or eggplant for the potatoes, replacing the paprika with oregano, and the salt and pepper with ½ teaspoon of tamari soy sauce. Bake for 35 minutes, or until the vegetables are tender.

Yield: 4 servings

4 large well-scrubbed potatoes

COATING

2 tablespoons finely ground toasted spelt flakes (page 4)

2 tablespoons finely grated low-fat Parmesan cheese

2 tablespoons canola margarine

½ teaspoon canola oil

⅛ teaspoon herb seasoning salt

Dash freshly ground white pepper

⅛ teaspoon paprika

Macaroni-and-Cheese Puff

This is a particularly versatile dish, suited to most entrées. For a vegetarian main dish, simply double the recipe ingredients.

1. Preheat the oven to 350°F. Lightly coat a 2-quart round casserole dish with cooking spray, and sprinkle with spelt bread crumbs. Set aside.

2. Place the prepared Béchamel Sauce in a 3-quart saucepan. Stir in the milk, cheese, and celery, and allow to simmer over low heat until needed, stirring frequently.

3. Place the egg whites in a 2-quart bowl, and beat with an electric mixer until the whites form stiff peaks. Set aside.

4. Cook the pasta for 8 minutes only. Drain well, and transfer to the prepared casserole dish. Add the sauce to the pasta, and stir to mix. Gently fold in the egg whites, and sprinkle with paprika.

5. Bake uncovered for 20 to 25 minutes, or until the mixture is nicely puffed. Serve immediately.

Yield: 4 servings

1 recipe prepared Basic Spelt Béchamel Sauce (page 102)

½ cup low-fat milk (or substitute)

2 cups coarsely shredded low-fat sharp Cheddar cheese

2 stalks celery with leaves, finely chopped

3 egg whites

2 cups spelt small shell or elbow pasta

1 tablespoon paprika

Scalloped Spinach and Bulgur Casserole

Yield: 4 servings

1 cup low-fat milk (or substitute)

½ cup spelt bulgur

4 egg whites

2 cups chopped fresh spinach

½ cup egg substitute

2 tablespoons chopped onion

½ teaspoon chopped fresh basil, or ¼ teaspoon dried basil

2 tablespoons Garlic Spelt Spread (page 95)

Spinach was probably brought from the Old World to the New World during the colonial period. Now this versatile vegetable is valued not only for its taste, but also for its many nutrients, including vitamin A, vitamin C, iron, and potassium.

1. Preheat the oven to 350°F. Coat a 2-quart casserole dish with nonstick cooking spray, and set aside.

2. Place the milk in a 1-quart saucepan over medium heat, and cook until hot, but not boiling. Place the bulgur in a 2-quart bowl, add the milk, and stir. Set aside for 5 minutes.

3. While the bulgur is soaking, place the egg whites in a 3-quart bowl, and beat with an electric mixer until the whites form stiff peaks. Set aside.

4. Add the spinach, egg substitute, onion, and basil to the bulgur mixture, and mix well. Carefully fold in the egg whites. Pour the mixture into the prepared dish, and dot the top with Garlic Spelt Spread. Bake uncovered for 35 minutes, or until a toothpick inserted in the center of the casserole comes out clean. Serve immediately.

Leek and Potatoes au Gratin

Yield: 4 servings

¼ cup whole-grain spelt flour

1 teaspoon herb seasoning salt

1 leek, thinly sliced

2 large potatoes, peeled and thinly sliced

2 tablespoons canola margarine

1 cup soymilk or low-fat milk

TOPPING

½ cup toasted spelt flakes

¼ cup tomato paste

1 tablespoon canola margarine or Garlic Spelt Spread (page 95)

The leek, like the onion, originated in central Asia, and is believed to have been first cultivated in prehistoric times. And no wonder, as this nutrient-packed vegetable adds a unique flavor to any number of dishes.

1. Preheat the oven to 400°F. Generously coat a 1-quart casserole dish with nonstick cooking spray, and sprinkle with finely ground spelt flakes. Set aside.

2. Place the flour and herb seasoning in a large plastic bag, and shake to mix. Add the leek and potato slices to the bag, and shake and turn the bag until the vegetables are well coated.

3. Place the margarine in a 10-inch skillet, and cook over medium heat until the margarine is hot, but not smoking. Add the coated vegetables, and cook, stirring frequently, for about 5 minutes, or until the flour is browned. Transfer the mixture to the prepared casserole dish.

4. To make the topping, place all of the topping ingredients in a 1-quart bowl, and mix thoroughly with a fork. Evenly spread the topping over the vegetable mixture, and pour the milk over the topping. Bake for about 45 minutes, or until the vegetables are soft. Serve immediately.

Serving Suggestions

- Before serving, gently stir the topping into the casserole mixture and sprinkle the top with chopped parsley.

- Top each serving with a tablespoon of nonfat sour cream or yogurt.

Variation

- Prepare the leeks and potatoes according to the basic recipe, but omit the spelt flake topping and the soymilk. Instead, after transferring the vegetables to the casserole dish, top them with 2½ cups of Basic Spelt Béchamel Sauce (page 102). Bake as directed, sprinkling 1 cup of shredded sharp Cheddar cheese over the vegetables during the last 10 minutes of baking.

Zucchini Casserole

This prize-winning recipe was created by Jackie Evangelista of Painesville, Ohio. Select small zucchini when making this dish, as small squash are tastier than large ones, and contain less water, too.

1. Preheat the oven to 350°F. Lightly coat a 13-x-9-inch glass baking dish with nonstick cooking spray, and set aside.

2. Combine all of the ingredients in a 3-quart bowl. Pour the mixture into the prepared dish, and bake uncovered for 30 to 40 minutes, or until lightly browned. Serve immediately.

Yield: 6 servings

3 small zucchini, thinly sliced

½ cup chopped onion

1½ teaspoons chopped fresh parsley

1 clove garlic, minced

1 cup white or whole-grain spelt flour

½ cup grated low-fat Parmesan cheese

4 eggs (or substitute)

⅓ cup canola oil

⅓ cup low-fat milk (or substitute)

1 teaspoon sea salt

Pepper to taste

2 teaspoons chopped fresh oregano, or 1 teaspoon dried oregano

Twice-Baked Potatoes

Yield: 4 servings

1 tablespoon canola margarine

2 large well-scrubbed potatoes, halved lengthwise

Caraway seeds to taste

2 tablespoons ground toasted spelt flakes (page 4)

3 tablespoons plain nonfat yogurt

1 tablespoon chopped fresh chives

Dash sea salt

Dash freshly ground white pepper

These crisp potatoes are stuffed with a flavorful mixture of spelt flakes, yogurt, and chives.

1. Preheat the oven to 400°F. Lightly coat a 13-x-9-inch baking sheet with nonstick cooking spray, and set aside.

2. Using your hands, rub the margarine on all surfaces of the potato halves. Stick 10 or 12 caraway seeds into the skin of each potato half. Lay the potatoes cut side down on the prepared baking sheet, and bake for about 40 minutes, or until tender.

3. While the potatoes are baking, combine the remaining ingredients in a 1-quart bowl. Set aside.

4. Transfer the cooked potatoes to a board, and use a small spoon to scoop out about half of the potato flesh, leaving a ¼- to ½-inch shell.

5. Transfer the scooped-out potato to a small bowl, and mash with a fork. Add to the spelt flake mixture, and stir well to combine.

6. Divide the stuffing mixture among the potato skins. Return the stuffed potatoes to the oven, and bake for an additional 10 minutes, or until the tops are lightly browned. Serve immediately.

Macaroni and Cheese With Herbed Vegetables

Yield: 4 servings

1 package (7¼ ounces) Vita-Spelt Macaroni and Cheese (or equivalent product)

2 cups chopped cooked carrots or mixed vegetables

1 tablespoon prepared Savory Garni (page 124)

½ teaspoon tamari soy sauce

With Vita-Spelt Macaroni and Cheese mix on hand, this creamy, colorful dish is a snap to make.

1. Prepare the macaroni and cheese according to package directions.

2. Add the carrots, Savory Garni, and tamari sauce to the macaroni mixture, and stir to combine. Serve immediately.

Cranberry-Spelt Onion Skins

These tasty stuffed onion skins are a delicious accompaniment to almost any entrée, but go particularly well with poultry.

1. Preheat the oven to 350°F. Coat a 9-inch square baking dish with nonstick cooking spray, and set aside.

2. Peel the thin outer skin from each of the onions. Place the whole onions, vinegar, and salt in a 2-quart saucepan, and add cold water to cover. Place the saucepan over medium-high heat, and bring the water to a boil. Reduce the heat to medium, and cook uncovered for about 18 minutes, or until the onions are barely tender.

3. Transfer the onions to a colander, and rinse under cold running water until the onions are cool enough to handle. Drain thoroughly.

4. Cut a ½-inch slice off the top of 1 onion, and reserve the slice. Using a small round-ended knife, work around the inside of the outermost layer of the onion until it separates from the next layer. Gently squeeze out the inside layers, leaving a single onion shell. Repeat with the remainder of that onion until you have 5 empty onion shells plus a core. Reserve the core, and repeat the process with the second onion until you have 10 onion shells. Set aside.

5. To make the stuffing, place 1 tablespoon of the margarine in a skillet, and melt over medium heat. Add the spelt flakes, and further toast the flakes for about 3 minutes, or until lightly browned. Transfer to a board, and use a rolling pin to grind the flakes into medium granules.

6. Finely chop the reserved onion slices and cores. Place the chopped onion in a 1-quart bowl, and add the toasted spelt flakes, the remaining tablespoon of margarine, and the seeds or nuts, parsley, cranberry sauce, apple, and mayonnaise. Use the back of a fork to thoroughly mash and mix the ingredients into a stuffing mixture.

7. Evenly divide the stuffing mixture among the onion shells, and place the shells in the prepared pan. Pour the water or other liquid into the bottom of the dish until the liquid covers the lower halves of the onions. Cover with aluminum foil, and bake for 35 minutes, or until a toothpick inserted in the stuffing comes out clean. Serve immediately.

Serving Suggestion

• Before serving, top each onion with a teaspoonful of nonfat yogurt or sour cream.

Yield: 5 servings

2 extra large yellow onions

2 tablespoons apple cider vinegar

Pinch sea salt

STUFFING

2 tablespoons canola margarine, divided

¾ cup toasted spelt flakes

2 tablespoons chopped pumpkin seeds, sunflower seeds, or walnuts

1 tablespoon chopped fresh parsley

¼ cup plus 2 tablespoons jellied cranberry sauce

1 small apple, peeled and grated

1 heaping tablespoon nonfat mayonnaise

1 cup water, Veggie Stock (page 37), or tomato juice

11

Desserts

No matter how satisfying the appetizer, entrée, and side dishes, many of us don't feel that a meal is complete until we have enjoyed dessert. And, of course, when spelt is one of the ingredients, desserts are more than just tempting. They brim with the goodness of this highly nutritious grain.

This chapter presents a wide variety of dessert recipes. First, you will find a delightful selection of puddings, cobblers, and crisps, ranging from creamy Blueberry Flummery, to chocolaty Bittersweet Noodle Kugel, to warm and spicy Apple Spelt Betty. With so many recipes to choose from, you're sure to find one to suit every taste.

Some occasions seem to demand a cake, and this chapter offers a number of tempting concoctions, both plain and fancy. Made moist and luscious with tropical fruits, exotic Coconut-Pineapple Cake is the perfect ending to a special-occasion meal. Carrot Spelt Torte and Raspberry Linzer Torte, too, are impressive enough for any holiday dinner. But perhaps your menu calls for a lighter, but equally delicious, dessert. If so, try Apple

Spice Cake or Oat 'n' Honey Cake. These and several other spelt-enriched delights are perfect not only at meal's end, but also at afternoon snack time, and whenever you crave a sweet pick-me-up.

Pies are favorites with nearly everyone, and this chapter boasts two refreshingly different recipes. Date-Nut Chess Pie is rich with egg yolks and flavored with a blend of dates, nuts, and maple syrup. Strawberry Cream Pie has a cream cheese filling and a fresh fruit topping. And, of course, both pies have crusts made crisp and flavorful with spelt flour.

Perhaps the most versatile of all desserts is the cookie, which seems to be at home at any event from a holiday feast to a weekday dinner to a picnic lunch. In the following pages, you will find recipes for Orange Spice Muffin Cookies, peanut butter-and-chocolate Spelties, Rum Raisin Refrigerator Cookies, and other finger-food treats that are sure to tame the cookie monsters in your house.

When making baked goods, it is important to be aware of a few guidelines that can make your baking experience more pleasurable and help ensure success. If you live in a high-altitude area, you will want to turn to Chapter 1 for tips on high-altitude cooking. Chapter 1 also includes information on using egg substitutes, and on replacing the sweeteners specified in the recipes with alternative products, should you wish to do so. In addition to those guidelines, you will want to keep in mind the following do's and don'ts.

• Always read through a recipe from beginning to end before you begin cooking or baking. This will help ensure that you have all of the necessary ingredients and equipment on hand, and that you understand all of the instructions.

• The first time you try a recipe, always follow it exactly, modifying only the baking time, which may vary from oven to oven. After you have enjoyed success, you may want to alter the recipe to suit your tastes, but do so only if you are an experienced baker.

• Try to keep your cooking area free of drafts. Consistent, controlled temperature is one of the keys to baking success.

• Never overmix. For best results, always mix just as specified in the recipe.

• Never use a baking pan or dish that is smaller than the size called for in the recipe.

• Whenever a recipe calls for a baking dish to have a paper liner or a dusting of bread crumbs, be sure to follow the instructions exactly, as these techniques are designed to diffuse heat more evenly through the dish. Similarly, cookie sheets—which are made of two sheets of metal divided by an air cushion—are also designed to diffuse heat. If a recipe calls for a cookie sheet, but you don't have one on hand, use a paper liner or a dusting of bread crumbs to ensure proper baking.

• Always preheat your oven. Cakes and other baked goods placed in still-cool ovens may fail to rise.

• Never crowd your oven with other dishes in order to save time. Delicate cakes will not rise properly when baked next to casseroles of steamy vegetables.

Once you begin cooking with spelt flour, and you enjoy the delightful taste this grain lends to baked goods and other desserts, you will probably want to use spelt in your own favorite dessert recipes. Fortunately, this can be easily done by substituting white spelt flour for regular white flour, and whole-grain spelt flour for whole-wheat flour. So take out your baking pans and preheat your oven, and get ready to enjoy sweet temptations made even better with the goodness of spelt!

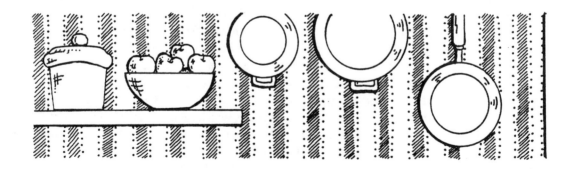

PUDDINGS, COBBLERS, AND CRISPS

Mocha Brownie Pudding

This prize-winning recipe was created by Jean Meyer of Gahanna, Ohio. Jean says that this family favorite is perfect on a cold winter night.

Yield: 6 servings

1. Preheat the oven to 350°F. Lightly coat an 8-inch square baking pan with nonstick vegetable cooking spray, and set aside.

2. To make the topping, combine the brown sugar and cocoa in a small bowl. Set aside.

3. Combine the flour, baking powder, cocoa, sugar, and salt in a 2-quart bowl. Set aside.

4. Combine the milk, vanilla, margarine, and walnuts in a 1-quart bowl. Fold the milk mixture into the flour mixture.

5. Spoon the batter into the prepared pan, and smooth the top with a knife or spatula. Sprinkle the topping over the batter. Then pour the coffee over the topping.

6. Bake uncovered for 35 to 40 minutes, or until a toothpick inserted in the center of the pudding comes out clean. Spoon the pudding into individual dessert dishes, and serve warm.

1 cup white or whole-grain spelt flour

2½ teaspoons nonaluminum baking powder

2 tablespoons cocoa or carob powder

¾ cup turbinado sugar (or other sweetener)

½ teaspoon sea salt

½ cup low-fat milk (or substitute)

1 teaspoon vanilla extract

2 tablespoons melted canola margarine

½ cup chopped walnuts

1 cup hot black coffee

TOPPING

½ cup packed brown sugar

2 tablespoons cocoa or carob powder

Serving Suggestion

• Top each serving with a dollop of whipped cream or nondairy whipped topping and a sprinkling of chopped walnuts.

Variation

• To make Brownie Pudding, replace the hot coffee with hot water.

Cherry⁄Nut Bread Pudding

Yield: 4 servings

1½ cups low-fat milk (or substitute)

4 slices white spelt bread, toasted

3 tablespoons canola margarine

¼ cup turbinado sugar (or other sweetener)

3 eggs (or substitute)

⅓ cup finely ground nuts, such as almonds, hazelnuts, or walnuts

Dash ground nutmeg

1 tablespoon fresh lemon juice

1 tablespoon grated fresh lemon peel

1 can (1 pound) pitted dark cherries, drained, or 20 fresh dark cherries, pitted

If you choose to use fresh cherries in this recipe, you can pit them in several ways. The easiest way is to use a special pitting tool, which can be found in some kitchen stores. If this handy device is not available, try using a clean ball-point pen from which the ink cartridge has been removed. Even a large hairpin will do in a pinch!

1. Preheat the oven to 350°F. Grease a round 2-quart casserole dish with a small amount of margarine, and sprinkle lightly with sugar. Set aside.

2. Place the milk in a 1-quart saucepan, and cook over medium-low heat until hot, but not boiling.

3. While the milk is heating, cut the toasted bread into small cubes, and place in a 3-quart bowl. Add the hot milk and the margarine, and beat with a wooden spoon until the milk and margarine are well mixed, and the bread is soupy in consistency.

4. Add the remaining ingredients to the bread mixture, and stir until well combined. Pour the mixture into the prepared dish.

5. Bake for 40 minutes, or until a toothpick inserted in the center of the pudding comes out clean. Allow the dish to cool slightly before spooning the pudding into individual dessert dishes. Serve warm.

Serving Suggestion

• Top each serving with a dollop of whipped cream or nondairy whipped topping, and garnish with a cherry.

Persimmon Pudding

The persimmon is a luscious fruit that is soft and deep yellow in color when ripe. Sweet and juicy, this fruit is a delicious addition to recipes.

1. Preheat the oven to 325°F. Coat a 1-quart baking dish with nonstick cooking spray, and set aside.

2. Peel and core the persimmons. Place the fruit in a sieve, and, using a wooden spoon, work it through the sieve. (If you prefer, place the fruit in a blender, and process on "purée" for 10 seconds.)

3. Place the persimmon pulp in a 2-quart bowl. Add the dates, sugar, rum extract, milk, and margarine, and mix well. Set aside.

4. Combine the flour, baking powder, salt, and nutmeg in a 1-quart bowl. Add this mixture to the persimmon mixture, and stir until smooth.

5. Pour the persimmon mixture into the prepared baking dish, and bake uncovered for 1 hour, or until the pudding pulls away from the sides of the dish. Spoon the pudding into deep dessert dishes, and serve warm.

Yield: 4 servings

2 ripe persimmons

6 pitted dates, finely chopped

¾ cup turbinado sugar (or other sweetener)

¼ teaspoon rum extract

1 cup low-fat milk (or substitute)

¼ cup melted canola margarine

1 cup whole-grain spelt flour

2 teaspoons nonaluminum baking powder

Dash sea salt

Dash ground nutmeg

Blueberry Flummery

The word "flummery" has several meanings. In this instance, it describes a type of blancmange—a soft, light custard.

1. Combine the 2 egg yolks and the sugar in a 1-quart bowl, and beat with a wire whisk until the mixture is creamy. Set aside.

2. Place the 2 egg whites in a 2-quart bowl, and beat with an electric mixer until the whites form stiff peaks. Set aside.

3. Combine the milk and vanilla in a 2-quart saucepan. Place the pan over medium heat, and cook, stirring constantly, until the mixture is warm, but not hot.

4. Sprinkle the ground bulgur and cornstarch over the milk mixture, and bring the mixture to a boil, stirring constantly. Reduce the heat to low, and simmer for 10 minutes, continuing to stir as the mixture cooks.

5. Gradually stir the egg yolk mixture into the milk mixture. Still stirring, cook for 2 more minutes. Do not allow the mixture to boil.

6. Remove the pan from the heat, and stir in the blueberries. Carefully fold in the beaten egg whites.

Yield: 4 servings

2 eggs, separated

¼ cup turbinado sugar (or other sweetener)

2½ cups low-fat milk (or substitute)

¼ teaspoon vanilla extract

2 tablespoons spelt bulgur, finely ground (page 4)

1 heaping teaspoon cornstarch

1 cup fresh or frozen blueberries, mashed

7. Spoon the flummery into 4 long-stemmed dessert glasses, and chill for at least 1 hour before serving.

Serving Suggestion

• Top each serving with a dollop of whipped cream or nondairy whipped topping, and a sprinkling of fresh blueberries.

Anise-Flavored Spelt Kernels in Raspberry Sauce

Yield: 4 servings

1 cup low-fat milk (or substitute)

½ cup cooked spelt kernels (page 3)

2 tablespoons turbinado sugar (or other sweetener)

1 tablespoon honey

¼ cup dark raisins

PASTRY CREAM

1 egg yolk (or substitute)

1 cup low-fat milk (or substitute)

1 tablespoon white spelt flour

1 tablespoon cornstarch

2 tablespoons turbinado sugar (or other sweetener)

1 tablespoon honey

Several drops anise extract

RASPBERRY SAUCE

2 cups fresh or frozen raspberries

2 tablespoons turbinado sugar (or other sweetener)

In this recipe, precooked spelt kernels are simmered in milk, sugar, and honey, allowing the flavors to penetrate the kernels. Anise extract imparts a subtle licorice flavor to this unusual dessert.

1. Place 1 cup of milk in a heavy 1-quart saucepan, and bring to a boil over high heat. Reduce the heat to low, and add the cooked spelt kernels, sugar, and honey. Cover the saucepan, and cook the mixture for 20 minutes, stirring frequently.

2. To prepare the pastry cream, place the egg yolk and milk in a 2-quart bowl, and lightly whisk together. Add the flour, cornstarch, sugar, and honey, and whisk until the mixture is smooth.

3. Transfer the pastry cream mixture to a 1-quart saucepan, and bring to a boil over medium heat, stirring constantly. Remove the pan from the heat, and stir in the anise extract. Set aside.

4. Place the kernel mixture in a sieve, and drain off and discard any remaining liquid. Transfer the kernels to a 2-quart bowl, and stir in the raisins. Fold in the pastry cream, and cover the bowl with plastic wrap to prevent a skin from forming. Refrigerate for 2 hours.

5. To prepare the sauce, place the raspberries and sugar in a blender or food processor, and process on "purée" for about 30 seconds, or until the mixture is smooth. Transfer the mixture to a fine sieve, and, using a wooden spoon, rub the purée through the sieve so that the seeds remain in the sieve. Discard the seeds.

6. To serve, arrange a few spoonfuls of sauce on the bottom of each of 4 deep dessert plates. Place a scoop of the chilled spelt kernel mixture in the center of each plate, and serve.

Bittersweet Noodle Kugel

A kugel is a noodle pudding that is cooked in a casserole or skillet. This one is delightfully flavored with orange marmalade and bittersweet chocolate.

1. Preheat the oven to 450°F. Fill a large, deep baking pan with 1 inch of water, and set aside. Coat a 1-quart round casserole dish with nonstick cooking spray, and sprinkle lightly with sugar. Set aside.

2. Place the milk in a 2-quart saucepan, and bring to a boil over medium heat, stirring constantly.

3. Stir the sugar and nutmeg into the hot milk. Add the noodles to the pan, stirring constantly to separate the noodles and to prevent the milk from burning. Still stirring, cook for 2 minutes. Continue stirring as you add the potato starch, and cook for an additional minute.

4. Remove the pan from the heat, and fold in the egg yolks and marmalade. Pour the mixture into the prepared casserole dish, and sprinkle with the chocolate. Cover the dish with aluminum foil, and place in the water-filled pan.

5. Bake for 30 minutes, or until a toothpick inserted in the center of the pudding comes out clean. Spoon the kugel into individual dessert dishes, and serve warm.

Yield: 4 servings

2 cups low-fat milk (or substitute)

1 tablespoon turbinado sugar (or other sweetener)

Dash nutmeg

4 ounces spelt angel hair pasta

1 teaspoon potato starch

2 egg yolks, beaten (or substitute)

2 tablespoons bittersweet orange marmalade

2 tablespoons grated bittersweet chocolate

Apple Delight
With Sweet Sauce Amandine

Yield: 16 servings

2 cups cold water

3 tablespoons fresh lemon juice

2 cups peeled, sliced McIntosh apple

¾ teaspoon baking soda

1 cup nonfat vanilla yogurt

½ cup chopped dates

1 egg (or substitute)

1½ teaspoons ground cinnamon

½ cup chopped almonds

CRUMB MIXTURE

2 cups white or whole-grain spelt flour

½ cup canola margarine

1½ cups brown sugar (or other sweetener)

SWEET SAUCE AMANDINE

2 cups low-fat milk or half-and-half

2 tablespoons white or whole-grain spelt flour

2 tablespoons melted canola margarine

2 egg yolks

¼ cup brown sugar (or other sweetener)

2 teaspoons pure almond extract

This prize-winning recipe was created by Ann Eldrich of Coldwater, Michigan. Ann says: "This is an old English family favorite, now made better with spelt flour."

1. Preheat the oven to 350°F. Coat a 9-inch square baking pan with nonstick cooking spray, and set aside.

2. To make the crumb mixture, place the flour, margarine, and brown sugar in a 2-quart bowl, and mix with your fingers until the ingredients form a crumbly dough. Set aside.

3. Combine the water and lemon juice in a 2-quart bowl. Add the apple slices to the bowl, and set aside for a few minutes, periodically pushing the slices into the liquid to prevent discoloration.

4. Stir the baking soda into the yogurt, and set aside.

5. Place half of the crumb mixture in the prepared baking pan, and sprinkle the dates evenly over the mixture. Set the pan aside.

6. Add the egg, cinnamon, and yogurt mixture to the remaining crumb mixture, and stir until the mixture is thoroughly blended. Set aside.

7. Drain the apples well, and place them on a paper towel to dry. When dry, arrange them in a layer over the dates. Pour the yogurt-crumb mixture over the apples, spreading it evenly. Finally, sprinkle the almonds over the pudding.

8. Bake uncovered for 40 minutes, or until a toothpick inserted in the center of the pudding comes out clean.

9. While the pudding is baking, place all of the sauce ingredients except for the almond extract in a 2-quart saucepan, and whisk the ingredients together until the mixture is smooth.

10. Place the saucepan over low heat, and cook, stirring constantly, for about 3 minutes, or until the sauce has thickened. Continue to simmer for an additional 3 minutes.

11. Remove the pan from the heat, and stir in the almond extract. Cover the pan to keep the sauce warm.

12. Spoon the pudding into individual dessert dishes, and serve warm or chilled, topping each serving with a few spoonfuls of sauce.

Apple Spelt Betty

This version of an old favorite replaces white flour with ground spelt flakes, boosting both nutritional value and taste for a truly special dessert.

Yield: 6 servings

1. Preheat the oven to 350°F. Coat an 8-inch square baking pan with nonstick cooking spray, and set aside.

2. Combine the sugar, salt, cinnamon, nutmeg, cloves, and lemon peel in a 1-quart bowl. Set aside.

3. Place the spelt flakes and margarine in a 1-quart bowl, and, using both hands, work the ingredients together until thoroughly mixed.

4. To assemble the dessert, place a third of the spelt flake mixture in the prepared pan, and pat the mixture over the bottom of the pan. Arrange half of the apple slices over the flake mixture. Sprinkle half of the sugar mixture over the apples, and sprinkle half of the lemon juice and half of the apple juice over the sugar. Repeat the layers, ending with the third layer of spelt flake mixture.

5. Cover the baking pan with aluminum foil, and bake for 40 minutes. Increase the heat to 400°F, remove the foil, and bake for an additional 10 minutes. Spoon the dessert into individual dishes, and serve warm.

¾ cup turbinado sugar (or other sweetener)

Pinch sea salt

1 teaspoon ground cinnamon

¼ teaspoon ground nutmeg

¼ teaspoon ground cloves

1 teaspoon grated fresh lemon peel

1½ cups ground toasted spelt flakes (page 4)

¼ cup canola margarine, softened

4 medium apples, peeled, cored, and thinly sliced

Juice of 1 lemon

2 tablespoons apple juice

Serving Suggestion

• Top each serving with a dollop of whipped cream, nondairy whipped topping, or nonfat vanilla yogurt.

Caramel Apple Crisp

Yield: 8 servings

1¼ cups white or whole-grain spelt flour

½ cup oat bran

1 teaspoon nonaluminum baking powder

½ teaspoon sea salt

¼ cup honey

½ cup canola margarine

1 cup coarsely chopped walnuts

⅔ cup evaporated milk

¼ cup honey or brown rice syrup

1 can (21 ounces) unsweetened apple pie filling

20 caramels, chopped

Vanilla ice cream (optional)

This prize-winning recipe was developed by Jacqueline Evangelista of Painesville, Ohio. Jacqueline says: "Your family will be delighted when you set this 'health food' in front of them."

1. Preheat the oven to 375°F. Lightly coat a 9-x-13-inch baking pan with nonstick cooking spray, and set aside.

2. Combine the flour, oat bran, baking powder, salt, and honey in a 3-quart bowl. Using a pastry blender, cut the margarine into the flour mixture until the mixture is crumbly.

3. Set aside 1½ cups of the flour mixture. Press the remainder of the mixture over the bottom of the prepared pan, wetting your hands occasionally to prevent sticking. Bake for 15 minutes, or until the crust is browned.

4. While the crust is baking, mix the walnuts into the reserved flour mixture. Set aside.

5. Place the evaporated milk and the honey or syrup in a 1-quart saucepan. Mix thoroughly, and place over low heat for 3 to 5 minutes, or just until the mixture is warm, but not hot.

6. Spoon the apple pie filling over the baked crust, spreading it evenly. Pour the warm honey mixture over the filling, and evenly sprinkle the caramel pieces over the top. Finally, sprinkle the walnut mixture over the caramels.

7. Return the pan to the oven, and bake for an additional 20 minutes, or until the topping has set. Cool at room temperature for 5 minutes. Cut into squares and serve warm, topping each square with a scoop of ice cream if desired.

Peach Cobbler

This cobbler, with its fruit filling and flaky spelt crust, is delicious when accompanied by a scoop of vanilla ice cream or frozen yogurt.

1. Preheat the oven to 425°F. Coat an 8-inch square baking pan with nonstick cooking spray, and generously sprinkle with turbinado sugar. Set aside.

2. Combine the sugar and pudding mix in a 2-quart saucepan. Add the peaches and honey, and, stirring constantly, cook over low heat for about 5 minutes, or until the fruit is tender.

3. Pour the peach mixture into the prepared pan. Dot the top with the canola margarine, and sprinkle with the cinnamon. Set aside.

4. To make the crust, sift the flour, baking powder, and salt into a 2-quart bowl. Using your fingertips, pinch the margarine into the flour until it is well distributed. Then stir in just enough of the milk to form a soft dough.

5. Transfer the dough to a floured board, and knead for a few minutes, or until the dough is pliable. Using a lightly floured rolling pin, roll the dough into a ¼-inch-thick 8-inch square.

6. Transfer the square of dough to the pan, placing it over the peach mixture. Using a sharp knife, cut several slits in the dough to allow steam to escape during baking.

7. Bake for 25 to 30 minutes, or until nicely browned. Spoon the cobbler into individual dessert dishes, and serve warm.

Yield: 6 servings

⅔ cup turbinado sugar (or other sweetener)

1 tablespoon instant vanilla pudding mix

3 cups skinned peach slices, fresh or canned

1 tablespoon honey

2 tablespoons canola margarine

1 teaspoon ground cinnamon

CRUST

1½ cups white spelt flour

1 tablespoon nonaluminum baking powder

Dash sea salt

3 tablespoons canola margarine

¼ cup low-fat milk (or substitute)

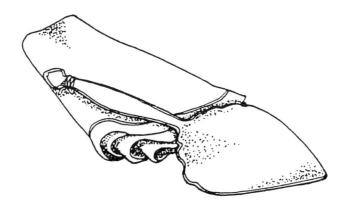

CAKES

Coconut⁄Pineapple Cake

Yield: 12 servings

½ cup canola margarine

¾ cup turbinado sugar (or other sweetener), divided

2½ teaspoons vanilla sugar

Dash sea salt

2 eggs, beaten (or substitute)

1 tablespoon fresh lemon juice

1½ cups sifted white spelt flour

2 teaspoons nonaluminum baking powder

½ cup shredded or flaked coconut

¼ cup plus 2 tablespoons canned pineapple juice

1½ cups canned pineapple chunks

This recipe can be made with either packaged coconut or fresh coconut. If using fresh, knock out two of the "eyes" at the stem end; pour out the milk, which can be used in other recipes; and crack the coconut open with a hammer, taking care to protect your eyes. The flesh, which will deteriorate fairly quickly, can be removed with a sharp knife. To flake it, simply grate it using the largest openings on a hand-held grater.

1. Preheat the oven to 350°F. Coat a 10-inch springform pan with nonstick cooking spray, and sprinkle with spelt flour. Set aside.

2. Place the margarine in a 2-quart bowl, and, using a fork, cream it until soft and smooth. Slowly add ½ cup of the turbinado sugar and the vanilla sugar, salt, eggs, and lemon juice, beating with the fork until the ingredients are thoroughly mixed. Set aside.

3. Sift the flour into another 2-quart bowl. Stir in the baking powder.

4. A little at a time, add the flour mixture to the margarine mixture, beating constantly. Add the coconut and pineapple juice, and thoroughly mix.

5. Spoon the batter into the prepared pan, and smooth it into a level surface. Arrange the pineapple chunks in a circular pattern over the batter, spacing them at ½-inch intervals. Push the chunks slightly into the batter. Sprinkle the remaining ¼ cup of sugar over the top.

6. Bake for 40 minutes, or until the cake is nicely browned and a toothpick inserted in the center comes out clean. Allow the cake to cool for 5 minutes. Unclasp the springform collar, and cool completely before slicing and serving.

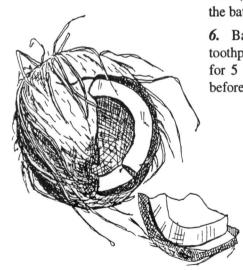

Apple Gingerbread

Most of us love the spicy aroma of warm gingerbread. To make sure that your gingerbread is as temptingly fragrant as possible, be sure that your powdered ginger is fresh. Like most seasonings, packaged ginger tends to lose its spiciness if stored for too long a time.

1. Preheat the oven to 350°F. Coat a 9-inch square cake pan with nonstick cooking spray, and set aside.

2. Place the apples in a 2-quart bowl. Add the lemon juice and marmalade, and toss to coat. Set aside.

3. Combine the flour, baking powder, ginger, cinnamon, salt, allspice, and cloves in a 2-quart bowl, and stir to mix. Set aside.

4. Place the margarine and sugar in a 3-quart bowl, and cream with a fork until thoroughly blended. Add the egg, and beat with a fork or electric mixer until blended. Add the maple syrup, and beat until the mixture is light and fluffy.

5. Gradually stir the flour mixture into the margarine mixture. Add about one third of the milk, and stir to mix. Add the remaining milk, one half at a time, stirring after each addition just until the mixture is blended into a batter.

6. Pour the batter into the prepared cake pan. Arrange the apple slices on the surface of the batter in three rows, slightly overlapping the slices.

7. Bake for 45 minutes, or until the edges of the cake pull away from the sides of the pan. Allow the cake to cool in the pan for 5 minutes. Remove the cake from the pan, cut into squares, and serve warm.

Yield: 8 servings

3 tart apples, peeled, cored, and cut lengthwise into ¼-inch slices

2 tablespoons fresh lemon juice

2 tablespoons orange marmalade

2½ cups whole-grain spelt flour

1 teaspoon nonaluminum baking powder

1 teaspoon ground ginger

1 teaspoon ground cinnamon

¾ teaspoon sea salt

½ teaspoon ground allspice

¼ teaspoon ground cloves

½ cup canola margarine, softened

¼ cup turbinado sugar (or other sweetener)

1 egg (or substitute)

⅓ cup maple syrup

¾ cup low-fat milk (or substitute)

Apple Spice Cake

Yield: 8 servings

½ cup canola margarine

1 packed cup brown sugar (or other sweetener)

3 eggs (or substitute)

2 cups white or whole-grain spelt flour

1½ teaspoons baking soda

1 tablespoon plus ½ teaspoon nonaluminum baking powder

½ teaspoon sea salt

1½ teaspoons ground cinnamon

½ teaspoon ground nutmeg

½ teaspoon ground allspice

1½ cups applesauce

1 cup dark raisins

½ cup chopped walnuts

This prize-winning recipe was created by Jean Meyer of Gahanna, Ohio. Jean says that this spicy cake is the perfect dessert on a crisp fall evening.

1. Preheat the oven to 350°F. Generously coat a 9-x-13-inch baking pan with nonstick cooking spray, and set aside.

2. Place the margarine in a 3-quart bowl, and cream with a fork until soft and smooth. Gradually add the brown sugar, continuing to cream. Add the eggs one at a time, creaming after each addition. Set aside.

3. Combine the flour, baking soda, baking powder, salt, cinnamon, nutmeg, and allspice in a 2-quart bowl. Stir to mix.

4. Alternately add small amounts of the flour mixture and the applesauce to the margarine mixture, stirring just until a batter is formed. Fold in the raisins and nuts, and pour the batter into the prepared pan.

5. Bake for 40 minutes, or until the cake is golden brown and a toothpick inserted in the center comes out clean. Remove the cake from the oven, and cool completely before cutting into squares and serving.

Serving Suggestion

• Top each serving with a dollop of whipped cream.

Oat 'n' Honey Cake

Yield: 8 servings

1 cup rolled oats

1½ cups boiling water

½ cup canola oil

1¾ cups white spelt flour

1 teaspoon baking soda

1 teaspoon ground cinnamon

¼ teaspoon sea salt

¼ teaspoon ground nutmeg

2 eggs, beaten (or substitute)

1 teaspoon vanilla extract

1¼ cups honey

This prize-winning recipe was created by Cheryl Townsley of Littleton, Colorado. Cheryl says: "This oatmeal cake is a family favorite, and the recipe may be doubled and baked in a larger cake pan."

1. Preheat the oven to 350°F. Spray a 9-x-9-inch square baking pan with nonstick cooking spray, and set aside.

2. Place the oats in a 2-quart saucepan, and add the boiling water. Stir in the oil, cover, and set aside for about 30 minutes.

3. Combine the flour, baking soda, cinnamon, salt, and nutmeg in a 2-quart bowl. Set aside.

4. Combine the eggs, vanilla, and honey in a 1-quart bowl. Add the egg mixture to the flour mixture, and stir to mix. Add the oat mixture, and stir until you have a smooth batter. Spread the batter in the prepared pan.

5. Bake for 40 minutes, or until a toothpick inserted in the center of the cake comes out clean. Allow the cake to cool in the pan for 5 minutes. Remove the cake from the pan, and cool completely before cutting into squares and serving.

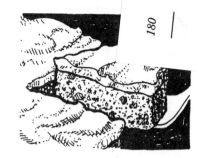

Variation

• Heat 20 ounces of undrained canned crushed pineapple. Dissolve ¾ tablespoon of arrowroot in a small amount of water, and stir it into the pineapple. If you like, also add ½ cup of chopped pecans to the mixture. Top the cake with the mixture while the cake is still warm.

Maple Coffee Cake

This prize-winning recipe was developed by Sally Cashman of Danbury, Connecticut. Maple syrup adds its distinctive taste to this delicious coffee cake.

1. Preheat the oven to 350°F. Generously coat a 1-pound loaf pan with nonstick cooking spray, and then line it with waxed paper. Set aside.

2. To make the nut mixture, combine the nut mixture ingredients in a 1-quart bowl. Set aside.

3. To make the batter, place the oil and maple syrup in a saucepan over low heat, and cook until the mixture is warm, but not hot. Transfer the mixture to a 2-quart bowl, and add the vanilla and eggs, 1 at a time, mixing after each addition. Set aside.

4. Sift the spelt flour, oatmeal flour, baking powder, and baking soda into a 1-quart bowl, and stir to mix. Alternately add small amounts of the flour mixture and the yogurt to the maple mixture, mixing thoroughly to form a stiff batter.

5. Spread half of the batter in the prepared pan. Top with half of the nut mixture, followed by the remaining batter. Spread the remaining nut mixture over the top of the batter.

6. Bake for 50 to 60 minutes, or until a toothpick inserted in the center of the loaf comes out clean. Allow the cake to cool in the pan for 5 minutes. Remove the cake from the pan, and cool completely before slicing and serving.

Yield: 10 servings

½ cup canola oil

⅓ cup maple syrup

1 teaspoon vanilla extract

3 eggs (or substitute)

1¾ cups white spelt flour

¼ cup oatmeal flour*

1 teaspoon nonaluminum baking powder

1 teaspoon baking soda

1 cup plain nonfat yogurt

NUT MIXTURE

¼ cup plus 2 tablespoons canola oil

½ cup granulated maple sugar

2 teaspoons ground cinnamon

1 cup chopped walnuts or pecans

*Oatmeal flour is available in health foods stores and many grocery stores.

Pear Cake

Yield: 8 servings

½ cup Vita-Spelt Pancake/Muffin Mix (or equivalent product)

½ cup whole-grain spelt flour

1 cup white spelt flour

2 tablespoons nonaluminum baking powder

½ cup canola margarine

½ cup turbinado sugar (or other sweetener)

3 eggs (or substitute)

1 tablespoon fresh lemon juice

½ cup finely ground hazelnuts

¼ cup plus 2 tablespoons canned pear juice

8 canned pear halves, drained

TOPPING

1 tablespoon turbinado sugar (or other sweetener)

¼ teaspoon ground cinnamon

1 tablespoon vanilla sugar

Vita-Spelt Pancake/Muffin Mix helps you make this delicious, rich-tasting cake in a snap.

1. Preheat the oven to 350°F. Coat a 9-inch springform pan with nonstick cooking spray, and sprinkle it lightly with finely ground spelt bread crumbs. Set aside.

2. To make the topping, combine the topping ingredients in a small bowl. Set aside.

3. Combine the pancake mix, the flours, and the baking powder in a 1-quart bowl. Set aside.

4. Place the margarine in a 2-quart bowl, and cream with a fork until the mixture is smooth. Add the sugar, eggs, and lemon juice, and whip with a fork or electric mixer until the mixture is creamy.

5. While continuously whipping with a fork or mixer, slowly add the flour mixture, hazelnuts, and pear juice to the margarine mixture until a thick batter is formed. Evenly spread the batter in the prepared pan.

6. Cut each pear half lengthwise into 2 equal-sized pieces, and arrange the pieces over the batter in a circle pattern. Push the pieces slightly into the batter. Sprinkle the topping over the batter.

7. Bake for 45 to 50 minutes, or until a toothpick inserted in the center of the cake comes out clean. Allow the cake to cool for 5 minutes. Then remove the collar of the pan, and cool completely before slicing and serving.

PIES

Date-Nut Chess Pie

While the origin of the word "chess" is unclear, we do know that the creamy chess pie is a Southern specialty that appears in many forms, including the Buttermilk Chess, Kentucky Bourbon Chess, and Pecan Chess. I hope that you enjoy this spelt-enriched version of a Southern classic.

1. Place the flours and the sugar in a 2-quart bowl, and stir to mix. Using a pastry blender, cut in the cold margarine. Using the pastry blender or your fingertips, work the mixture into a crumbly dough resembling large kernels. (This process layers the margarine and flour, creating "leaves" that will form flakes when baked.)

2. Add the egg substitute, water, and lemon juice to the flour mixture, and lightly combine the dough with your hands until it just begins to form clumps, but does not yet form a ball. If the dough is too dry, sprinkle it with a little more water. The dough should feel pliable like clay, but not sticky.

3. Turn the dough out onto a lightly floured board, and quickly knead it into a ball. Wrap the ball in plastic wrap, and store overnight in the refrigerator.

4. The next day, preheat the oven to 350°F. Lightly coat an 8-inch pie pan with nonstick cooking spray, and set aside.

5. Place the chilled dough in the center of a lightly floured board. Using a lightly floured rolling pin, roll the dough into a 10-inch circle. Transfer the dough to the prepared pie pan, and crimp the edges using either your fingers or the back of a fork. Set aside.

6. Combine all of the filling ingredients in a 2-quart bowl. Spoon the mixture into the pie shell, and bake for about 40 minutes, or until the filling puffs and a toothpick inserted in the center of the pie comes out clean. Allow the pie to cool completely before cutting into wedges and serving.

Yield: 8 servings

CRUST

¼ cup white spelt flour

¼ cup whole-grain spelt flour

1 tablespoon turbinado sugar (or other sweetener)

¼ cup cold canola margarine

2 tablespoons egg substitute

1½ teaspoons ice water

1½ teaspoons fresh lemon juice

FILLING

2 egg yolks (or substitute)

1 tablespoon nonfat sour cream

¾ cup coarsely chopped pecans or walnuts

½ cup chopped dates

½ cup turbinado sugar (or other sweetener)

1 tablespoon maple syrup

1 teaspoon vanilla extract

Strawberry Cream Pie

Yield: 8 servings

CRUST

½ cup unsalted hulled sunflower seeds

1 cup finely crushed Spelt Honey Graham Crackers (6 to 8 crackers) (page 186)

¼ cup melted canola margarine

FILLING

⅓ cup turbinado sugar (or other sweetener)

9 ounces nonfat cream cheese, softened

2 eggs, beaten (or substitute)

¼ cup strawberry jelly

6 to 8 whole strawberries, sliced (topping)

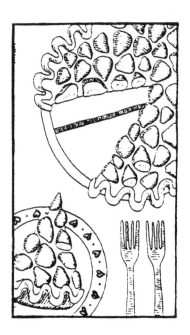

The easy-to-make crust and delicious fruit filling make this pie a summertime favorite.

1. Preheat the oven to 375°F.

2. Place the sunflower seeds in a blender or food processor, and process on "grind" for 1 minute, or until finely ground. Transfer the ground seeds to a 1-quart bowl. Add the remaining crust ingredients, and stir to blend.

3. Press the crust mixture over the bottom and sides of an 8-inch pie pan, and bake for 5 minutes, or until the crust is evenly browned. Reduce the oven temperature to 325°F, and set the pie crust aside until needed.

4. Place the filling ingredients in a 2-quart bowl, and thoroughly beat together with a fork until the mixture is smooth. Spoon the mixture into the prepared shell.

5. Bake for about 20 minutes, or just until the filling is firm. Allow the pie to cool completely before arranging the strawberry slices over the top in a circular pattern. Cut into wedges and serve.

Variations

• For Raspberry Cream Pie, replace the strawberries with fresh raspberries, and the strawberry jelly with raspberry jam.

• For Citrus Cream Pie, replace the strawberries with fresh orange slices, and the strawberry jelly with orange marmalade.

TORTES

Raspberry Linzer Torte

This prize-winning recipe was created by Janet Hill of Sacramento, California. Janet says: "This streamlined combination of chocolate and raspberry is a favorite with kids of all ages."

1. Preheat the oven to 325°F.

2. Place the margarine and brown sugar in a 2-quart bowl, and beat with a fork until the mixture is creamy. Add the egg, and stir to blend.

3. Combine the flour, almonds, cinnamon, and cloves in a 1-quart bowl. Using a fork, gradually beat the flour mixture into the margarine mixture, mixing until a dough is formed.

4. Transfer two-thirds of the dough to an ungreased 9-inch springform pan, evenly spreading the dough over the bottom and 1 inch up the sides. Set aside.

5. Combine the jam and the lemon juice in a small bowl. Spread the mixture over the dough in the pan. Then sprinkle with the chocolate or carob chips.

6. Form the remaining dough into a ball, and place between 2 sheets of waxed paper. Using a rolling pin, roll the dough into a 9-inch circle. Remove the paper, and place the dough on top of the torte, lightly pressing the edges of the top crust to the edges of the bottom crust to seal.

7. Brush the torte with the egg white, and bake for 45 minutes, or until golden brown. Place the pan on a wire rack, and allow the torte to cool for 20 minutes. Unclasp the springform collar, and cool completely. If desired, sprinkle the cooled torte with confectioners' sugar. Cut into wedges and serve.

Variations

• To make a chocolate-flavored crust, substitute cocoa powder for the cinnamon and cloves.

• If desired, after rolling out the top crust, cut it into strips and arrange in a lattice pattern over the filling. Bake as directed above.

Yield: 8 servings

1 cup canola margarine, softened

⅔ cup packed brown sugar (or other sweetener)

1 egg (or substitute)

1⅓ cups white or whole-grain spelt flour

1½ cups ground almonds

1 teaspoon ground cinnamon

½ teaspoon ground cloves

⅔ cup raspberry jam

1 teaspoon fresh lemon juice

1 cup chocolate or carob chips

1 egg white, lightly beaten (glaze)

¼ cup confectioners' sugar (optional)

Carrot Spelt Torte

Yield: 12 servings

6 eggs, separated

1¼ cups turbinado sugar (or other sweetener)

1 tablespoon plus 2 teaspoons vanilla sugar (optional)

Grated fresh peel of 1 lemon

½ teaspoon wild cherry extract

3 cups finely ground hazelnuts

2½ cups finely grated carrots

¼ cup white spelt flour

TOPPING

¼ cup plus 2 tablespoons apricot jam

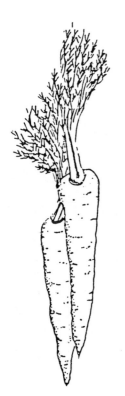

With a scrumptious taste and light texture, this is a dessert for special occasions. Be sure to use whole eggs when making this recipe, as egg substitute simply does not work in this delightful creation.

1. Preheat the oven to 350°F. Coat a 9-inch springform pan with nonstick cooking spray, and lightly coat it with spelt flour. Set aside.

2. Place the egg whites in a 2-quart bowl, and beat with an electric mixer until the whites form stiff peaks. Set aside.

3. Place the egg yolks in a 3-quart bowl. Add the turbinado sugar and, if desired, the vanilla sugar, and beat with an electric mixer until the mixture is fluffy. Add the lemon peel and cherry extract, and mix well.

4. Gently fold the egg whites, hazelnuts, carrots, and flour into the egg yolk mixture, adding a little of each ingredient at a time, and alternating between ingredients. Pour the batter into the prepared pan.

5. Bake for about 1 hour, or until the top of the torte is lightly browned. Allow the torte to cool for 5 minutes. Unclasp the springform collar, and cool completely. Carefully spread the jam over the cooled torte, completely sealing the torte. Cut into wedges and serve.

COOKIES AND BARS

Orange Spice Muffin Cookies

This prize-winning recipe was created by Gloria Piantek of Plainsboro, New Jersey. Gloria says that eating these cookies is just like eating the tops of muffins—and leaving the bottoms behind!

1. Preheat the oven to 350°F. Coat a 16-x-14-inch cookie sheet with nonstick cooking spray, and set aside.

2. Place the egg white, sugar, oil, and vanilla extract in a 3-quart bowl, and beat with a wire whisk until the mixture is creamy. Stir in the orange peel, ginger, oranges, carrots, dates, and ⅓ cup of the walnuts. Add the pancake mix, and stir until a soft dough forms.

3. For each cookie, spoon about 2 tablespoons of the dough onto the prepared sheet, spacing the cookies about 2 inches apart. Top each cookie with a few walnut pieces, and bake for about 15 minutes, or until golden brown.

4. Allow the cookies to cool on the sheet for several minutes. Then transfer the cookies to a rack. If you choose to glaze the cookies, place the glaze ingredients in a small bowl, and stir until smoooth. Drizzle the glaze over the cookies while they are cooling. Cool completely before serving or storing in an airtight container.

Yield: 16 to 18 cookies

1 egg white

⅓ cup turbinado sugar, divided

⅓ cup canola oil

2 teaspoons vanilla extract

1 tablespoon grated fresh orange peel

1½ teaspoons chopped candied ginger

½ cup chopped orange segments (about 2 oranges)

⅓ cup shredded carrots

⅓ cup chopped dates

½ cup coarsely chopped walnuts, divided

1⅔ cups Vita-Spelt Pancake/Muffin Mix (or equivalent product)

OPTIONAL CITRUS GLAZE

½ cup confectioners' sugar

1½ teaspoons melted canola margarine

¾ to 1 tablespoon lemon or orange juice

Spelt Honey Graham Crackers

Yield: 18 crackers

2½ cups whole-grain spelt flour

½ teaspoon sea salt

¾ teaspoon baking soda

½ cup canola margarine, softened

¼ cup canola oil

½ cup honey

3 tablespoons cold water.

Eada Phelps of Silverton, Oregon, developed this prize-winning recipe. Eada says: "These tasty 'graham' crackers also make perfect crumbs for a pie crust."

1. Preheat the oven to 375°F.

2. Place the flour, salt, and baking soda in a 2-quart bowl, and stir to mix. Set aside.

3. Place the margarine, oil, honey, and water in a 3-quart bowl, and beat together with a fork. Add the flour mixture to the margarine mixture, and blend with a wooden spoon until a smooth dough is formed.

4. Spread half of the dough over each of two 13-x-9-inch ungreased baking sheets, using a rolling pin to flatten and smooth the surfaces. With a sharp knife, mark off nine 4-x-3-inch rectangles, and prick the center of each with a fork.

5. Bake for 6 to 8 minutes, or until the crackers are golden brown. Cut the crackers apart while still hot. Cool completely before serving or storing in an airtight container.

Razz-Ma-Tazz Cookies

Yield: 18 to 20 cookies

1 cup pecan halves

1 cup rolled oats

1 cup white or whole-grain spelt flour

½ teaspoon ground cinnamon

Pinch sea salt

½ cup canola oil

¼ cup barley malt syrup

¼ cup maple syrup

½ cup unsweetened raspberry jam

This prize-winning recipe was created by Emily Marx of Lombard, Illinois. The addition of raspberry jam to the ever-popular oatmeal cookie makes these treats a favorite with kids.

1. Preheat the oven to 325°F. Spread the pecans on a cookie sheet or baking pan, and toast for 5 minutes. Set the nuts aside to cool, and increase the oven temperature to 350°F.

2. Coat a 16-x-14-inch cookie sheet with nonstick cooking spray. Set aside.

3. Place the pecans in a blender or food processor, and process on "grind" for about 1 minute, or until coarsely chopped. Set aside.

4. Place the oats in a blender or food processor, and process on "grind" for about 30 seconds, or until coarsely chopped. Set aside.

5. Combine the nuts, oats, flour, cinnamon, and salt in a 3-quart bowl. Set aside.

6. Combine the oil, barley malt syrup, and maple syrup in a 1-quart bowl. Add the oil mixture to the flour mixture, and blend until a moist, but not sticky, dough is formed. If necessary, add additional flour while blending.

7. Using wet hands, form the dough into 1½- to 2-inch balls, and place them on the prepared sheet, spacing the cookies about 1½ inches apart. Flatten each cookie with the palm of your hand, and using a finger, make an indentation in the center of each one. Place about ½ teaspoon of raspberry jam in each indentation.

8. Bake for 10 to 15 minutes, or until the cookies are golden brown. Allow the cookies to cool on the sheet for 15 minutes. Then transfer the cookies to a rack, and cool completely before serving or storing in an airtight container.

Spelties

This prize-winning recipe was created by Jean Meyer of Gahanna, Ohio. Jean says: "Spelties are a sure cure for the 'chocoholic' in your life."

Yield: 3 dozen bars

½ cup canola margarine

1 cup turbinado sugar (or other sweetener)

3 eggs (or substitute)

½ cup extra-chunky peanut butter

1½ teaspoons vanilla extract

1 cup white or whole-grain spelt flour

2 tablespoons plus 1½ teaspoons nonaluminum baking powder

½ teaspoon sea salt

1 cup chocolate chips

1. Preheat the oven to 350°F. Coat a 9-x-12-inch baking pan with nonstick cooking spray, and set aside.

2. Place the margarine and sugar in a 2-quart bowl, and, using a fork, cream the mixture until it is light and fluffly. Add 1 egg at a time, creaming thoroughly after each addition. Add the peanut butter and vanilla, creaming until the mixture is smooth.

3. Combine the flour, baking powder, and salt in a 3-quart bowl. Add the margarine mixture to the flour mixture, and stir until smooth. Add the chocolate chips, and stir to mix.

4. Spread the mixture over the entire surface of the prepared pan, and bake for 30 to 35 minutes, or until browned.

5. Remove the pan from the oven, and place it on a wire rack for 5 minutes to cool. While the slab is still warm, use a sharp knife to cut it into 36 bars, each 1 x 3 inches in size. Cool completely before serving or storing in an airtight container.

Rum Raisin Refrigerator Cookies

Yield: 24 cookies

2 cups white spelt flour

1 teaspoon nonaluminum baking powder

1 cup turbinado sugar (or other sweetener)

2 eggs (or substitute)

¼ teaspoon imitation rum extract

1 cup canola margarine, chilled and cut into 1-x-1-x-¼-inch pieces

½ cup dark raisins, chopped

This recipe uses a make-ahead dough, which is rolled into a log and stored in the refrigerator for up to a week. Then, whenever you want some fresh-baked cookies, just take out the dough and you'll be ready to go!

1. Sift the flour and baking powder onto a large board. Using a large spoon, make a well in the flour, being careful not to make the well so deep that you can see the board.

2. Pour the sugar into the well. Using a large spoon, make a well in the sugar. Break the egg into the well, and add the rum extract.

3. Using a fork, start mixing the egg and sugar together. Slowly mix in some flour from the rim, mixing until the well in the flour is filled with a creamy mixture.

4. Place the chilled margarine pieces on top of the creamy mixture. Top the margarine with half of the flour by using a scraper or other utensil to move the flour from the bottom outer portion of the mound to the center.

5. Spread the raisins on a work surface. Sprinkle them lightly with a small amount of flour, and roll them around to coat. Place the raisins in the flour well, and use your hands to quickly knead all of the ingredients into a pliable dough.

6. Using your hands, roll the dough into a 12-inch log. Wrap the log tightly, first in plastic wrap, and then in aluminum foil. Place the log in the refrigerator for at least 3 hours, or until needed.

7. When you are ready to bake, preheat the oven to 350°F, and line several 14-x-9½-inch cookie sheets with baking paper. Set aside.

8. Unwrap the chilled dough, and place the log on a board. Using a sharp knife, cut off ½-inch slices and arrange them on the prepared sheets, placing only 6 cookies on each sheet.

9. Bake for about 15 minutes, or until the cookies are golden brown. Allow the cookies to cool on the sheet for 5 minutes. Then transfer the cookies to a rack, and cool completely before serving or storing in an airtight container.

Variations

• Substitute finely ground nuts for the raisins.

• Omit the raisins, and knead a few additional tablespoons of flour into the dough. Using a rolling pin, roll the dough into a ¼- to ½-inch-thick sheet, and use decorative cookie cutters to make festive shapes. Bake as directed above.

• To create pinwheel cookies, first make a batch of dough as directed above, omitting the raisins. Then make a second batch of dough—again, without the raisins. This time, though, use whole-grain spelt flour, reducing the amount to 1½ cups, and mixing into it ¾ cup of unsweetened cocoa or carob powder. Roll each batch into a 12-x-10-inch rectangle. Place 1 rectangle on top of the other, and roll the dough up, jelly-roll style, starting at the long end. Refrigerate for at least 3 hours, and slice and bake as directed on the previous page.

Bitter Almond-Banana Logs

Vita-Spelt Pancake/Muffin Mix will help you make these delicious and highly nutritious cookies in just 20 minutes.

1. Using a sharp knife, cut each hazelnut in half. Place the hazelnut halves flat side down on a wooden board, and slice each half into slivers. Set aside.

2. Preheat the oven to 350°F. Generously coat a 16-x-14-inch cookie sheet with nonstick cooking spray, and set aside.

3. Place the egg white in a 1-quart bowl, and beat with an electric mixer until the mixture forms stiff peaks. Set aside.

4. Place the banana in a 1-quart bowl, and thoroughly mash with a fork. Add the juice, sugar, almond extract, and oil, and stir to blend. Fold in the egg white.

5. Combine the pancake mix and the ground hazelnuts in a 2-quart bowl. Slowly add the banana mixture to the dry mixture, and stir just until the dry mixture is moistened.

6. Using a wet spoon, cut 1 tablespoon from the dough. With wet hands, roll the dough into a 2½- to 3-inch-long log. Press a few hazelnut slivers into the center, and place the log on the prepared sheet. Repeat with the remaining dough, spacing the cookies about 1 inch apart.

7. Bake for 12 minutes, or until the cookies are evenly browned. Allow the cookies to cool on the sheet for 5 minutes. Then transfer the cookies to a rack, and cool completely before serving or storing in an airtight container.

Yield: 16 to 18 cookies

18 hazelnuts

1 egg white

1 large banana

⅓ cup banana juice or combination banana-peach juice*

¼ cup turbinado sugar (or other sweetener)

½ teaspoon bitter almond extract

2 tablespoons canola oil

1⅔ cups Vita-Spelt Pancake/Muffin Mix (or equivalent product)

1¼ cups finely ground hazelnuts

*These juices are available in most health foods stores.

Snickerdoodles

Yield: 34 cookies

1½ cups white spelt flour

Dash sea salt

½ teaspoon nonaluminum baking powder

½ teaspoon ground cinnamon

Dash ground allspice

½ cup canola margarine, softened

½ cup turbinado sugar (or other sweetener)

2 tablespoons honey

2 eggs, beaten (or substitute)

½ cup finely chopped hazelnuts

½ cup finely chopped prunes

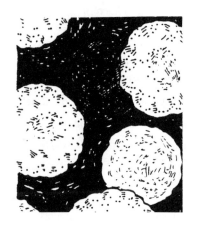

There are many different recipes for snickerdoodles—a drop cookie made from a sweet white dough. This one combines spelt flour with chopped hazelnuts and prunes for a super-nutritious, super-delicious cookie that your whole family will love.

1. Preheat the oven to 350°F. Lightly coat a 16-x-14-inch cookie sheet with nonstick cooking spray, and set aside.

2. Sift the flour, salt, baking powder, cinnamon, and allspice into a 1-quart bowl. Set aside.

3. Place the margarine, sugar, and honey in a 2-quart bowl, and, using a fork, cream the mixture until it is light and fluffy. Add the eggs, and continue to mix until the mixture is smooth. Set aside.

4. Combine the nuts and prunes in a small bowl. (This will prevent the prunes from lumping together when added to the dough.) Set aside.

5. Add the flour mixture to the margarine mixture a little at a time, stirring thoroughly after each addition until the dough is smooth. Stir in the nut mixture.

6. Drop teaspoonfuls of the dough onto the prepared sheet, spacing the cookies 1 inch apart. Using the back of a fork, slightly flatten the spoonfuls of dough.

7. Bake for 10 to 12 minutes, or until the cookies are golden. Allow the cookies to cool on the sheet for 5 minutes. Then transfer the cookies to a rack, and cool completely before serving or storing in an airtight container.

Variation

• For slightly sweeter cookies, substitute hickory nuts for the hazelnuts, and dates for the prunes.

Hi-Energy Cookies

This versatile recipe produces one dozen raisin cookies, one dozen peanut butter cookies, and one dozen chocolate cookies—something for everyone! Better yet, with their wholesome ingredients, these treats will not only satisfy your sweet tooth, but also supply you with the energy you need for your busy life.

1. Preheat the oven to 350°F. Line a 16-x-14-inch cookie sheet with baking paper, and set aside.

2. Place 1 tablespoon of the margarine in a 10-inch skillet, and melt over medium heat. Add the spelt flakes, and sauté, stirring constantly, until the flakes are lightly browned. Sprinkle the allspice over the flakes, and mix well. Remove the pan from the heat, and set aside.

3. Place the remaining ½ cup of margarine in a 2-quart bowl, and, using an electric mixer set at medium speed, cream the margarine until light and smooth. Add the sugar, egg, and vanilla, and continue to cream for 2 minutes, or until the mixture is creamy. Set aside.

4. Place the flour and baking powder in a 1-quart bowl, and stir to mix. Add the flour mixture, the spelt flakes, and the nuts to the margarine mixture, and use a wooden spoon to stir the ingredients into a dough.

5. Divide the dough into 3 equal portions, placing each portion in a separate bowl. Add the raisins to the first portion, the peanut butter and coconut to the second portion, and the chocolate to the third portion. Then knead each piece separately by hand, just enough to completely mix in the flavoring ingredients.

6. Using a wet spoon, cut 1 tablespoon from the dough. With wet hands, roll the dough into a ball. Place the ball on the prepared sheet, and, using the back of a fork, flatten it until it forms a 1½-inch cookie. Repeat with the remaining dough, spacing the cookies about 2 inches apart.

7. Bake on the middle oven rack for 12 to 15 minutes, or until brown. Allow the cookies to cool on the sheet for 5 minutes. Then transfer the cookies to a rack, and cool completely before serving or storing in an airtight container.

Yield: 36 cookies

½ cup plus 1 tablespoon canola margarine, divided

1¼ cups toasted spelt flakes

½ teaspoon ground allspice

½ cup turbinado sugar (or other sweetener)

1 egg (or substitute)

¼ teaspoon vanilla extract

½ cup whole-grain spelt flour

1 teaspoon nonaluminum baking powder

1 cup finely ground hazelnuts

RAISIN COOKIES

¼ cup chopped dark raisins

PEANUT BUTTER-COCONUT COOKIES

2 tablespoons smooth peanut butter

¼ cup finely grated coconut

BITTERSWEET CHOCOLATE COOKIES

¼ cup grated bittersweet chocolate

Spiced Honey and Almond Squares

Yield: 30 squares

1 cup honey

½ cup turbinado sugar (or other sweetener)

1 egg, beaten (or substitute)

¼ teaspoon imitation brandy extract

3 cups whole-grain spelt flour, divided

1 tablespoon plus 1½ teaspoons nonaluminum baking powder

1 teaspoon ground cinnamon

¼ teaspoon ground nutmeg

¼ teaspoon ground cloves

¼ teaspoon ground ginger

1 cup finely ground almonds

Grated peel of 1 lemon

The color and flavor of honey vary according to the flowers on which the bees feed. Some honey is quite dark and strongly flavored, while other honey is lighter in color and taste. For this recipe, light clover honey is best.

1. Place the honey and sugar in a 1-quart saucepan, and bring to a boil over medium-high heat, stirring constantly with a wooden spoon. Transfer the mixture to a 3-quart heatproof bowl, and allow to cool for 20 minutes.

2. Stir the egg and brandy extract into the cooled honey mixture, mixing well. Slowly add 2¾ cups of the flour, and the baking powder, cinnamon, nutmeg, cloves, and ginger, stirring until a smooth dough is formed. Add the almonds and lemon peel, and mix well.

3. Turn the mixture onto a floured board and, using your hands, knead in enough of the remaining ¼ cup of flour to form a soft nonsticky dough. Shape the dough into a ball, wrap it in plastic wrap, and refrigerate for 2 hours.

4. Preheat the oven to 350°F. Lightly flour a large sheet of aluminum foil, and place the chilled dough on the foil. Using a rolling pin, roll the dough into a 12-x-10-inch rectangle of even thickness. Transfer the foil and dough to a baking sheet just larger than the dough.

5. Bake on the middle rack for about 15 minutes, or until the top is golden brown and the center springs back when lightly touched. Tranfer the foil to a board, and allow to cool for about 5 minutes. Using a sharp knife, cut the dough into 3-inch squares, and cool completely.

6. Remove the foil from each of the squares, and transfer the squares to an airtight container, arranging them in single layers separated by sheets of waxed paper. Allow the squares to soften in the container for 3 or 4 days, and serve.

Index